FAVORITE BRAND NAME

Best-Loved CASSEROLES

Publications International, Ltd.

Microwave Cooking: Microwave ovens vary in wattage. Use the cooking times as guidelines and check for doneness before adding more time.

CONTENTS

Breakfast & BRUNCH

PARMESAN AND ROASTED RED PEPPER STRATA

1 loaf (16 ounces) French bread, cut into
  ½-inch-thick slices
2 jars (7½ ounces each) roasted red peppers,
  drained and cut into ½-inch pieces
1 cup grated Parmesan cheese
1 cup sliced green onions
3 cups (12 ounces) shredded mozzarella cheese
8 eggs
¾ cup reduced-fat (2%) milk
1 container (7 ounces) prepared pesto
2 teaspoons minced garlic
¾ teaspoon salt

1. Grease 13×9-inch baking dish. Arrange half of bread slices in single layer on bottom of prepared baking dish. Top bread with half of red peppers, ½ cup Parmesan, ½ cup green onions and 1½ cups mozzarella. Repeat layers with remaining bread, red peppers, Parmesan, green onions and mozzarella.

2. Combine eggs, milk, pesto, garlic and salt in medium bowl; whisk to combine. Pour egg mixture evenly over strata. Cover and refrigerate overnight.

3. Preheat oven to 375°F. Bake, uncovered, 30 minutes or until hot and bubbly.   *Makes 6 servings*

Left: *Parmesan
and Roasted Red
Pepper Strata*

Above: *No-Fuss
Tuna Quiche
(page 24)*

5

FETA BRUNCH BAKE

1 medium red bell pepper
2 bags (10 ounces each) fresh spinach,
    washed and stemmed
6 eggs
6 ounces crumbled feta cheese
⅓ cup chopped onion
2 tablespoons chopped fresh parsley
¼ teaspoon dried dill weed
    Dash ground black pepper

Preheat broiler. Place bell pepper on foil-lined broiler pan. Broil, 4 inches from heat, 15 to 20 minutes or until blackened on all sides, turning every 5 minutes with tongs. Place in paper bag; close bag and set aside to cool about 15 to 20 minutes. Cut into ½-inch pieces.

To blanch spinach, heat 1 quart water in 2-quart saucepan over high heat to a boil. Add spinach and return to a boil; boil 2 to 3 minutes until crisp-tender. Drain and immediately plunge into cold water. Drain; let stand until cool enough to handle. Squeeze spinach to remove excess water. Finely chop.

Preheat oven to 400°F. Grease 1-quart baking dish. Beat eggs in large bowl with electric mixer at medium speed until foamy. Stir in bell pepper, spinach, cheese, onion, parsley, dill weed and black pepper. Pour egg mixture into prepared dish. Bake 20 minutes or until set. Let stand 5 minutes before serving. Garnish as desired.   *Makes 4 servings*

BETTY JO'S SAUSAGE AND CHEESE GRITS

WESSON® No-Stick Cooking Spray
1 pound mild or hot cooked sausage,
    crumbled and drained
1½ cups grits
2½ cups shredded Cheddar cheese
3 tablespoons WESSON® Vegetable Oil
1½ cups milk
3 eggs, slightly beaten

Preheat oven to 350°F. Lightly spray a 13×9×2-inch baking dish with Wesson® Cooking Spray. Evenly spread crumbled sausage on bottom of dish; set aside. Bring 4½ cups water to a boil in a large saucepan. Stir in grits and lower heat. Cook 5 minutes until thickened, stirring occasionally. Add cheese and Wesson® Oil; stir until cheese has melted. Stir in milk and eggs; blend well. Evenly spoon mixture over sausage; bake, uncovered, 1 hour or until grits have set.   *Makes 6 to 8 servings*

Feta Brunch Bake

EGG & SAUSAGE CASSEROLE

- **½ pound pork sausage**
- **3 tablespoons margarine or butter, divided**
- **2 tablespoons all-purpose flour**
- **¼ teaspoon salt**
- **¼ teaspoon black pepper**
- **1¼ cups milk**
- **2 cups frozen hash brown potatoes**
- **4 eggs, hard-boiled and sliced**
- **½ cup cornflake crumbs**
- **¼ cup sliced green onions**

Preheat oven to 350°F. Spray 2-quart oval baking dish with nonstick cooking spray.

Crumble sausage into large skillet; brown over medium-high heat until no longer pink, stirring to separate meat. Drain sausage on paper towels. Discard fat and wipe skillet with paper towel.

Melt 2 tablespoons margarine in same skillet over medium heat. Stir in flour, salt and pepper until smooth. Gradually stir in milk; cook and stir until thickened. Add sausage, potatoes and eggs; stir to combine. Pour into prepared dish.

Melt remaining 1 tablespoon margarine. Combine cornflake crumbs and melted margarine in small bowl; sprinkle evenly over casserole.

Bake, uncovered, 30 minutes or until hot and bubbly. Sprinkle with onions. *Makes 6 servings*

Cook's Tip

To remove a sausage casing, use a paring knife to slit the casing at one end. Be careful not to cut through the sausage. Grasp the cut edge and gently pull the casing away from the sausage.

Egg & Sausage Casserole

Breakfast & BRUNCH

SPINACH SENSATION

½ **pound bacon slices**
1 **cup (8 ounces) sour cream**
3 **eggs, separated**
2 **tablespoons all-purpose flour**
⅛ **teaspoon black pepper**
1 **package (10 ounces) frozen chopped spinach, thawed and squeezed dry**
½ **cup (2 ounces) shredded sharp Cheddar cheese**
½ **cup dry bread crumbs**
1 **tablespoon margarine or butter, melted**

Preheat oven to 350°F. Spray 2-quart round baking dish with nonstick cooking spray.

Place bacon in single layer in large skillet; cook over medium heat until crisp. Remove from skillet; drain on paper towels. Crumble and set aside.

Combine sour cream, egg yolks, flour and pepper in large bowl; set aside. Beat egg whites in medium bowl with electric mixer at high speed until stiff peaks form. Stir ¼ of egg whites into sour cream mixture; fold in remaining egg whites.

Arrange half of spinach in prepared dish. Top with half of sour cream mixture. Sprinkle ¼ cup cheese over sour cream mixture. Sprinkle bacon over cheese. Repeat layers, ending with remaining ¼ cup cheese.

Combine bread crumbs and margarine in small bowl; sprinkle evenly over cheese.

Bake, uncovered, 30 to 35 minutes or until egg mixture is set. Let stand 5 minutes before serving.

Makes 6 servings

RANCH–STYLE SAUSAGE & APPLE QUICHE

1 **(9-inch) pastry shell, 1½ inches deep**
½ **pound bulk spicy pork sausage**
½ **cup chopped onion**
¾ **cup shredded, peeled tart apple**
1 **tablespoon lemon juice**
1 **tablespoon sugar**
⅛ **teaspoon red pepper flakes**
1 **cup (4 ounces) shredded Cheddar cheese**
3 **eggs**
1½ **cups half-and-half**
¼ **teaspoon salt**
Dash black pepper

Preheat oven to 450°F. Line pastry shell with foil; partially fill with uncooked beans or rice to weight shell. Bake 10 minutes. Remove foil and beans; continue baking pastry shell 5 minutes or until lightly browned. Let cool. *Reduce oven temperature to 375°F.*

Crumble sausage into large skillet; add onion. Stir over medium heat until sausage is browned and onion is tender. Spoon off and discard pan drippings. Add apple, lemon juice, sugar and red pepper flakes. Cook and stir on medium-high heat 4 minutes or until apple is barely tender and all liquid is evaporated. Let cool. Spoon sausage mixture into pastry shell; top with cheese. Whisk eggs, half-and-half, salt and black pepper in medium bowl. Pour over sausage mixture. Bake 35 to 45 minutes or until filling is puffed and knife inserted in center comes out clean. Let stand 10 minutes before serving.

Makes 6 servings

Spinach Sensation

HAM AND EGG ENCHILADAS

2 tablespoons butter or margarine
1 small red bell pepper, chopped
3 green onions with tops, sliced
½ cup diced ham
8 eggs
8 (7- to 8-inch) flour tortillas
2 cups (8 ounces) shredded Colby-Jack
    cheese or Monterey Jack cheese with
    jalapeño peppers, divided
1 can (10 ounces) enchilada sauce
½ cup prepared salsa
    Sliced avocado, fresh cilantro and red
    pepper slices for garnish

1. Preheat oven to 350°F.

2. Melt butter in large nonstick skillet over medium heat. Add bell pepper and onions; cook and stir 2 minutes. Add ham; cook and stir 1 minute.

3. Lightly beat eggs with wire whisk in medium bowl. Add eggs to skillet; cook until eggs are set, but still soft, stirring occasionally.

4. Spoon about ⅓ cup egg mixture evenly down center of each tortilla; top with 1 tablespoon cheese. Roll tortillas up and place seam side down in shallow 11×7-inch baking dish.

5. Combine enchilada sauce and salsa in small bowl; pour evenly over enchiladas.

6. Cover enchiladas with foil; bake 20 minutes. Uncover; sprinkle with remaining 1½ cups cheese. Continue baking 10 minutes or until enchiladas are hot and cheese is melted. Garnish, if desired.

Makes 4 servings

Cook's Tip

The microwave is a great way to soften and warm tortillas. Stack tortillas wrapped in plastic in oven and microwave at HIGH (100%) power ½ to 1 minute. Rotate ¼ turn once during heating.

Ham and Egg Enchiladas

LOW FAT TURKEY BACON FRITTATA

1 package (12 ounces) BUTTERBALL®
  Turkey Bacon, heated and chopped
6 ounces uncooked angel hair pasta, broken
2 teaspoons olive oil
1 small onion, sliced
1 red bell pepper, cut into thin strips
4 containers (4 ounces each) egg substitute
1 container (5 ounces) fat free ricotta
  cheese
1 cup (4 ounces) shredded fat free
  mozzarella cheese
1 cup (4 ounces) shredded reduced fat Swiss
  cheese
½ teaspoon salt
½ teaspoon black pepper
1 package (10 ounces) frozen spinach,
  thawed and squeezed dry

Cook and drain pasta. Heat oil in large skillet over medium heat until hot. Cook and stir onion and bell pepper until tender. Combine egg substitute, cheeses, salt, pepper and cooked pasta in large bowl. Add vegetables, spinach and turkey bacon. Spray 10-inch quiche dish with nonstick cooking spray; pour mixture into dish. Bake in preheated 350°F oven 30 minutes. Cut into wedges. Serve with spicy salsa, if desired. *Makes 8 servings*

Preparation Time: 15 minutes plus baking time

OVEN BREAKFAST HASH

2 pounds baking potatoes, unpeeled
  (5 or 6 medium)
1 pound BOB EVANS® Original Recipe Roll
  Sausage
1 (12-ounce can) evaporated milk
⅓ cup chopped green onions
1 tablespoon Worcestershire sauce
½ teaspoon salt
¼ teaspoon black pepper
¼ cup dried bread crumbs
1 tablespoon melted butter or margarine
½ teaspoon paprika

Cook potatoes in boiling water until fork-tender. Drain and coarsely chop or mash. Preheat oven to 350°F. Crumble and cook sausage in medium skillet until browned. Drain and transfer to large bowl. Stir in potatoes, milk, green onions, Worcestershire sauce, salt and pepper. Pour into greased 2½- or 3-quart casserole dish. Sprinkle with bread crumbs; drizzle with melted butter. Sprinkle with paprika. Bake, uncovered, 30 to 35 minutes or until casserole bubbles and top is browned. Refrigerate leftovers.
Makes 6 to 8 servings

Low Fat Turkey Bacon Frittata

Breakfast &
BRUNCH

SPAM™ BREAKFAST BURRITOS

- 1 (12-ounce) can SPAM® Luncheon Meat, cubed
- 4 eggs
- 2 tablespoons milk
- 1 tablespoon butter or margarine
- 6 (6-inch) flour tortillas
- 1 cup (4 ounces) shredded Cheddar cheese, divided
- 1 cup (4 ounces) shredded Monterey Jack cheese, divided
  CHI-CHI'S® Salsa or Taco Sauce

Heat oven to 400°F. In medium bowl, beat together SPAM®, eggs and milk. Melt butter in large skillet; add egg mixture. Cook, stirring, to desired doneness. Divide SPAM™ mixture and half of cheeses over tortillas. Roll up burritos; place seam side down in 12×8-inch baking dish. Sprinkle remaining cheeses over top of burritos. Bake 5 to 10 minutes or until cheese is melted. Serve with salsa.

Makes 6 servings

CHILI–CORN QUICHE

- 1 9-inch pastry shell, 1½ inches deep
- 1 can (8¾ ounces) corn, drained, *or* 1 cup frozen corn, cooked
- 1 can (4 ounces) diced green chilies, drained
- ¼ cup thinly sliced green onions with tops
- 1 cup (4 ounces) shredded Monterey Jack cheese
- 3 eggs
- 1½ cups half-and-half
- ½ teaspoon salt
- ½ teaspoon ground cumin

Preheat oven to 450°F. Line pastry shell with foil; partially fill with uncooked beans or rice to weight shell. Bake 10 minutes. Remove foil and beans; continue baking pastry shell 5 minutes or until lightly browned. Let cool. *Reduce oven temperature to 375°F.*

Combine corn, green chilies and green onions in small bowl. Spoon into pastry shell; top with cheese. Whisk eggs, half-and-half, salt and cumin in medium bowl. Pour over cheese. Bake 35 to 45 minutes or until filling is puffed and knife inserted in center comes out clean. Let stand 10 minutes before serving.

Makes 6 servings

CHEESE STRATA

3 tablespoons butter or margarine
6 slices bread, crusts removed
3 cups (12 ounces) grated cheddar cheese, divided
6 eggs
2 cups milk
1 tablespoon LAWRY'S® Minced Onion with Green Onion Flakes
1 teaspoon LAWRY'S® Seasoned Salt
¼ teaspoon LAWRY'S® Garlic Powder with Parsley

Lightly grease 13×9×2-inch baking dish with butter; arrange bread slices in bottom of dish. Sprinkle with half of cheddar cheese. In medium bowl, beat together eggs, milk, Minced Onion with Green Onion Flakes, Seasoned Salt and Garlic Powder with Parsley. Pour mixture over bread and cheese. Sprinkle with remaining cheddar cheese. Bake, uncovered, in 350°F oven 35 minutes or until light golden brown. Let stand 5 minutes before serving.
Makes 6 servings

Herb Strata: Add 2 tablespoons LAWRY'S® Pinch of Herbs to Cheese Strata egg and milk mixture.

Italian-Herb Strata: To HERB STRATA variation, add ¼ cup sliced black olives to each cheese layer and top with diced tomatoes. Serve with LAWRY'S® Original-Style Spaghetti Sauce Spices & Seasonings prepared as directed on package.

PINWHEEL CHEESE QUICHE

2 tablespoons margarine or butter
2 cups sliced mushrooms
6 green onions, sliced (about 2 cups)
1 package (8 ounces) refrigerated crescent rolls, separated into 8 triangles
1 envelope LIPTON® RECIPE SECRETS® Golden Herb with Lemon Soup Mix
½ cup half and half
4 eggs, beaten
1 cup (about 4 ounces) shredded Monterey Jack or mozzarella cheese

Preheat oven to 375°F.

In 12-inch skillet, melt margarine over medium heat and cook mushrooms and green onions, stirring occasionally, 5 minutes or until tender. Remove from heat and set aside.

In 9-inch pie plate sprayed with nonstick cooking spray, arrange crescent roll triangles in a spoke pattern with narrow tips hanging over rim of pie plate about 2 inches. Press dough onto bottom and up side of pie plate forming full crust.

In medium bowl, combine golden herb with lemon soup mix, half and half and eggs. Stir in cheese and mushroom mixture. Pour into prepared pie crust. Bring tips of dough over filling towards center. Bake uncovered 30 minutes or until knife inserted in center comes out clean.   *Makes about 6 servings*

Tip: Also terrific with LIPTON® Recipe Secrets® Savory Herb with Garlic Soup Mix.

Breakfast &
BRUNCH

CHEDDAR AND LEEK STRATA

8 eggs, lightly beaten
2 cups milk
½ cup ale or beer
2 cloves garlic, minced
¼ teaspoon salt
¼ teaspoon black pepper
1 loaf (16 ounces) sourdough bread, cut into ½-inch cubes
2 small leeks, coarsely chopped
1 red bell pepper, chopped
1½ cups (6 ounces) shredded Swiss cheese
1½ cups (6 ounces) shredded sharp Cheddar cheese

1. Combine eggs, milk, ale, garlic, salt and black pepper in large bowl. Beat until well blended.

2. Place ½ of bread cubes on bottom of greased 13×9-inch baking dish. Sprinkle ½ of leeks and ½ of bell pepper over bread cubes. Top with ¾ cup Swiss cheese and ¾ cup Cheddar cheese. Repeat layers with remaining ingredients, ending with Cheddar cheese.

3. Pour egg mixture evenly over top. Cover tightly with plastic wrap or foil. Weight top of strata down with slightly smaller baking dish. Refrigerate strata at least 2 hours or overnight.

4. Preheat oven to 350°F. Bake uncovered 40 to 45 minutes or until center is set. Garnish with fresh sage, if desired. Serve immediately.

Makes 12 servings

BAKED HAM & CHEESE MONTE CRISTO

6 slices bread, divided
2 cups (8 ounces) shredded Cheddar cheese, divided
1⅓ cups FRENCH'S® French Fried Onions, divided
1 package (10 ounces) frozen broccoli spears, thawed, drained and cut into 1-inch pieces
2 cups (10 ounces) cubed cooked ham
5 eggs
2 cups milk
½ teaspoon ground mustard
½ teaspoon seasoned salt
¼ teaspoon coarsely ground black pepper

Preheat oven to 325°F. Cut 3 bread slices into cubes; place in greased 12×8-inch baking dish. Top bread with 1 cup cheese, ⅔ *cup* French Fried Onions, the broccoli and ham. Cut remaining bread slices diagonally into halves. Arrange bread halves down center of casserole, overlapping slightly, crusted points all in one direction. In medium bowl, beat eggs, milk and seasonings; pour evenly over casserole. Bake, uncovered, at 325°F for 1 hour or until center is set. Top with remaining 1 cup cheese and ⅔ *cup* onions; bake, uncovered, 5 minutes or until onions are golden brown. Let stand 10 minutes before serving.

Makes 6 to 8 servings

Cheddar and Leek Strata

CHEESY COUNTRY SPAM™ PUFF

6 slices white bread, torn into small pieces
1¼ cups milk
3 eggs
1 tablespoon spicy mustard
½ teaspoon garlic powder
½ teaspoon paprika
1 (12-ounce) can SPAM® Luncheon Meat, cubed
2 cups (8 ounces) shredded sharp Cheddar cheese, divided
½ cup chopped onion
½ cup (2 ounces) shredded Monterey Jack cheese

Heat oven to 375°F. In large bowl, combine bread, milk, eggs, mustard, garlic powder and paprika. Beat at medium speed of electric mixer 1 minute or until smooth. Stir in SPAM®, 1 cup Cheddar cheese and onion. Pour into greased 12×8-inch baking dish. Bake 25 minutes. Top with remaining 1 cup Cheddar cheese and Monterey Jack cheese. Bake 5 minutes longer or until cheese is melted. Let stand 10 minutes before serving. *Makes 6 servings*

HEARTY BREAKFAST CUSTARD CASSEROLE

1 pound (2 medium-large) Colorado baking potatoes
Salt and pepper
8 ounces low-fat bulk pork sausage, cooked and crumbled *or* 6 ounces finely diced lean ham *or* 6 ounces turkey bacon, cooked and crumbled
⅓ cup julienne-sliced roasted red pepper *or* 1 jar (2 ounces) sliced pimientos, drained
3 eggs
1 cup low-fat milk
3 tablespoons chopped fresh chives or green onion tops *or* ¾ teaspoon dried thyme or oregano leaves
Salsa and low-fat sour cream or plain yogurt (optional)

Heat oven to 375°F. Grease 8- or 9-inch square baking dish or other small casserole. Peel potatoes and slice very thinly; arrange half of potatoes in baking dish. Sprinkle with salt and pepper. Cover with half of sausage. Arrange remaining potatoes on top; sprinkle with salt and pepper. Top with remaining sausage and red pepper. Beat eggs, milk and chives until blended. Pour over potatoes. Cover baking dish with foil and bake 35 to 45 minutes or until potatoes are tender. Uncover and bake 5 to 10 minutes more. Serve with salsa and sour cream, if desired. *Makes 4 to 5 servings*

Favorite recipe from **Colorado Potato Administrative Committee**

Cheesy Country Spam™ Puff

ROASTED PEPPER AND SOURDOUGH BRUNCH CASSEROLE

3 cups sourdough bread cubes
1 jar (12 ounces) roasted pepper strips, drained
1 cup (4 ounces) shredded reduced-fat sharp Cheddar cheese
1 cup (4 ounces) shredded reduced-fat Monterey Jack cheese
1 cup nonfat cottage cheese
12 ounces cholesterol-free egg substitute
1 cup fat-free (skim) milk
¼ cup chopped fresh cilantro
¼ teaspoon black pepper

1. Spray 11×9-inch baking pan with nonstick cooking spray. Place bread cubes in pan. Arrange roasted peppers evenly over bread cubes. Sprinkle Cheddar and Monterey Jack cheeses over peppers.

2. Place cottage cheese in food processor or blender; process until smooth. Add egg substitute; process 10 seconds. Combine cottage cheese mixture and milk in small bowl; pour over ingredients in baking pan. Sprinkle with cilantro and black pepper. Refrigerate, covered, 4 to 12 hours.

3. Preheat oven to 375°F. Bake, uncovered, 40 minutes or until hot and bubbly and golden brown on top.   *Makes 8 servings*

MOM'S FAVORITE BRUNCH CASSEROLE

6 eggs
1 cup plain yogurt
1 cup (4 ounces) shredded Cheddar cheese
½ teaspoon pepper
1 cup finely chopped ham*
½ can (8 ounces) pasteurized process cheese

*Substitute 1 pound bulk pork sausage, browned and drained, for ham.

1. Preheat oven to 350°F. Lightly grease 12×8-inch baking dish.

2. Combine eggs and yogurt in medium bowl; beat with wire whisk until well blended. Stir in Cheddar cheese and pepper.

3. Place ham in prepared baking dish; pour egg mixture over ham. Bake 25 to 30 minutes or until egg mixture is set. Use process cheese to decorate top of casserole; let stand 2 to 3 minutes or until cheese is slightly melted.   *Makes 10 servings*

Roasted Pepper and Sourdough Brunch Casserole

NO–FUSS TUNA QUICHE

1 unbaked 9-inch deep-dish pastry shell
1½ cups low-fat milk
3 extra large eggs
⅓ cup chopped green onions
1 tablespoon chopped drained pimiento
1 teaspoon dried basil leaves, crushed
½ teaspoon salt
1 can (6 ounces) STARKIST® Tuna, drained and broken into chunks
½ cup (2 ounces) shredded low-fat Cheddar cheese
8 spears (4 inches each) broccoli

Preheat oven to 450°F. Bake pastry shell for 5 minutes; remove to rack to cool. *Reduce oven temperature to 325°F.* For filling, in large bowl whisk together milk and eggs. Stir in onions, pimiento, basil and salt. Fold in tuna and cheese. Pour into prebaked pastry shell. Bake at 325°F for 30 minutes.

Meanwhile, in a saucepan steam broccoli spears over simmering water for 5 minutes. Drain; set aside. After 30 minutes baking time, arrange broccoli spears, spoke-fashion, over quiche. Bake 25 to 35 minutes more or until a knife inserted 2 inches from center comes out clean. Let stand for 5 minutes. Cut into 8 wedges, centering a broccoli spear in each wedge.   *Makes 8 servings*

Note: If desired, 1 cup chopped broccoli may be added to the filling before baking.

MUSHROOM & ONION EGG BAKE

1 tablespoon vegetable oil
4 green onions, chopped
4 ounces mushrooms, sliced
1 cup low-fat cottage cheese
1 cup sour cream
6 eggs
2 tablespoons all-purpose flour
¼ teaspoon salt
⅛ teaspoon freshly ground pepper
   Dash hot pepper sauce

1. Preheat oven to 350°F. Grease shallow 1-quart baking dish.

2. Heat oil in medium skillet over medium heat. Add onions and mushrooms; cook and stir until tender.

3. In blender or food processor, process cottage cheese until almost smooth. Add sour cream, eggs, flour, salt, pepper and hot pepper sauce; process until combined. Stir in onions and mushrooms. Pour into greased dish. Bake about 40 minutes or until knife inserted near center comes out clean.

Makes about 6 servings

No-Fuss Tuna Quiche

MEXICAN OMELET ROLL–UPS WITH AVOCADO SAUCE

8 eggs
2 tablespoons milk
1 tablespoon margarine or butter
1½ cups (6 ounces) shredded Monterey Jack cheese
1 large tomato, seeded and chopped
¼ cup chopped fresh cilantro
8 (7-inch) corn tortillas
1½ cups salsa
2 medium avocados, chopped
¼ cup reduced-calorie sour cream
2 tablespoons diced green chilies
1 tablespoon fresh lemon juice
1 teaspoon hot pepper sauce
¼ teaspoon salt

Preheat oven to 350°F. Spray 13×9-inch baking dish with nonstick cooking spray.

Whisk eggs and milk in medium bowl until blended. Melt margarine in large skillet over medium heat; add egg mixture to skillet. Cook and stir 5 minutes or until eggs are set, but still soft. Remove from heat. Stir in cheese, tomato and cilantro.

Spoon about ⅓ cup egg mixture evenly down center of each tortilla. Roll up tortillas and place seam side down in prepared dish. Pour salsa evenly over tortillas.

Cover tightly with foil and bake 20 minutes or until heated through.

Meanwhile, process avocados, sour cream, chilies, lemon juice, pepper sauce and salt in food processor or blender until smooth. Serve tortillas with avocado sauce. *Makes 8 servings*

Food Fact

Avocado trees were first discovered in Florida back in the 1830's; today, however, California produces over 80 percent of America's avocado crop.

Mexican Omelet Roll-Up with Avocado Sauce

Breakfast &
BRUNCH

SPINACH & EGG CASSEROLE

1 box (10 ounces) **BIRDS EYE**® frozen
    Chopped Spinach
1 can (15 ounces) Cheddar cheese soup
1 tablespoon mustard
½ pound deli ham, cut into ¼-inch cubes
4 hard-boiled eggs, chopped or sliced

• Preheat oven to 350°F.

• In large saucepan, cook spinach according to package directions; drain well.

• Stir in soup, mustard and ham.

• Pour into 9×9-inch baking pan. Top with eggs.

• Bake 15 to 20 minutes or until heated through.

Makes 4 servings

Serving Suggestion: Sprinkle with paprika for added color.

Birds Eye Idea: Cook eggs the day before and refrigerate. They will be much easier to peel.

Prep Time: 10 minutes
Cook Time: 15 to 20 minutes

LEAN PICADILLO PIE

1½ pounds lean ground pork
½ cup chopped onion
½ cup chopped green bell pepper
1 clove garlic, minced
1 can (14½ ounces) whole tomatoes,
    undrained, cut up
¾ cup chopped dried apricots or raisins
12 pimiento-stuffed green olives, sliced
3 tablespoons chili powder
2 tablespoons chopped almonds
2 cans (14½ ounces each) chicken broth
2 cups cornmeal

Heat large nonstick skillet over medium heat; cook and stir pork, onion, bell pepper and garlic 5 minutes or until pork is lightly browned. Pour off any drippings. Stir in tomatoes, dried apricots, olives, chili powder and almonds. Cover and simmer 10 minutes. Bring chicken broth to a boil in large saucepan. Gradually stir in cornmeal; mix well. Spoon cornmeal mixture into 13×9-inch baking dish sprayed with nonstick cooking spray. Top with pork mixture. Cover with foil. Bake at 350°F for 30 minutes. Cut into squares to serve.

Makes 12 servings

Prep Time: 20 minutes
Cook Time: 30 minutes

Favorite recipe from **National Pork Producers Council**

Spinach & Egg Casserole

Breakfast & BRUNCH

SOUTH-OF-THE-BORDER QUICHE SQUARES

1 pound **BOB EVANS® Zesty Hot Roll Sausage**
1 package (8-ounces) refrigerated crescent dinner roll dough
1 cup (4 ounces) shredded Monterey Jack cheese, divided
1 cup (4 ounces) shredded Cheddar cheese, divided
½ cup diced green chiles
½ cup chopped green onions
1 cup diced fresh or drained canned tomatoes
8 eggs, beaten
1 cup half-and-half
1 cup milk
2 tablespoons Dijon mustard
1 tablespoon chopped fresh parsley
½ teaspoon chili powder

Preheat oven to 350°F. Crumble and cook sausage in medium skillet over medium heat until browned. Drain well on paper towels. Unroll dough and press perforations together. Press dough on bottom and 1 inch up sides of greased 13×9×2-inch baking pan. Bake 8 minutes or until light golden. Remove from oven; sprinkle with half of cheeses. Top with chiles, onions, tomatoes, sausage and remaining cheeses. Blend eggs, half-and-half, milk, mustard, parsley and chili powder in medium bowl. Pour mixture evenly over cheese layer. Bake 25 to 30 minutes or until set. Cool 5 minutes before cutting into 8 pieces. Serve hot. Refrigerate leftovers.   *Makes 8 servings*

SPAGHETTI & EGG CASSEROLE

12 ounces uncooked spaghetti
3 tablespoons **FILIPPO BERIO® Olive Oil**
¾ cup sliced onion
4 eggs, beaten
3 tablespoons grated Parmesan cheese
Additional grated Parmesan cheese (optional)
Additional beaten egg (optional)

Preheat oven to 350°F. Cook pasta according to package directions until al dente (tender but still firm). Drain. Meanwhile, in medium skillet, heat olive oil over medium heat until hot. Add onion; cook and stir 5 minutes or until softened. Remove with slotted spoon to large bowl. When oil is cool, grease 9-inch square baking pan with a portion of oil from skillet.

Add 4 beaten eggs and 3 tablespoons Parmesan cheese to onion; mix well. Add pasta; toss until lightly coated. Pour into prepared pan. Bake 10 to 20 minutes or until egg mixture is firm.

Sprinkle with additional Parmesan cheese or brush with additional beaten egg, if desired. Broil, 4 to 5 inches from heat, until golden brown.

Makes 6 servings

South-of-the-Border Quiche Squares

Breakfast & BRUNCH

VEGETABLE MEDLEY QUICHE

Nonstick cooking spray
2 cups frozen diced potatoes with onions and peppers, thawed
1 can (10¾ ounces) condensed cream of mushroom soup, divided
1 package (16 ounces) frozen mixed vegetables (such as zucchini, carrots and beans), thawed and drained
4 eggs, beaten
½ cup grated Parmesan cheese, divided
¼ cup reduced-fat (2%) milk
¼ teaspoon dried dill weed
¼ teaspoon dried thyme
¼ teaspoon dried oregano
Dash of salt and pepper

Spray 9-inch pie plate with cooking spray; press potatoes onto bottom and side to form crust. Spray potatoes lightly with cooking spray. Bake at 400°F 15 minutes.

Combine half of soup, mixed vegetables, eggs and cheese in small bowl; mix well. Pour egg mixture into potato shell; sprinkle with remaining cheese. Bake at 375°F 35 to 40 minutes or until set.

Combine remaining soup, milk and seasonings in small saucepan; mix well. Simmer 5 minutes until heated through. Serve sauce with quiche.

Makes 6 servings

SPAM™ HASH BROWN BAKE

1 (32-ounce) package frozen hash brown potatoes, thawed slightly
½ cup butter or margarine, melted
1 teaspoon salt
1 teaspoon black pepper
½ teaspoon garlic powder
2 cups (8 ounces) shredded Cheddar cheese
1 (12-ounce) can SPAM® Luncheon Meat, cubed
1 (10¾-ounce) can cream of chicken soup
1½ cups sour cream
½ cup milk
½ cup chopped onion
1 (4.25-ounce) jar CHI-CHI'S® Diced Green Chilies, drained
2 cups crushed potato chips

Heat oven to 350°F. In large bowl, combine potatoes, melted butter, salt, pepper and garlic powder. In separate large bowl, combine cheese, SPAM®, soup, sour cream, milk, onion and green chilies. Add SPAM™ mixture to potato mixture; mix well. Pour into 2-quart baking dish. Sprinkle with potato chips. Bake 45 to 60 minutes or until thoroughly heated.

Makes 8 servings

Vegetable Medley Quiche

Breakfast &
BRUNCH

FRENCH TOAST STRATA

**4 ounces day-old French or Italian bread,
cut into ¾-inch cubes (4 cups)**
⅓ cup golden raisins
**1 package (3 ounces) cream cheese, cut into
¼-inch cubes**
3 eggs
1½ cups milk
½ cup maple-flavored pancake syrup
1 teaspoon vanilla
2 tablespoons sugar
1 teaspoon ground cinnamon
**Additional maple-flavored pancake syrup
(optional)**

Spray 11×7-inch baking dish with nonstick cooking
spray. Place bread cubes in even layer in prepared
dish; sprinkle raisins and cream cheese evenly over
bread.

Beat eggs in medium bowl with electric mixer at
medium speed until blended. Add milk, ½ cup
pancake syrup and vanilla; mix well. Pour egg mixture
evenly over bread mixture. Cover; refrigerate at least
4 hours or overnight.

Preheat oven to 350°F. Combine sugar and
cinnamon in small bowl; sprinkle evenly over strata.

Bake, uncovered, 40 to 45 minutes or until puffed,
golden brown and knife inserted in center comes out
clean. Cut into squares and serve with additional
pancake syrup, if desired.   *Makes 6 servings*

LIT'L LINKS SOUFFLÉ

8 slices white bread
2 cups (8 ounces) shredded Cheddar cheese
1 pound HILLSHIRE FARM® Lit'l Polskas
6 eggs
2¾ cups milk
¾ teaspoon dry mustard

Spread bread in bottom of greased 13×9-inch
baking pan. Sprinkle cheese over top of bread.

Arrange Lit'l Polskas on top of cheese. Beat eggs
with milk and mustard in large bowl; pour over links.
Cover pan with aluminum foil; refrigerate overnight.

Preheat oven to 300°F. Bake egg mixture 1½ hours
or until puffy and brown.   *Makes 4 to 6 servings*

French Toast Strata

SAVORY BREAD PUDDING

**8 slices day-old, thick-cut white bread,
   crusts trimmed**
**2 tablespoons unsalted butter substitute,
   softened**
**2 cups (8 ounces) shredded ALPINE LACE®
   Reduced Fat Swiss Cheese, divided**
1 cup grated peeled apple
½ cup egg substitute or 2 large eggs
2 large egg whites
2 cups low fat 2% milk
½ teaspoon salt
¼ teaspoon freshly ground black pepper

1. Preheat the oven to 400°F. Spray a 13×9×2-inch rectangular or 3-quart oval baking dish with nonstick cooking spray. Thinly spread the bread slices with the butter. Cut each bread slice into 4 triangles, making a total of 32. In a small bowl, toss 1¾ cups of the cheese with the grated apple.

2. In a medium-size bowl, using an electric mixer set on high, beat the egg substitute (or the whole eggs), the egg whites, milk, salt and pepper together until frothy and light yellow.

3. To assemble the pudding: Line the bottom of the dish with 16 of the bread triangles. Cover with the apple-cheese mixture, then pour over half the egg mixture. Arrange the remaining 16 triangles around the edge and down the center of the dish, overlapping slightly as you go.

4. Pour the remaining egg mixture over the top, then sprinkle with the remaining ¼ cup of cheese. Bake, uncovered, for 35 minutes or until crisp and golden brown. *Makes 8 servings*

Food Fact

**Eggs function as a thickener for cooked foods,
such as custards, puddings, quiches and sauces.**

Savory Bread Pudding

CHILES RELLENOS EN CASSEROLE

3 eggs, separated
¾ cup milk
¾ cup all-purpose flour
½ teaspoon salt
1 tablespoon butter or margarine
½ cup chopped onion
8 peeled roasted Anaheim chiles *or* 2 cans (7 ounces each) whole green chiles, drained
8 ounces Monterey Jack cheese, cut into 8 slices

CONDIMENTS
    Sour cream
    Sliced green onions
    Pitted black olive slices
    Guacamole
    Salsa

Preheat oven to 350°F. Place egg yolks, milk, flour and salt in blender or food processor; process until smooth. Pour into bowl and let stand. Melt butter in small skillet over medium heat. Add onion; cook until tender. If using canned chiles, pat dry with paper towels. Slit each chile lengthwise and carefully remove seeds. Place 1 strip cheese and 1 tablespoon onion in each chile; reshape chiles to cover cheese. Place 2 chiles in each of 4 greased 1½-cup gratin dishes or place in single layer in 13×9-inch baking dish. Beat egg whites until soft peaks form; fold into yolk mixture. Dividing mixture evenly, pour over chiles in gratin dishes (or pour entire mixture over casserole).

Bake 20 to 25 minutes or until topping is puffed and knife inserted in center comes out clean. Broil 4 inches below heat 30 seconds or until topping is golden brown. Serve with condiments.

Makes 4 servings

BRUNCH STRATA

1 can (10¾ ounces) condensed cream of celery soup
8 eggs, beaten
1 cup reduced-fat (2%) milk
1 can (4 ounces) sliced mushrooms
¼ cup sliced green onions
1 teaspoon dry mustard
½ teaspoon salt
¼ teaspoon black pepper
    Nonstick cooking spray
6 slices white bread, cut into 1-inch cubes
4 links precooked breakfast sausage, thinly sliced

Combine soup, eggs, milk, mushrooms, green onions, mustard, salt and pepper in medium bowl; mix well. Spray 2-quart baking dish with cooking spray, combine bread cubes, sausage and soup mixture; toss to coat. Bake at 350°F 30 to 35 minutes or until set.

Makes 6 servings

Brunch Strata

CHILI CHEESE PUFF

¾ cup all-purpose flour
1½ teaspoons baking powder
9 eggs
1 pound (16 ounces) shredded Monterey Jack cheese
2 cups (16 ounces) 1% cottage cheese
2 cans (4 ounces each) diced green chilies, drained
1½ teaspoons sugar
¼ teaspoon salt
⅛ teaspoon hot pepper sauce
1 cup salsa

Preheat oven to 350°F. Spray 13×9-inch baking dish with nonstick cooking spray.

Combine flour and baking powder in small bowl.

Whisk eggs in large bowl until blended; add Monterey Jack cheese, cottage cheese, chilies, sugar, salt and hot pepper sauce. Add flour mixture; stir just until combined. Pour into prepared dish.

Bake, uncovered, 45 minutes or until egg mixture is set. Let stand 5 minutes before serving. Serve with salsa. *Makes 8 servings*

RANCH QUICHE LORRAINE

2 cups crushed butter-flavored crackers
6 tablespoons butter or margarine, melted
2 cups shredded Swiss cheese
4 eggs
2 cups heavy cream
1 package (1.2 ounces) **HIDDEN VALLEY®** Original **Ranch®** with Bacon salad dressing mix
1 tablespoon dehydrated minced onion

Preheat oven to 375°F. In medium bowl, combine crackers and butter. Press crumb mixture evenly into 10-inch pie pan or quiche dish. Bake until golden, about 7 minutes. Remove and cool pan on wire rack.

Increase oven temperature to 425°F. Sprinkle cheese over cooled pie crust. In medium bowl, whisk eggs until frothy. Add cream, salad dressing mix and onion. Pour egg mixture over cheese. Bake 15 minutes. *Reduce temperature to 350°F.* Continue baking until knife inserted in center comes out clean. Cool on wire rack 10 minutes before slicing. *Makes 8 servings*

Chili Cheese Puff

DENVER SPOONBREAD

3 tablespoons butter or margarine, divided
2 tablespoons grated Parmesan cheese
½ cup chopped onion
¼ cup chopped green bell pepper
¼ cup chopped red bell pepper
2½ cups milk
1 cup yellow cornmeal
1 teaspoon salt
1½ cups (6 ounces) shredded Cheddar cheese
4 eggs, separated*

*Egg whites must be free from any yolk to reach proper volume when beaten.

1. Preheat oven to 350°F.

2. Grease 1½-quart soufflé dish with 1 tablespoon butter. Sprinkle bottom and side of dish evenly with Parmesan cheese.

3. Melt remaining 2 tablespoons butter in medium heavy saucepan over medium heat. Add onion and bell peppers; cook 5 to 7 minutes or until tender, stirring occasionally. Transfer mixture to small bowl; set aside.

4. Combine milk, cornmeal and salt in same saucepan. Bring to a boil over high heat. Reduce heat to medium; cook and stir 5 minutes or until mixture thickens. Remove from heat. Stir in Cheddar cheese until melted. Stir in onion mixture.

5. Beat egg whites in clean large bowl with electric mixer at high speed until stiff but not dry; set aside.

6. Beat egg yolks in separate large bowl. Stir into cornmeal mixture. Stir ⅓ of egg whites into cornmeal mixture. Fold remaining egg whites into cornmeal mixture until blended. Pour into prepared soufflé dish.

7. Bake about 50 minutes or until puffed and golden brown. Serve immediately. Garnish, if desired.

Makes 6 servings

Cook's Tip

When onions are cut, they release sulfur compounds that bring tears to the eyes. Try chewing on a piece of bread while peeling and chopping onions to help minimize the tears.

Denver Spoonbread

SPINACH AND CHEESE BRUNCH SQUARES

1 box (11 ounces) pie crust mix
⅓ cup cold water
1 package (10 ounces) frozen chopped spinach, thawed and well drained
1⅓ cups FRENCH'S® French Fried Onions
1 cup (4 ounces) shredded Swiss cheese
1 container (8 ounces) low-fat sour cream
5 eggs
1 cup milk
1 tablespoon FRENCH'S® Deli Brown Mustard
½ teaspoon salt
⅛ teaspoon ground black pepper

Preheat oven to 450°F. Line 13×9×2-inch baking pan with foil; spray with nonstick cooking spray. Combine pie crust mix and water in large bowl until moistened and crumbly. Using floured bottom of measuring cup, press mixture firmly into bottom of prepared pan. Prick with fork. Bake 20 minutes or until golden. *Reduce oven temperature to 350°F.*

Layer spinach, French Fried Onions and cheese over crust. Combine sour cream, eggs, milk, mustard, salt and pepper in medium bowl; mix until well blended. Pour over vegetable and cheese layers. Bake 30 minutes or until knife inserted in center comes out clean. Let stand 10 minutes. Cut into squares to serve. *Makes 8 main-course servings*

Prep Time: 20 minutes
Cook Time: 50 minutes
Stand Time: 10 minutes

ENCHILADA BREAKFAST SPAM™ CASSEROLE

8 (8-inch) flour tortillas
1 (12-ounce) can SPAM® Luncheon Meat, cubed
1 cup chopped onions
1 cup chopped green bell pepper
1 tomato, chopped
2 cups (8 ounces) shredded Cheddar cheese, divided
4 eggs
2 cups whipping cream
1 (4.25-ounce) jar CHI-CHI'S® Diced Green Chilies
CHI-CHI'S® Picante Sauce

In center of each tortilla, place about ¼ cup SPAM®, 1 tablespoon onion, 1 tablespoon bell pepper, 1 tablespoon tomato and 1 tablespoon cheese. Roll up tightly. Repeat procedure to make 8 enchiladas. Place enchiladas seam side down in greased 13×9-inch baking dish. In medium bowl, beat together eggs, cream and green chilies. Pour over enchiladas. Cover. Refrigerate overnight. Heat oven to 350°F. Bake, uncovered, 40 to 50 minutes or until egg mixture is set. Sprinkle with remaining cheese. Bake 5 minutes longer or until cheese is melted. Serve with picante sauce. *Makes 8 servings*

Spinach and Cheese Brunch Square

Breakfast &
BRUNCH

HAM & CHEESE GRITS SOUFFLÉ

3 cups water
¾ cup quick-cooking grits
½ teaspoon salt
½ cup (2 ounces) shredded mozzarella cheese
2 ounces ham, finely chopped
2 tablespoons minced chives
2 eggs, separated
   Dash hot pepper sauce

1. Preheat oven to 375°F. Grease 1½-quart soufflé dish or deep casserole.

2. Bring water to a boil in medium saucepan. Stir in grits and salt. Cook, stirring frequently, about 5 minutes or until thickened. Stir in cheese, ham, chives, egg yolks and hot pepper sauce.

3. In small clean bowl, beat egg whites until stiff but not dry; fold into grits mixture. Pour into prepared dish. Bake about 30 minutes or until puffed and golden. Serve immediately.   *Makes 4 to 6 servings*

SAUSAGE AND CHEESE POTATO CASSEROLE

1 pound BOB EVANS® Italian Roll Sausage
4 cups cubed unpeeled red skin potatoes
1 cup (4 ounces) shredded Monterey Jack cheese
¼ cup chopped green onions
1 (4-ounce) can chopped green chiles, drained
6 eggs
¾ cup milk
¼ teaspoon salt
⅛ teaspoon black pepper
½ cup grated Parmesan cheese

Preheat oven to 350°F. Crumble and cook sausage in medium skillet until browned. Drain off any drippings. Spread potatoes in greased 13×9-inch baking pan. Top with cooked sausage, Monterey Jack cheese, green onions and chiles. Whisk eggs, milk, salt and pepper in medium bowl until frothy. Pour egg mixture over sausage layer; bake 30 minutes. Remove from oven. Sprinkle with Parmesan cheese; bake 15 minutes more or until eggs are set. Refrigerate leftovers.

Makes 6 to 8 servings

ASPARAGUS FRITTATA CASSEROLE

3 large eggs
1½ cups 1% milk
1 teaspoon salt
1 box (10 ounces) BIRDS EYE® frozen Deluxe
    Asparagus Spears, thawed
½ cup shredded Monterey Jack or Cheddar
    cheese

- Preheat oven to 400°F.

- In medium bowl, beat eggs. Add milk and salt; blend well.

- Pour mixture into greased 9×9-inch baking pan; top with asparagus.

- Sprinkle with cheese.

- Bake 15 minutes or until egg mixture is set.

Makes 4 servings

Prep Time: 5 to 7 minutes
Cook Time: 15 minutes

BEEF & ZUCCHINI QUICHE

1 unbaked 9-inch pie shell
½ pound lean ground beef
1 medium zucchini, shredded
3 green onions, sliced
¼ cup sliced mushrooms
1 tablespoon all-purpose flour
3 eggs, beaten
1 cup milk
¾ cup (3 ounces) shredded Swiss cheese
1½ teaspoons chopped fresh thyme or
    ½ teaspoon dried thyme leaves
½ teaspoon salt
    Dash of freshly ground black pepper
    Dash of ground red pepper

Preheat oven to 475°F.

Line pie shell with foil; fill with dried beans or rice. Bake 8 minutes. Remove from oven; carefully remove foil and beans. Return pie shell to oven. Continue baking 4 minutes; set aside. *Reduce oven temperature to 375°F.*

Brown ground beef in medium skillet. Drain. Add zucchini, onions and mushrooms; cook, stirring occasionally, until vegetables are tender. Stir in flour; cook 2 minutes, stirring constantly. Remove from heat.

Combine eggs, milk, cheese and seasonings in medium bowl. Stir into ground beef mixture; pour into crust.

Bake 35 minutes or until knife inserted near center comes out clean. *Makes 6 servings*

SAUSAGE & APPLE QUICHE

1 unbaked (9-inch) pastry shell
½ pound bulk spicy pork sausage
½ cup chopped onion
¾ cup shredded peeled tart apple
1 tablespoon lemon juice
1 tablespoon sugar
⅛ teaspoon red pepper flakes
1 cup (4 ounces) shredded Cheddar cheese
3 eggs
1½ cups half-and-half
¼ teaspoon salt
Ground black pepper

1. Preheat oven to 425°F.

2. Place piece of foil inside pastry shell; partially fill with uncooked beans or rice. Bake 10 minutes. Remove foil and beans; continue baking pastry shell 5 minutes or until lightly browned. Let cool. *Reduce oven temperature to 375°F.*

3. Crumble sausage into large skillet; add onion. Cook and stir over medium heat until meat is browned and onion is tender. Spoon off and discard pan drippings.

4. Add apple, lemon juice, sugar and red pepper to skillet. Cook and stir on medium-high heat 4 minutes or until apple is just tender and all liquid is evaporated. Let cool.

5. Spoon sausage mixture into pastry shell; top with cheese. Whisk eggs, half-and-half, salt and dash of black pepper in medium bowl. Pour over sausage mixture.

6. Bake 35 to 45 minutes or until filling is puffed and knife inserted in center comes out clean. Let stand 10 minutes before cutting.   *Makes 6 servings*

Food Fact

A quiche is a savory tart or pie with an egg custard filling. Quiches are usually flavored with cheese and sometimes meat, seafood or vegetables.

Sausage & Apple Quiche

Poultry PARADISE

CAMPBELL'S® HEALTHY REQUEST® STROGANOFF–STYLE CHICKEN

2 tablespoons vegetable oil
1 pound skinless, boneless chicken breasts, cut
   into strips
2 cups sliced mushrooms (about 6 ounces)
1 medium onion, chopped (about ½ cup)
1 can (10¾ ounces) CAMPBELL'S® HEALTHY
   REQUEST® Condensed Cream of Chicken
   Soup
½ cup plain nonfat yogurt
¼ cup water
4 cups hot cooked medium egg noodles (about
   3 cups uncooked), cooked without salt
Paprika

1. In medium skillet over medium-high heat, heat **half** the oil. Add chicken in 2 batches and cook until browned, stirring often. Set chicken aside.

2. Reduce heat to medium. Add remaining oil. Add mushrooms and onion and cook until tender.

3. Add soup, yogurt and water. Heat to a boil. Return chicken to pan and heat through. Serve over noodles. Sprinkle with paprika. *Makes 4 servings*

Left:
Campbell's® Healthy Request® Stroganoff-Style Chicken

Above: *Turkey and Biscuit (page 100)*

ARTICHOKE–OLIVE CHICKEN BAKE

1½ cups uncooked rotini pasta
1 tablespoon olive oil
1 medium onion, chopped
½ green bell pepper, chopped
2 cups shredded cooked chicken
1 can (14½ ounces) diced tomatoes with Italian-style herbs, undrained
1 can (14 ounces) artichoke hearts, drained and quartered
1 can (6 ounces) sliced black olives, drained
1 teaspoon dried Italian seasoning
2 cups (8 ounces) shredded mozzarella cheese

Preheat oven to 350°F. Spray 2-quart round casserole with nonstick cooking spray.

Cook pasta according to package directions. Drain and set aside.

Meanwhile, heat oil in large deep skillet over medium heat until hot. Add onion and pepper; cook and stir 1 minute. Add chicken, tomatoes with juice, pasta, artichokes, olives and Italian seasoning; mix until combined.

Place half of chicken mixture in prepared dish; sprinkle with half of cheese. Top with remaining chicken mixture and cheese.

Bake, covered, 35 minutes or until hot and bubbly.

Makes 8 servings

CHICKEN À LA KING

1 pound boneless skinless chicken breasts, cut into strips
2 tablespoons butter or margarine
1 jar (12 ounces) home-style chicken gravy
1 package (10 ounces) frozen green peas
1 cup milk
1 jar (4½ ounces) sliced mushrooms, drained
2 tablespoons dry sherry (optional)
½ teaspoon salt
⅛ teaspoon pepper
1½ cups MINUTE® White Rice, uncooked
1 jar (4 ounces) pimiento pieces

COOK and stir chicken in hot butter in large skillet until lightly browned.

ADD gravy, peas, milk, mushrooms, sherry, salt and pepper. Bring to boil. Reduce heat; cover. Simmer 2 minutes. Return to full boil.

STIR in rice and pimiento; cover. Remove from heat. Let stand 5 minutes. Fluff with fork.

Makes 4 servings

Artichoke-Olive Chicken Bake

CHICKEN POT PIE

1 can (14½ ounces) chicken broth
½ teaspoon salt
¼ teaspoon black pepper
1 to 1½ cups 2% milk
3 tablespoons margarine or butter
1 medium onion, chopped
1 cup sliced celery
⅓ cup all-purpose flour
2 cups diced, cooked chicken
2 cups frozen mixed vegetables (broccoli, carrots and cauliflower combination), thawed
½ teaspoon dried thyme leaves
1 tablespoon chopped fresh parsley or 1 teaspoon dried parsley
1 (9-inch) refrigerated pastry crust
1 egg, slightly beaten

Pour chicken broth, salt and pepper into glass measure; add enough milk to equal 2½ cups.

Melt margarine in large saucepan over medium heat. Add onion and celery. Cook and stir 3 minutes. Stir in flour until well blended. Gradually stir in broth mixture. Cook, stirring constantly, until sauce thickens and boils. Add chicken, vegetables, thyme and parsley. Pour into 1½-quart deep casserole.

Preheat oven to 400°F. Roll out pastry 1 inch larger than diameter of casserole on lightly floured surface. Cut slits in pastry for venting steam. Place pastry on top of casserole. Roll edges and cut away extra pastry; flute edges. Reroll scraps to cut into decorative designs. Place on top of pastry. Brush pastry with beaten egg. Bake about 30 minutes until crust is golden brown and filling is bubbling.

Makes 4 servings

Food Fact

The term *poultry* refers to any domesticated bird raised for its eggs or meat. Chicken, turkey, capon, game hen, duck and goose are all examples.

Chicken Pot Pie

CHICKEN MARENGO

2 tablespoons olive or vegetable oil
2½ to 3 pounds skinned frying chicken pieces
   or 1½ pounds boneless, skinless chicken
   breast halves
½ cup chopped onion
½ cup chopped green bell pepper
½ cup sliced fresh mushrooms
1 clove garlic, minced
1 can (14½ ounces) **CONTADINA®** Diced
   Tomatoes, undrained
1 can (6 ounces) **CONTADINA®** Tomato
   Paste
½ cup dry red wine
½ cup chicken broth
1 teaspoon Italian herb seasoning
½ teaspoon salt
⅛ teaspoon ground black pepper

1. Heat oil in large skillet. Add chicken; cook until browned on all sides. Remove chicken from skillet, reserving any drippings in skillet.

2. Add onion, bell pepper, mushrooms and garlic to skillet; sauté for 5 minutes.

3. Add tomatoes and juice, tomato paste, wine, broth, Italian seasoning, salt and black pepper. Return chicken to skillet. Bring to a boil. Reduce heat to low; cover.

4. Cook for 30 to 40 minutes or until chicken is no longer pink in center. Serve over hot cooked rice or pasta, if desired.   *Makes 6 servings*

Note: Red wine can be omitted. Increase chicken broth to 1 cup.

Prep Time: 10 minutes
Cook Time: 50 minutes

CHICKEN WITH ZUCCHINI AND TOMATOES

8 broiler-fryer chicken thighs, boned,
   skinned
1 tablespoon olive oil
2 small zucchini, cut in ¼-inch slices
1 can (14½ ounces) stewed tomatoes
½ teaspoon Italian seasoning
¼ teaspoon salt
⅛ teaspoon pepper

In large skillet, heat oil over medium-high heat. Add chicken and cook, turning, 10 minutes or until browned. Drain off excess fat. Add zucchini, tomatoes, Italian seasoning, salt and pepper. Reduce heat to medium-low; cover and cook about 10 minutes more or until chicken is no longer pink in center and zucchini is tender.   *Makes 4 servings*

Favorite recipe from **Delmarva Poultry Industry, Inc.**

Chicken Marengo

CHICKEN TETRAZZINI

8 ounces vermicelli or other thin noodles
2 teaspoons butter or margarine
8 ounces fresh mushrooms, sliced
¼ cup chopped green onions
1 can (14½ ounces) fat-free reduced-sodium
chicken broth
1 cup low-fat (1%) milk, divided
2 tablespoons dry sherry
¼ cup all-purpose flour
¼ teaspoon ground nutmeg
¼ teaspoon salt
⅛ teaspoon white pepper
1 jar (2 ounces) chopped pimiento, drained
4 tablespoons grated Parmesan cheese,
divided
½ cup reduced-fat sour cream
2 cups cooked skinless chicken breasts, cut
into bite-sized pieces

1. Preheat oven to 350°F. Cook noodles according to package directions. Drain; set aside.

2. Melt margarine in large nonstick skillet over medium-high heat. Add mushrooms and onions; cook and stir until onions are tender. Add chicken broth, ½ cup milk and sherry to onion mixture. Pour remaining ½ cup milk into small jar with tight-fitting lid; add flour, nutmeg, salt and pepper. Shake well. Slowly stir flour mixture into skillet. Bring to a boil; cook 1 minute. Reduce heat; stir in pimiento and 2 tablespoons Parmesan cheese. Stir in sour cream; blend well. Add chicken and noodles; mix well.

3. Lightly coat 1½-quart casserole with nonstick cooking spray. Spread mixture evenly into prepared casserole. Sprinkle with remaining 2 tablespoons Parmesan cheese. Bake 30 to 35 minutes until hot. Let cool slightly before serving.   *Makes 6 servings*

CREAMY CHICKEN BROCCOLI BAKE

4 boneless skinless chicken breast halves
(about 1¼ pounds), cubed
1½ cups MINUTE® White Rice, uncooked
1¼ cups milk
1 package (10 ounces) frozen chopped
broccoli, thawed, drained
½ pound (8 ounces) VELVEETA® Process
Cheese Spread, cut up
½ cup MIRACLE WHIP® or MIRACLE
WHIP LIGHT® Dressing

MIX all ingredients.

SPOON into 12×8-inch baking dish.

BAKE at 375°F for 30 minutes or until chicken is cooked through.   *Makes 6 servings*

Prep Time: 15 minutes
Bake Time: 30 minutes

Chicken Tetrazzini

CHICKEN & VEGETABLE TORTILLA ROLL-UPS

1 pound boneless skinless chicken breasts, cooked
1 cup chopped broccoli
1 cup diced carrots
1 can (10¾ ounces) condensed cream of celery soup
¼ cup reduced-fat (2%) milk
1 tablespoon dry sherry
½ cup grated Parmesan cheese
6 (10-inch) flour tortillas

Preheat oven to 350°F. Cut chicken into 1-inch pieces; set aside.

Combine broccoli and carrots in 1-quart microwavable dish. Cover and microwave at HIGH 2 to 3 minutes or until vegetables are crisp-tender; set aside.

Combine soup, milk and sherry in small saucepan over medium heat; cook and stir 5 minutes. Stir in Parmesan cheese, chicken, broccoli and carrots; season to taste with salt and pepper. Cook 2 minutes or until cheese is melted. Remove from heat.

Spoon ¼ cup chicken mixture onto each tortilla. Roll up and place seam side down in 13×9-inch baking dish coated with nonstick cooking spray. Bake covered 20 minutes or until heated through.

Makes 6 servings

CHICKEN–MAC CASSEROLE

1½ cups elbow macaroni, cooked in unsalted water and drained
6 slices bacon, fried crisp and crumbled
2 cups (10 ounces) cubed cooked chicken
1⅓ cups FRENCH'S® French Fried Onions, divided
1 can (10¾ ounces) condensed cream of mushroom soup
1 cup sour cream
1 package (10 ounces) frozen chopped spinach, thawed and well drained
⅛ teaspoon garlic powder
1½ cups (6 ounces) shredded Cheddar cheese, divided

Preheat oven to 375°F. Return cooked macaroni to saucepan; stir in bacon, chicken and ⅔ cup French Fried Onions. In medium bowl, combine soup, sour cream, spinach, garlic powder and 1 cup Cheddar cheese. Spoon half the macaroni mixture into greased 12×8-inch baking dish; cover with half the spinach mixture. Repeat layers. Bake, covered, at 375°F for 30 minutes or until heated through. Top with remaining cheese and ⅔ cup onions. Bake, uncovered, 3 minutes or until onions are golden brown.

Makes 6 to 8 servings

Chicken & Vegetable Tortilla Roll-Ups

Poultry
PARADISE

CAMPBELL'S® NO–GUILT CHICKEN POT PIE

1 can (10¾ ounces) CAMPBELL'S®
    Condensed 98% Fat Free Cream of
    Chicken Soup
1 package (about 9 ounces) frozen mixed
    vegetables, thawed (about 2 cups)
1 cup cubed cooked chicken
½ cup milk
1 egg
1 cup reduced fat all-purpose baking mix

1. Preheat oven to 400°F. In 9-inch pie plate mix soup, vegetables and chicken.

2. Mix milk, egg and baking mix. Pour over chicken mixture. Bake 30 minutes or until golden.

Makes 4 servings

Campbell's® No-Guilt Turkey Pot Pie:
Substitute 1 cup cubed cooked turkey for chicken.

Tip: For a variation, substitute CAMPBELL'S® Condensed Cream of Chicken Soup *or* Cream of Chicken Soup with Herbs.

Prep Time: 10 minutes
Cook Time: 30 minutes

SKILLET CHICKEN CORDON BLEU

1 tablespoon butter or margarine
¾ pound boneless skinless chicken breasts,
    cut into strips
2 ounces OSCAR MAYER® Boiled Ham, cut
    into strips (about ½ cup)
1 can (10¾ ounces) condensed cream of
    chicken soup
1 package (10 ounces) frozen cut green
    beans, thawed
1 cup water
1 tablespoon Dijon mustard
1½ cups MINUTE® White Rice, uncooked
⅔ cup (about 3 ounces) KRAFT® Shredded
    Swiss Cheese

MELT butter in large skillet on medium-high heat. Add chicken and ham; cook and stir until chicken is browned.

STIR in soup, beans, water and mustard. Bring to boil.

STIR in rice; cover. Remove from heat. Let stand 5 minutes. Stir. Sprinkle with cheese; cover. Let stand 3 minutes or until cheese is melted.

Makes 4 servings

Prep Time: 10 minutes
Cook Time: 15 minutes

Campbell's® No-Guilt Chicken Pot Pie

PARADISE

CREAMY CHICKEN AND PASTA WITH SPINACH

6 ounces uncooked egg noodles
1 tablespoon olive oil
¼ cup chopped onion
¼ cup chopped red bell pepper
1 package (10 ounces) frozen spinach, thawed and drained
2 boneless skinless chicken breast halves (¾ pound), cooked and cut into 1-inch pieces
1 can (4 ounces) sliced mushrooms, drained
2 cups (8 ounces) shredded Swiss cheese
1 container (8 ounces) sour cream
¾ cup half-and-half
2 eggs, slightly beaten
½ teaspoon salt
    Red onion and fresh spinach for garnish

Preheat oven to 350°F. Prepare egg noodles according to package directions; set aside.

Heat oil in large skillet over medium-high heat. Add onion and bell pepper; cook and stir 2 minutes or until onion is tender. Add spinach, chicken, mushrooms and cooked noodles; stir to combine.

Combine cheese, sour cream, half-and-half, eggs and salt in medium bowl; blend well.

Add cheese mixture to chicken mixture; stir to combine. Pour into 13×9-inch baking dish coated with nonstick cooking spray. Bake, covered, 30 to 35 minutes or until heated through. Garnish with red onion and fresh spinach, if desired.

Makes 8 servings

Food Fact

Most pastas are prepared with wheat flours or other cereal grains and water. If an egg is added to this mix, the product is then called a noodle.

Creamy Chicken and Pasta with Spinach

Poultry
PARADISE

SPINACH QUICHE

1 medium leek
  Water
¼ cup butter or margarine
2 cups finely chopped cooked chicken
½ package (10 ounces) frozen chopped spinach or broccoli, cooked and drained
1 unbaked ready-to-use pie crust (10 inches in diameter)
1 tablespoon all-purpose flour
1½ cups (6 ounces) shredded Swiss cheese
4 eggs
1½ cups half-and-half or evaporated milk
2 tablespoons brandy (optional)
½ teaspoon salt
¼ teaspoon pepper
¼ teaspoon ground nutmeg

Preheat oven to 375°F. Cut leek in half lengthwise; wash and trim, leaving 2 to 3 inches of green tops intact. Cut leek halves crosswise into thin slices. Place in small saucepan; add enough water to cover. Bring to a boil over high heat; reduce heat and simmer 5 minutes. Drain; reserve leek.

Melt butter in large skillet over medium heat. Add chicken; cook until chicken is golden, about 5 minutes. Add spinach and leek to chicken mixture; cook 1 to 2 minutes longer. Remove from heat.

Spoon chicken mixture into pie crust. Sprinkle flour and cheese over chicken mixture. Combine eggs, half-and-half, brandy, salt, pepper and nutmeg in medium bowl. Pour egg mixture over cheese.

Bake 35 to 40 minutes or until knife inserted into center comes out clean. Let stand 5 minutes before serving. Serve hot or cold.   *Makes 6 servings*

PIZZA CHICKEN BAKE

3½ cups uncooked bow tie pasta
1 tablespoon vegetable oil
1 cup sliced mushrooms
1 jar (26 ounces) herb-flavored spaghetti sauce
1 teaspoon pizza seasoning blend
3 boneless skinless chicken breast halves (about ¾ pound), quartered
1 cup (4 ounces) shredded mozzarella cheese

Preheat oven to 350°F. Spray 2-quart round casserole with nonstick cooking spray.

Cook pasta according to package directions. Drain and place in prepared dish.

Meanwhile, heat oil in large skillet over medium-high heat until hot. Add mushrooms; cook and stir 2 minutes. Remove from heat. Stir in spaghetti sauce and pizza seasoning.

Pour half of spaghetti sauce mixture into casserole; stir until pasta is well coated. Arrange chicken on top of pasta. Pour remaining spaghetti sauce mixture evenly over chicken.

Bake, covered, 50 minutes or until chicken is no longer pink in centers. Remove from oven; sprinkle with cheese. Cover and let stand 5 minutes before serving.   *Makes 4 servings*

Pizza Chicken Bake

HOME–STYLE CHICKEN 'N BISCUITS

5 slices bacon, fried crisp and crumbled
1½ cups (7 ounces) cubed cooked chicken
1 package (10 ounces) frozen mixed vegetables, thawed and drained
1½ cups (6 ounces) shredded Cheddar cheese, divided
2 medium tomatoes, chopped (about 1 cup)
1 can (10¾ ounces) condensed cream of chicken soup
¾ cup milk
1½ cups biscuit baking mix
⅔ cup milk
1⅓ cups FRENCH'S® French Fried Onions, divided

Preheat oven to 400°F. In large bowl, combine bacon, chicken, mixed vegetables, 1 cup cheese, tomatoes, soup and ¾ cup milk. Pour chicken mixture into greased 12×8-inch baking dish. Bake, covered, at 400°F for 15 minutes. Meanwhile, in medium bowl, combine baking mix, ⅔ cup milk and ⅔ cup French Fried Onions to form soft dough. Spoon biscuit dough in 6 mounds around edges of casserole. Bake, uncovered, 15 to 20 minutes or until biscuits are golden brown. Top biscuits with remaining cheese and ⅔ cup onions; bake 1 to 3 minutes or until onions are golden brown.

Makes 6 servings

Microwave Directions: Prepare chicken mixture as directed, except reduce ¾ cup milk to ½ cup; pour into 12×8-inch microwave-safe dish. Cook, covered, on HIGH 10 minutes or until heated through. Stir chicken mixture halfway through cooking time. Prepare biscuit dough as directed. Stir casserole and spoon biscuit dough over hot chicken mixture as directed. Cook, uncovered, 7 to 8 minutes or until biscuits are done. Rotate dish halfway through cooking time. Top biscuits with remaining cheese and ⅔ cup onions; cook, uncovered, 1 minute or until cheese melts. Let stand 5 minutes.

OVEN CHICKEN & RICE

1 can (10¾ ounces) condensed cream of mushroom soup
1 cup long-grain or converted rice
1 teaspoon dried dill weed, divided
¼ teaspoon black pepper
1 (3-pound) chicken, cut up and skinned
½ cup crushed multi-grain crackers
1 teaspoon paprika
2 tablespoons butter or margarine, melted
Fresh dill sprigs for garnish

Preheat oven to 375°F. Combine soup, 1⅓ cups water, rice, ¾ teaspoon dill weed and pepper in 13×9-inch baking dish. Arrange chicken pieces on top of rice mixture. Cover tightly with foil. Bake 45 minutes.

Sprinkle chicken pieces with crackers, paprika and remaining ¼ teaspoon dill. Drizzle with butter. Bake 5 to 10 minutes or until chicken is tender. Season to taste with salt and pepper. Garnish with dill sprig, if desired.

Makes 4 to 5 servings

Oven Chicken & Rice

BROCCOLI–FILLED CHICKEN ROULADE

2 cups broccoli florets
1 tablespoon water
¼ cup fresh parsley
1 cup diced red bell pepper
4 ounces fat-free cream cheese, softened
2 tablespoons grated Parmesan cheese
2 tablespoons lemon juice
2 tablespoons olive oil
1 teaspoon paprika
¼ teaspoon salt
1 egg
½ cup fat-free (skim) milk
4 cups cornflake cereal, crushed
1 tablespoon dried basil leaves
8 boneless skinless chicken breast halves

1. Place broccoli and water in microwavable dish; cover. Microwave at HIGH 2 minutes. Let stand, covered, 2 minutes. Drain water from broccoli. Place broccoli in food processor or blender. Add parsley; process 10 seconds, scraping side of bowl if necessary. Add bell pepper, cream cheese, Parmesan cheese, lemon juice, oil, paprika and salt. Pulse 2 to 3 times or until bell pepper is minced.

2. Preheat oven to 375°F. Spray 11×7-inch baking pan with nonstick cooking spray. Lightly beat egg in small bowl. Add milk; blend well. Place cornflake crumbs in shallow bowl. Add basil; blend well.

3. Pound chicken breasts between two pieces of plastic wrap to ¼-inch thickness using flat side of meat mallet or rolling pin. Spread each chicken breast with ⅛ of the broccoli mixture, spreading to within ½ inch of edges. Roll up chicken breast from short end, tucking in sides if possible; secure with toothpicks. Dip roulades in milk mixture; roll in cornflake crumb mixture. Place in prepared baking pan. Bake 20 minutes or until chicken is no longer pink in center and juices run clear. Garnish, if desired. *Makes 8 servings*

Cook's Tip

When skinning and deboning chicken breasts, freeze the bones and skin in plastic bags; soon you will have enough to make a flavorful chicken stock.

Broccoli-Filled Chicken Roulade

CHICKEN–POTATO POT PIE

2 cans (14½ ounces each) chicken broth
1 bay leaf
½ teaspoon white pepper
2 cups cubed Colorado potatoes
1 package (16 ounces) frozen mixed
   vegetables
1 rib celery, chopped
3 tablespoons butter or margarine
3 tablespoons all-purpose flour
3 cups cubed cooked chicken
4 hard-cooked eggs, sliced
   Pastry for 9-inch pie

Combine broth, bay leaf and pepper in large Dutch oven; bring to a boil. Add potatoes; cover. Reduce heat to medium and cook 5 minutes. Add frozen vegetables and celery; return to a boil. Cover. Reduce heat and simmer 8 to 12 minutes. Remove and discard bay leaf. Drain vegetables, reserving broth. Melt butter in Dutch oven over medium heat; add flour, stirring until smooth. Cook 1 minute, stirring constantly. Gradually add reserved broth; cook and stir until mixture is thickened and bubbly. Stir in vegetables, chicken and eggs; spoon mixture into round 2½-quart casserole. Roll out pastry; place over chicken mixture. Trim edges; seal and flute. Cut slits in pastry to allow steam to escape. Bake at 400°F for 20 minutes or until hot and pastry is golden brown. *Makes 6 to 8 servings*

Favorite recipe from **Colorado Potato Administrative Committee**

CHICKEN & BISCUITS

¼ cup butter or margarine
4 boneless skinless chicken breast halves
   (about 1¼ pounds), cut into ½-inch
   pieces
½ cup chopped onion
½ teaspoon dried thyme leaves
½ teaspoon paprika
¼ teaspoon black pepper
1 can (about 14 ounces) chicken broth,
   divided
⅓ cup all-purpose flour
1 package (10 ounces) frozen peas and
   carrots
1 can (12 ounces) refrigerated biscuits

Preheat oven to 375°F. Melt butter in large skillet over medium heat. Add chicken, onion, thyme, paprika and pepper. Cook 5 minutes or until chicken is browned.

Combine ¼ cup chicken broth with flour; stir until smooth. Set aside.

Add remaining chicken broth to chicken mixture in skillet; bring to a boil. Gradually add flour mixture, stirring constantly to prevent lumps from forming. Simmer 5 minutes. Add peas and carrots; continue cooking 2 minutes.

Transfer to 1½-quart casserole; top with biscuits. Bake 25 to 30 minutes or until biscuits are golden brown. *Makes 4 to 6 servings*

Chicken & Biscuits

CLASSIC CHICKEN MARSALA

- 2 tablespoons unsalted butter
- 1 tablespoon vegetable oil
- 4 boneless skinless chicken breast halves (about 1¼ pounds)
- 4 slices mozzarella cheese (1 ounce each)
- 12 capers, drained
- 4 flat anchovy fillets, drained
- 1 tablespoon chopped fresh parsley
- 1 clove garlic, minced
- 3 tablespoons marsala wine
- ⅔ cup whipping cream
  Dash each salt and pepper
  Hot cooked pasta (optional)

Heat butter and oil in large skillet over medium-high heat until melted and bubbly. Add chicken; reduce heat to medium. Cook, uncovered, 5 to 6 minutes per side or until chicken is golden brown. Remove from heat. Top each chicken breast with 1 cheese slice, 3 capers and 1 anchovy fillet.

Return skillet to heat. Sprinkle chicken with parsley. Cover and cook over low heat 3 minutes or until cheese is almost melted and chicken is no longer pink in center. Remove chicken with slotted spatula to serving dish; keep warm.

Add garlic to drippings remaining in skillet; cook and stir over medium heat 30 seconds. Stir in wine; cook and stir 45 seconds, scraping up any brown bits in skillet. Stir in cream. Cook and stir 3 minutes or until sauce thickens slightly. Stir in salt and pepper. Spoon sauce over chicken. Serve with pasta, if desired. Garnish as desired. *Makes 4 servings*

EXOTIC APPLE–CHICKEN BAKE

- 1 cup butter, divided
- 2 Washington Winesap apples, cored and diced
- 1 large onion, diced
- ½ cup raisins
- 1 cup walnuts or almonds, coarsely chopped
- 1 can (16 ounces) apricot halves
- 1 cup bread crumbs
- 1 teaspoon salt
- ½ teaspoon each ground nutmeg, coriander, cloves and cinnamon
- 2 to 3 whole chicken breasts, split
  Flour
  Salt and pepper
  Washington Winesap apple wedges (optional)

Melt ½ cup butter in skillet. Add diced apples and onion; cook until transparent. Mix in raisins and nuts. Drain apricots; reserve syrup. Add to apple mixture with bread crumbs and seasonings; blend well. Melt remaining ½ cup butter in second skillet. Roll chicken breasts in flour; brown in butter. Spread dressing in baking dish; place chicken breasts, skin side up, on dressing. Salt and pepper lightly and cover with foil. Bake at 350°F. 20 minutes; remove foil. Bake at 250°F. 15 to 20 minutes longer. Garnish with apple wedges, if desired. *Makes 4 to 6 servings*

Favorite recipe from **Washington Apple Commission**

Classic Chicken Marsala

COUNTRY CHICKEN POT PIE

- **2 tablespoons butter or margarine**
- **¾ pound boneless skinless chicken breasts, cut into 1-inch pieces**
- **¾ teaspoon salt**
- **8 ounces fresh green beans, cut into 1-inch pieces (2 cups)**
- **½ cup chopped red bell pepper**
- **½ cup thinly sliced celery**
- **3 tablespoons all-purpose flour**
- **½ cup chicken broth**
- **½ cup half-and-half**
- **1 teaspoon dried thyme leaves**
- **½ teaspoon rubbed sage**
- **1 cup frozen pearl onions**
- **½ cup frozen corn**
- **Pastry for single-crust 10-inch pie**

Preheat oven to 425°F. Spray 10-inch deep-dish pie plate with nonstick cooking spray.

Melt butter in large deep skillet over medium-high heat. Add chicken; cook and stir 3 minutes or until no longer pink in center. Sprinkle with salt. Add beans, bell pepper and celery; cook and stir 3 minutes.

Sprinkle flour evenly over chicken and vegetables; cook and stir 1 minute. Stir in broth, half-and-half, thyme and sage; bring to a boil over high heat. Reduce heat to low and simmer 3 minutes or until sauce is very thick. Stir in onions and corn. Return to a simmer; cook and stir 1 minute.

Transfer mixture to prepared pie plate. Place pie crust over chicken mixture; turn edge under and crimp to seal. Cut 4 slits in pie crust to allow steam to escape.

Bake 20 minutes or until crust is light golden brown and mixture is hot and bubbly. Let stand 5 minutes before serving.   *Makes 6 servings*

SWISS CHICKEN & RICE

- **1 package (4.9 ounces) RICE-A-RONI® Chicken and Broccoli Flavor**
- **1 tablespoon margarine or butter**
- **4 skinless, boneless chicken breast halves, pounded to ½ inch thick**
- **1 clove garlic, minced**
- **1 tablespoon honey mustard or Dijon mustard**
- **4 slices Swiss cheese**

1. Prepare Rice-A-Roni® Mix as package directs.

2. In second large skillet, melt margarine over medium heat. Add chicken and garlic. Cook 5 minutes. Turn; cook 2 minutes.

3. Spread mustard over chicken. Top with cheese. Continue cooking 3 to 4 minutes or until chicken is no longer pink inside and cheese is melted.

4. Serve rice topped with chicken.

Makes 4 servings

Country Chicken Pot Pie

CHICKEN BREASTS DIAVOLO

6 chicken breast halves, boned, skinned and slightly flattened
½ cup finely minced fresh parsley
1 teaspoon lemon pepper seasoning
Dash salt
Dash garlic powder
3 tablespoons olive oil
3 (6-ounce) jars marinated artichoke hearts
1 tablespoon fresh lemon juice
1 (26-ounce) jar NEWMAN'S OWN® Diavolo Sauce
½ cup red wine (preferably Chianti)
1½ cups shredded mozzarella cheese
1½ cups onion-garlic flavor croutons (tossed with 1 tablespoon olive oil)
6 cups hot cooked pasta or rice

Preheat oven to 350°F. Sprinkle chicken breasts with parsley, lemon pepper seasoning, salt and garlic powder. Roll each breast, seasoned side in; secure with wooden toothpicks. Cook chicken in olive oil in large skillet until golden brown on all sides. Remove from pan with tongs and place in 13×9-inch baking dish. Carefully remove toothpicks.

Drain artichoke hearts; sprinkle with lemon juice and distribute among rolled chicken breasts.

Combine Newman's Own® Diavolo Sauce with wine; pour over chicken and artichokes. Sprinkle cheese evenly over top. Sprinkle with crouton mixture. Bake 30 to 40 minutes until golden brown and bubbly. Spoon chicken over pasta or rice.

Makes 6 servings

WALNUT CHICKEN

1 pound boneless skinless chicken thighs
3 tablespoons soy sauce
2 tablespoons minced fresh ginger
1 tablespoon cornstarch
1 tablespoon rice wine
2 cloves garlic, minced
¼ to ½ teaspoon red pepper flakes
3 tablespoons vegetable oil
½ cup walnut halves or pieces
1 cup frozen cut green beans, thawed
½ cup sliced water chestnuts
2 green onions with tops, cut into 1-inch pieces
¼ cup water
Hot cooked rice

Rinse chicken and pat dry with paper towels. Cut into 1-inch cubes. Combine soy sauce, ginger, cornstarch, wine, garlic and red pepper in large bowl; stir until smooth. Add chicken; toss. Marinate 10 minutes.

Heat wok or large skillet over high heat about 1 minute or until hot. Drizzle oil into wok and heat 30 seconds. Add walnuts; stir-fry about 1 minute or until lightly browned. Remove to small bowl. Add chicken mixture to wok; stir-fry about 5 to 7 minutes or until chicken is no longer pink in center. Add beans, water chestnuts, onions and water; stir-fry until heated through. Serve over rice. Sprinkle with walnuts.

Makes 4 servings

Walnut Chicken

CHICKEN PRIMAVERA BUFFET

12 ounces uncooked thin spaghetti
¼ cup prepared pesto
¼ cup prepared fat-free Italian salad dressing
½ teaspoon red pepper flakes
2 cups water
1 cup thinly sliced carrots
1 cup broccoli florets
1 cup snow peas
1 can (4 ounces) sliced water chestnuts, drained
Nonstick cooking spray
8 boneless skinless chicken breast halves

1. Preheat oven to 350°F. Cook pasta according to package directions; drain. Place in large bowl.

2. Combine pesto, Italian dressing and red pepper flakes in small bowl. Reserve 1 tablespoon pesto mixture. Add remaining pesto mixture to pasta; toss to coat well.

3. In large saucepan, bring water to a boil over high heat. Add carrots, broccoli and snow peas; cook 3 minutes. Drain vegetables. Add water chestnuts and vegetables to pasta; toss to blend well. Spray 13×9-inch baking pan with nonstick cooking spray. Transfer pasta and vegetables to baking pan.

4. Spray large skillet with nonstick cooking spray; heat over medium heat until hot. Add chicken; cook until browned on both sides. Cover; cook 10 minutes or until no longer pink in center and juices run clear. Place chicken on pasta and vegetables. Pour juices from skillet over chicken. Spread reserved pesto mixture over chicken. Bake 45 minutes or until heated through. *Makes 8 servings*

Food Fact

Non-egg pastas contain no cholesterol. Noodles (pasta made with eggs) are low in cholesterol.

Chicken Primavera Buffet

Poultry
PARADISE

CHICKEN 'N' RICE FILLED CABBAGE ROLLS

12 large green cabbage leaves
¾ cup chopped onion
1 clove garlic, minced
1 tablespoon vegetable oil
1 can (15 ounces) tomato sauce
½ cup water
3 tablespoons firmly packed light brown sugar
3 tablespoons fresh lemon juice
⅛ teaspoon ground allspice
3 cups finely chopped cooked chicken
1 cup cooked white rice
1 egg
¾ teaspoon salt
⅛ teaspoon black pepper

Bring 6 cups water to a boil in Dutch oven over high heat. Add cabbage leaves and reduce heat to low. Simmer, covered, 10 to 12 minutes or until cabbage leaves are tender. Drain; rinse under cold running water.

Cook and stir onion and garlic in oil in large skillet over medium heat 6 to 8 minutes or until tender. Remove ½ cup onion mixture. Add tomato sauce, ½ cup water, brown sugar, lemon juice and allspice to onion mixture in skillet. Cook, uncovered, 10 minutes, stirring occasionally.

Combine reserved onion mixture, chicken, rice, egg, salt and black pepper; mix well. Place about ⅓ cup mixture in center of each cabbage leaf. Fold sides over filling; roll up.

Preheat oven to 350°F. Spread ½ cup tomato sauce over bottom of 13×9-inch baking dish. Arrange cabbage rolls, seam side down, over sauce. Spoon remaining sauce evenly over cabbage rolls; cover. Bake 1 hour and 15 minutes or until very tender.

Makes 4 to 6 servings

SAUSAGE, SWEET POTATO AND APPLE CASSEROLE

2 sweet potatoes, peeled and cut into 1-inch cubes
2 apples, peeled, cored and cut into 1-inch cubes
1 onion, cut into ⅓-inch strips
2 tablespoons vegetable oil
1 envelope (1¼ ounces) savory herb with garlic flavor dry soup mix
1 pound HILLSHIRE FARM® Gourmet Cooked Sausage—Turkey with Scallions and Herbs, diagonally cut into ⅓-inch pieces

Preheat oven to 400°F.

Spray 13×9-inch baking pan with nonstick cooking spray. Combine potatoes, apples, onion, oil and soup mix in large bowl. Stir until evenly coated. Place potato mixture into prepared pan. Bake, covered, 30 minutes. Add Gourmet Sausage to potato mixture; bake 5 to 10 minutes or until sausage is heated through and potatoes are tender.

Makes 4 to 5 servings

Sausage, Sweet Potato and Apple Casserole

PEPPERIDGE FARM® TURKEY & STUFFING BAKE

1 can (14½ ounces) SWANSON® Chicken
    Broth (1¾ cups)
    Generous dash pepper
1 stalk celery, chopped (about ½ cup)
1 small onion, coarsely chopped (about
    ¼ cup)
4 cups PEPPERIDGE FARM® Herb
    Seasoned Stuffing
4 servings sliced roasted *or* deli turkey
    (about 12 ounces)
1 jar (12 ounces) FRANCO-AMERICAN®
    Slow Roast™ Turkey Gravy

1. In medium saucepan mix broth, pepper, celery and onion. Over high heat, heat to a boil. Reduce heat to low. Cover and cook 5 minutes or until vegetables are tender. Add stuffing. Mix lightly.

2. Spoon into 2-quart shallow baking dish. Arrange turkey over stuffing. Pour gravy over turkey.

3. Bake at 350°F. for 30 minutes or until hot.

Makes 4 servings

Tip: For a variation, add ½ cup chopped nuts with the stuffing.

Prep Time: 15 minutes
Cook Time: 30 minutes

WILD RICE COUNTRY CASSEROLE

1 cup chopped onion
¼ cup butter or margarine
1¼ pounds ground turkey
¼ teaspoon black pepper
4 cups frozen potatoes O'Brien with onions
    and peppers, thawed
3 cups cooked wild rice
2 cups shredded mild Cheddar cheese,
    divided
1 can (10¾ ounces) condensed cream of
    chicken soup
1 cup sour cream
⅓ cup bread crumbs

Preheat oven to 350°F. In large skillet, sauté onion in butter; remove from skillet. In same skillet, brown turkey. Sprinkle with pepper. Spread potatoes in greased 13×9-inch baking pan. Combine onion, turkey, wild rice, 1½ cups cheese, soup and sour cream in large bowl. Spread onion mixture over potatoes. Sprinkle remaining ½ cup cheese and bread crumbs on top. Bake 40 minutes.

Makes 8 servings

Favorite recipe from **Minnesota Cultivated Wild Rice Council**

Pepperidge Farm® Turkey & Stuffing Bake

TURNIP SHEPHERD'S PIE

1 pound small turnips,* peeled and cut into
   ½-inch cubes
1 pound lean ground turkey
⅓ cup dry bread crumbs
¼ cup chopped onion
¼ cup ketchup
1 egg
½ teaspoon salt
½ teaspoon pepper
½ teaspoon beau monde seasoning
⅓ cup half-and-half
1 tablespoon butter or margarine
   Salt and pepper
1 tablespoon chopped fresh parsley
¼ cup shredded sharp Cheddar cheese

*For Rutabaga Shepherd's Pie, use 1 pound rutabagas in place of
turnips.

Preheat oven to 400°F. Place turnips in large saucepan; cover with water. Cover and bring to a boil; reduce heat to medium-low. Simmer 20 minutes or until fork-tender.

Mix turkey, crumbs, onion, ketchup, egg, salt, pepper and seasoning. Pat on bottom and side of 9-inch pie pan. Bake 20 to 30 minutes until turkey is no longer pink. Blot with paper towel to remove any drippings.

Drain turnips. Beat turnips with electric mixer until smooth, blending in half-and-half and butter. Season to taste with salt and pepper. Fill turkey shell with turnip mixture; sprinkle with parsley and cheese. Bake until cheese melts. Garnish as desired.

Makes 4 main-dish servings

Cook's Tip

Avoid cooking turnips or turnip greens in aluminum or iron pans; the metal may darken the flesh of the turnips or impart a metallic flavor to the greens.

Turnip Shepherd's Pie

CAMPBELL'S® TURKEY ASPARAGUS GRATIN

1 can (10¾ ounces) CAMPBELL'S®
  Condensed Cream of Asparagus Soup
½ cup milk
¼ teaspoon onion powder
⅛ teaspoon pepper
3 cups hot cooked corkscrew macaroni
  (about 2½ cups uncooked)
1½ cups cubed cooked turkey *or* chicken
1½ cups cooked cut asparagus
1 cup shredded Cheddar *or* Swiss cheese
  (4 ounces)

1. In 2-quart casserole mix soup, milk, onion powder and pepper. Stir in macaroni, turkey, asparagus and *½ cup* cheese.

2. Bake at 400°F. for 25 minutes or until hot.

3. Stir. Sprinkle remaining cheese over turkey mixture. Bake 5 minutes more or until cheese is melted. *Makes 4 servings*

Tip: For 1½ cups cooked cut asparagus, cook ¾ pound fresh asparagus, trimmed and cut into 1-inch pieces *or* 1 package (about 9 ounces) frozen asparagus cuts.

Prep Time: 20 minutes
Cook Time: 30 minutes

TURKEY-TORTILLA BAKE

9 (6-inch) corn tortillas
½ pound lean ground turkey
½ cup chopped onion
¾ cup mild or medium taco sauce
1 can (4 ounces) chopped green chilies,
  drained
½ cup frozen corn, thawed
½ cup (2 ounces) shredded reduced-fat
  Cheddar cheese

1. Preheat oven to 400°F. Place tortillas on large baking sheet, overlapping tortillas as little as possible. Bake 4 minutes; turn tortillas. Continue baking 2 minutes or until crisp. Cool completely on wire rack.

2. Heat medium nonstick skillet over medium heat until hot. Add turkey and onion. Cook and stir 5 minutes or until turkey is browned and onion is tender. Add taco sauce, chilies and corn. Reduce heat and simmer 5 minutes.

3. Break 3 tortillas and arrange over bottom of 1½-quart casserole. Spoon half the turkey mixture over tortillas; sprinkle with half the cheese. Repeat layers. Bake 10 minutes or until cheese is melted and casserole is heated through. Break remaining tortillas and sprinkle over casserole. Garnish with sour cream, if desired. *Makes 4 servings*

Prep and Cook Time: 30 minutes

Turkey-Tortilla Bake

CAMPBELL'S® COUNTRY TURKEY CASSEROLE

1 can (10¾ ounces) CAMPBELL'S® Condensed Cream of Celery Soup *or* 98% Fat Free Cream of Celery Soup
1 can (10¾ ounces) CAMPBELL'S® Condensed Cream of Potato Soup
1 cup milk
¼ teaspoon dried thyme leaves, crushed
⅛ teaspoon pepper
4 cups cooked cut-up vegetables*
2 cups cubed cooked turkey *or* chicken
4 cups prepared PEPPERIDGE FARM® Herb Seasoned Stuffing

Use a combination of green beans cut into 1-inch pieces and sliced carrots.

1. In 3-quart shallow baking dish mix soups, milk, thyme, pepper, vegetables and turkey. Spoon stuffing over turkey mixture.

2. Bake at 400°F. for 25 minutes or until hot.

Makes 5 servings

Tip: For prepared stuffing, heat 1¼ cups water and 4 tablespoons margarine **or** butter to a boil. Remove from heat and add 4 cups PEPPERIDGE FARM® Herb Seasoned Stuffing. Mix lightly.

Prep Time: 20 minutes
Cook Time: 25 minutes

WILD RICE TURKEY CASSEROLE

3 cups cooked wild rice
1¼ pounds turkey breast, cooked and chopped
2 boxes (10 ounces each) cut green beans, thawed
1½ cups shredded Cheddar cheese
1 can (10½ ounces) cream of celery soup
1 cup milk
1 teaspoon poultry seasoning
1 teaspoon salt
½ teaspoon ground red pepper
½ teaspoon black pepper
3 cups mashed potatoes

Preheat oven to 350°F. In large bowl, combine all ingredients except potatoes. Spread into 13×9-inch pan. Spread potatoes over top. Bake 45 minutes or until browned.

Makes 8 servings

Favorite recipe from **Minnesota Cultivated Wild Rice Council**

Campbell's® Country Turkey Casserole

TURKEY MEATBALL & OLIVE CASSEROLE

2 cups uncooked rotini pasta
½ pound ground turkey
¼ cup dry bread crumbs
1 egg, slightly beaten
2 teaspoons dried minced onion
2 teaspoons white wine Worcestershire sauce
½ teaspoon dried Italian seasoning
½ teaspoon salt
⅛ teaspoon black pepper
1 tablespoon vegetable oil
1 can (10¾ ounces) condensed cream of celery soup, undiluted
½ cup low-fat plain yogurt
¾ cup pimiento-stuffed green olives, sliced
3 tablespoons Italian-style bread crumbs
1 tablespoon butter or margarine, melted
Paprika (optional)

Preheat oven to 350°F. Spray 2-quart round casserole with nonstick cooking spray.

Cook pasta according to package directions. Drain and set aside.

Meanwhile, combine turkey, bread crumbs, egg, onion, Worcestershire, Italian seasoning, salt and pepper in medium bowl. Shape mixture into ½-inch meatballs.

Heat oil in medium skillet over high heat until hot. Add meatballs in single layer; cook until lightly browned on all sides and still pink in centers, turning frequently. *Do not overcook.* Remove from skillet; drain on paper towels.

Mix soup and yogurt in large bowl. Add pasta, meatballs and olives; stir gently to combine. Transfer to prepared dish.

Combine bread crumbs and butter in small bowl; sprinkle evenly over casserole. Sprinkle lightly with paprika, if desired.

Bake, covered, 30 minutes. Uncover and bake 12 minutes or until meatballs are no longer pink in centers and casserole is hot and bubbly.

Makes 6 to 8 servings

Turkey Meatball & Olive Casserole

CAMPBELL'S® EASY TURKEY & BISCUITS

1 can (10¾ ounces) CAMPBELL'S®
    Condensed Cream of Celery Soup *or*
    98% Fat Free Cream of Celery Soup
1 can (10¾ ounces) CAMPBELL'S®
    Condensed Cream of Potato Soup
1 cup milk
¼ teaspoon dried thyme leaves, crushed
¼ teaspoon pepper
4 cups cooked cut-up vegetables*
2 cups cubed cooked turkey, chicken *or* ham
1 package (7½ or 10 ounces) refrigerated
    buttermilk biscuits (10 biscuits)

*Use a combination of broccoli flowerets, cauliflower flowerets and sliced carrots **or** broccoli flowerets and sliced carrots **or** broccoli flowerets, sliced carrots and peas.*

1. In 3-quart shallow baking dish mix soups, milk, thyme, pepper, vegetables and turkey.

2. Bake at 400°F. for 15 minutes or until hot.

3. Stir. Arrange biscuits over turkey mixture. Bake 15 minutes more or until biscuits are golden.

Makes 5 servings

Tip: To microwave vegetables, in 2-quart shallow microwave-safe baking dish arrange vegetables and ¼ cup water. Cover. Microwave on HIGH 10 minutes.

Prep Time: 15 minutes
Cook Time: 30 minutes

TURKEY BROCCOLI BAKE

1 bag (16 ounces) frozen broccoli cuts,
    thawed, drained
2 cups cubed cooked turkey or chicken
2 cups soft bread cubes
8 ounces sliced American cheese, divided
1 jar (12 ounces) HEINZ® HomeStyle Turkey
    or Chicken Gravy
½ cup undiluted evaporated milk
    Dash pepper

In buttered 9-inch square baking dish, layer broccoli, turkey, bread cubes and cheese. Combine gravy, milk and pepper; pour over cheese. Bake in 375°F oven, 40 minutes. Let stand 5 minutes.

Makes 6 servings

Campbell's® Easy Turkey & Biscuits

TURKEY–VEGETABLE CRESCENT PIE

2 cans (about 14 ounces) fat-free
    reduced-sodium chicken broth
1 medium onion, diced
1¼ pounds turkey tenderloins, cut into
    ¾-inch pieces
3 cups diced red potatoes
1 teaspoon chopped fresh rosemary *or*
    ½ teaspoon dried rosemary
¼ teaspoon salt
⅛ teaspoon black pepper
1 bag (16 ounces) frozen mixed vegetables
1 bag (10 ounces) frozen mixed vegetables
⅓ cup fat-free (skim) milk plus additional,
    if necessary
3 tablespoons cornstarch
1 package (8 ounces) refrigerated
    reduced-fat crescent rolls

1. Bring broth to a boil in large saucepan. Add onion; reduce heat and simmer 3 minutes. Add turkey; return to a boil. Reduce heat; cover and simmer 7 to 9 minutes or until turkey is no longer pink. Remove turkey from saucepan with slotted spoon; place in 13×9-inch baking dish.

2. Increase heat and return broth to a boil. Add potatoes, rosemary, salt and pepper; simmer 2 minutes. Return to a boil and stir in mixed vegetables; return to a boil. Reduce heat and simmer, covered, 7 to 8 minutes or until potatoes are tender. Remove vegetables with slotted spoon. Drain in colander set over bowl; reserve broth. Transfer vegetables to baking dish with turkey.

3. Preheat oven to 375°F. Blend ⅓ cup milk with cornstarch in small bowl until smooth. Add enough milk to reserved broth to equal 3 cups. Heat in large saucepan over medium-high heat; whisk in cornstarch mixture, stirring constantly until mixture comes to a boil. Boil 1 minute; remove from heat. Pour over turkey-vegetable mixture in baking dish.

4. Roll out crescent roll dough and separate at perforations; arrange dough pieces decoratively over top of turkey-vegetable mixture. Bake 13 to 15 minutes or until crust is golden brown.

Makes 8 servings

Turkey-Vegetable Crescent Pie

CAMPBELL'S® TURKEY & BROCCOLI ALFREDO

6 ounces *uncooked* fettuccine
1 cup fresh *or* frozen broccoli flowerets
1 can (10¾ ounces) CAMPBELL'S®
   Condensed Cream of Mushroom Soup *or*
   98% Fat Free Cream of Mushroom Soup
½ cup milk
½ cup grated Parmesan cheese
1 cup cubed cooked turkey
¼ teaspoon freshly ground pepper

1. Prepare fettuccine according to package directions. Add broccoli for last 4 minutes of cooking time. Drain.

2. In same pan mix soup, milk, cheese, turkey, pepper and fettuccine mixture and heat through, stirring occasionally.   *Makes 4 servings*

Variation: Substitute 8 ounces uncooked spaghetti for fettuccine.

Prep Time: 10 minutes
Cook Time: 15 minutes

TURKEY AND BISCUITS

2 cans (10¾ ounces each) condensed cream
   of chicken soup, undiluted
¼ cup dry white wine
¼ teaspoon poultry seasoning
2 packages (8 ounces each) frozen cut
   asparagus, thawed
3 cups cubed cooked turkey or chicken
   Paprika (optional)
1 can (11 ounces) refrigerated flaky biscuits

Preheat oven to 350°F. Spray 13×9-inch baking dish with nonstick cooking spray.

Combine soup, wine and poultry seasoning in medium bowl.

Arrange asparagus in single layer in prepared dish. Place turkey evenly over asparagus. Spread soup mixture over turkey. Sprinkle lightly with paprika, if desired.

Cover tightly with foil and bake 20 minutes. Remove from oven. *Increase oven temperature to 425°F.* Top with biscuits and bake, uncovered, 8 to 10 minutes or until biscuits are golden brown.

Makes 6 servings

Campbell's® Turkey & Broccoli Alfredo

CAMPBELL'S® TURKEY STUFFING DIVAN

1¼ cups boiling water
4 tablespoons margarine or butter, melted
4 cups PEPPERIDGE FARM® Herb Seasoned Stuffing
2 cups cooked broccoli cuts
2 cups cubed cooked turkey
1 can (10¾ ounces) CAMPBELL'S® Condensed Cream of Celery Soup or 98% Fat Free Cream of Celery Soup
½ cup milk
1 cup shredded Cheddar cheese (4 ounces)

1. Mix water and margarine. Add stuffing. Mix lightly.

2. Spoon into 2-quart shallow baking dish. Arrange broccoli and turkey over stuffing. In small bowl mix soup, milk and ½ *cup* cheese. Pour over broccoli and turkey. Sprinkle remaining cheese over soup mixture.

3. Bake at 350°F. for 30 minutes or until hot.

Makes 6 servings

Variation: Substitute 1 can (10¾ ounces) CAMPBELL'S® Condensed Cream of Chicken Soup *or* 98% Fat Free Cream of Chicken Soup for Cream of Celery Soup. Substitute 2 cups cubed cooked chicken for turkey.

Tip: For 2 cups cooked broccoli cuts use about 1 pound fresh broccoli, trimmed, cut into 1-inch pieces (about 2 cups) *or* 1 package (10 ounces) frozen broccoli cuts.

Prep Time: 15 minutes
Cook Time: 30 minutes

Cook's Tip

When roasting a turkey with a pop-up timer, use the timer only as a guide for doneness. Using a meat thermometer is the best indicator to measure accurate internal temperature.

Campbell's® Turkey Stuffing Divan

Hearty
MEALS

MAIN–DISH PIE

1 package (8 rolls) refrigerated crescent rolls
1 pound lean ground beef
1 medium onion, chopped
1 can (12 ounces) beef or mushroom gravy
1 box (10 ounces) BIRDS EYE® frozen Green Peas,
    thawed
½ cup shredded Swiss cheese
6 slices tomato

• Preheat oven to 350°F.

• Unroll dough and separate rolls. Spread to cover bottom of ungreased 9-inch pie pan. Press together to form lower crust. Bake 10 minutes.

• Meanwhile, in large skillet, brown beef and onion; drain excess fat.

• Stir in gravy and peas; cook until heated through.

• Pour into partially baked crust. Sprinkle with cheese.

• Bake 10 to 15 minutes or until crust is brown and cheese is melted.

• Arrange tomato slices over pie; bake 2 minutes more.

Makes 6 servings

Prep Time: 10 minutes
Cook Time: 20 to 25 minutes

Left: *Main-Dish Pie*

Top: *Country Sausage Macaroni and Cheese (page 156)*

105

BEEF STROGANOFF CASSEROLE

 1 pound lean ground beef
¼ teaspoon salt
⅛ teaspoon black pepper
 1 teaspoon vegetable oil
 8 ounces sliced mushrooms
 1 large onion, chopped
 3 cloves garlic, minced
¼ cup dry white wine
 1 can (10¾ ounces) condensed cream of
    mushroom soup, undiluted
½ cup sour cream
 1 tablespoon Dijon mustard
 4 cups cooked egg noodles

Preheat oven to 350°F. Spray 13×9-inch baking dish with nonstick cooking spray.

Place beef in large skillet; season with salt and pepper. Brown beef over medium-high heat until no longer pink, stirring to separate beef. Drain fat from skillet; set beef aside.

Heat oil in same skillet over medium-high heat until hot. Add mushrooms, onion and garlic; cook and stir 2 minutes or until onion is tender. Add wine. Reduce heat to medium-low and simmer 3 minutes. Remove from heat; stir in soup, sour cream and mustard until well combined. Return beef to skillet.

Place noodles in prepared dish. Pour beef mixture over noodles; stir until noodles are well coated. Bake, uncovered, 30 minutes or until heated through. Sprinkle with chopped parsley, if desired.

Makes 6 servings

SPINACH–POTATO BAKE

 1 pound extra-lean (90% lean) ground beef
½ cup sliced fresh mushrooms
 1 small onion, chopped
 2 cloves garlic, minced
 1 package (10 ounces) frozen chopped
    spinach, thawed and well drained
½ teaspoon ground nutmeg
 1 pound russet potatoes, peeled, cooked and
    mashed
¼ cup reduced-fat sour cream
¼ cup fat-free (skim) milk
    Salt and freshly ground pepper
½ cup (2 ounces) shredded Cheddar cheese

Preheat oven to 400°F. Spray deep 9-inch casserole dish with nonstick cooking spray.

Brown ground beef in large skillet. Drain. Add mushrooms, onion and garlic; cook until tender. Stir in spinach and nutmeg; cover. Heat thoroughly, stirring occasionally.

Combine potatoes, sour cream and milk. Add to ground beef mixture; season to taste with salt and pepper. Spoon into prepared casserole dish; sprinkle with cheese.

Bake 15 to 20 minutes or until slightly puffed and cheese is melted.

Makes 6 servings

Beef Stroganoff Casserole

CHEESE–STUFFED BEEF ROLLS

1 jar (15½ ounces) spaghetti sauce
1 egg, slightly beaten
¼ teaspoon dried oregano, crumbled
¼ teaspoon garlic powder
1 container (15 ounces) ricotta cheese
¼ cup (1 ounce) grated Parmesan cheese
1 cup (4 ounces) shredded mozzarella
   cheese, divided
1⅓ cups FRENCH'S® French Fried Onions,
   divided
6 thin slices deli roast beef (about ½ pound)
2 medium zucchini, sliced (about 3 cups)

Preheat oven to 375°F. Spread ½ cup spaghetti sauce in bottom of 12×8-inch baking dish. In large bowl, thoroughly combine egg, seasonings, ricotta cheese, Parmesan cheese, ½ cup mozzarella cheese and ⅔ cup French Fried Onions. Spoon equal amounts of cheese mixture on 1 end of each beef slice. Roll up beef slices jelly-roll style and arrange, seam-side down, in baking dish. Place zucchini along both sides of dish. Pour remaining spaghetti sauce over beef rolls and zucchini. Bake, covered, at 375°F for 40 minutes or until heated through. Top beef rolls with remaining ½ cup mozzarella cheese and remaining ⅔ cup onions. Bake, uncovered, 3 minutes or until onions are golden brown.

Makes 6 servings

Microwave Directions: In large microwave-safe bowl, prepare cheese mixture as above. Cook, covered, on HIGH 2 to 4 minutes or until warmed through. Stir cheese mixture halfway through cooking time. Spread ½ cup spaghetti sauce in bottom of 12×8-inch microwave-safe dish. Prepare beef rolls and place in dish as above. Arrange zucchini along both sides of dish. Pour remaining spaghetti sauce over beef rolls and zucchini. Cook, loosely covered, 14 to 16 minutes or until heated through. Rotate dish halfway through cooking time. Top beef rolls with remaining mozzarella cheese and onions; cook, uncovered, 1 minute or until cheese melts. Let stand 5 minutes.

BISCUIT–TOPPED HEARTY STEAK PIE

1½ pounds top round steak, cooked and cut
   into 1-inch cubes
1 package (9 ounces) frozen baby carrots
1 package (9 ounces) frozen peas and pearl
   onions
1 large baking potato, cooked and cut into
   ½-inch pieces
1 jar (18 ounces) home-style brown gravy
½ teaspoon dried thyme leaves
½ teaspoon black pepper
1 can (10 ounces) refrigerated flaky
   buttermilk biscuits

Preheat oven to 375°F. Spray 2-quart square casserole with nonstick cooking spray. Combine steak, frozen vegetables and potato in prepared dish. Stir in gravy, thyme and pepper. Bake, uncovered, 40 minutes. Remove from oven. *Increase oven temperature to 400°F.* Top with biscuits and bake 8 to 10 minutes or until biscuits are golden brown.

Makes 6 servings

Biscuit-Topped Hearty Steak Pie

BROCCOLI AND BEEF PASTA

1 pound lean ground beef
2 cloves garlic, minced
1 can (about 14 ounces) beef broth
1 medium onion, thinly sliced
1 cup uncooked rotini pasta
½ teaspoon dried basil leaves
½ teaspoon dried oregano leaves
½ teaspoon dried thyme leaves
1 can (15 ounces) Italian-style tomatoes,
   undrained
2 cups broccoli florets *or* 1 package
   (10 ounces) frozen broccoli, thawed
3 ounces shredded Cheddar cheese or
   grated Parmesan cheese

1. Combine meat and garlic in large nonstick skillet; cook over high heat until meat is no longer pink, breaking meat apart with wooden spoon. Pour off drippings. Place meat in large bowl; set aside.

2. Add broth, onion, pasta, basil, oregano and thyme to skillet. Bring to a boil. Reduce heat to medium-high and boil 10 minutes; add tomatoes with juice. Increase heat to high and bring to a boil; stir in broccoli. Cook, uncovered, 6 to 8 minutes, stirring occasionally, until broccoli is crisp-tender and pasta is tender. Return meat to skillet and stir 3 to 4 minutes or until heated through.

3. With slotted spoon, transfer to serving platter. Sprinkle with cheese. Cover with lid or tent with foil several minutes, until cheese melts. Meanwhile, bring liquid left in skillet to a boil over high heat. Boil until thick and reduced to 3 to 4 tablespoons. Spoon over pasta. *Makes 4 servings*

CLASSIC HAMBURGER CASSEROLE

1 pound ground beef
1 package (9 ounces) frozen cut green
   beans, thawed and drained
1 can (10¾ ounces) condensed tomato soup
¼ cup water
½ teaspoon seasoned salt
⅛ teaspoon pepper
2 cups hot mashed potatoes
1⅓ cups FRENCH'S® French Fried Onions,
   divided
½ cup (2 ounces) shredded Cheddar cheese

Preheat oven to 350°F. In medium skillet, brown ground beef; drain. Stir in green beans, soup, water and seasonings; pour into 1½-quart casserole. In medium bowl, combine mashed potatoes and ⅔ *cup* French Fried Onions. Spoon potato mixture in mounds around edge of casserole. Bake, uncovered, at 350°F for 25 minutes or until heated through. Top potatoes with cheese and remaining ⅔ *cup* onions; bake, uncovered, 5 minutes or until onions are golden brown. *Makes 4 to 6 servings*

Broccoli and Beef Pasta

BEEF BURGUNDY AND MUSHROOMS

8 ounces uncooked yolk-free egg noodles
¼ cup water
2 tablespoons all-purpose flour
1 can (10 ounces) beef broth
2 tablespoons dry red wine
½ teaspoon Worcestershire sauce
¾ teaspoon sugar
   Nonstick cooking spray
1½ teaspoons extra virgin olive oil
1 package (16 ounces) sliced fresh
   mushrooms
4 cloves garlic, minced
1 pound beef sirloin, cut into thin strips
1 bay leaf
½ cup chopped green onions with tops
¼ cup chopped fresh parsley
   Black pepper

1. Cook noodles according to package directions. Drain; set aside.

2. Meanwhile, combine water and flour in small bowl; whisk until smooth. Slowly whisk in beef broth, wine, Worcestershire sauce and sugar; set aside.

3. Spray large skillet with nonstick cooking spray; add oil. Heat over high heat until hot. Add mushrooms and garlic; cook 2 minutes. Reduce heat to medium-high; cook 3 to 4 minutes or until tender. Place in separate bowl; set aside.

4. Recoat skillet with nonstick cooking spray. Brown sirloin strips over high heat 2 to 3 minutes. Add green onions, bay leaf, mushrooms and broth mixture. Bring to a boil. Reduce heat to medium-low; simmer, uncovered, 30 minutes or until meat is tender. Discard bay leaf. Remove from heat; add parsley. Sprinkle with pepper to taste. Let stand 10 minutes before serving. Spoon over egg noodles.

Makes 4 servings

BEEF STROGANOFF WITH RICE

½ cup UNCLE BEN'S® CONVERTED®
   Brand Original Rice
12 ounces sirloin steak
1 teaspoon olive oil
1 small onion, sliced
2 cups sliced mushrooms
½ cup reduced-fat sour cream
¼ teaspoon dill weed
½ cup sliced green onions

1. Cook rice according to package directions.

2. Meanwhile, cut beef into thin strips. Heat oil in large skillet over medium heat. Add beef, onion and mushrooms. Cook and stir 5 minutes or until beef is cooked through. Add sour cream, dill weed and cooked rice.

3. Garnish stroganoff with green onions.

Makes 4 servings

Beef Burgundy and Mushrooms

Hearty
MEALS

CAMPBELL'S® BEEF & MOZZARELLA BAKE

1 pound ground beef
1 can (11⅛ ounces) CAMPBELL'S®
    Condensed Italian Tomato Soup
1 can (10¾ ounces) CAMPBELL'S®
    Condensed Cream of Mushroom Soup
1¼ cups water
1 teaspoon dried basil leaves, crushed
¼ teaspoon pepper
⅛ teaspoon garlic powder *or* 1 clove garlic,
    minced
1½ cups shredded mozzarella cheese
    (6 ounces)
4 cups hot cooked medium shell macaroni
    (about 3 cups uncooked)

1. In medium skillet over medium-high heat, cook beef until browned, stirring to separate meat. Pour off fat.

2. Add soups, water, basil, pepper, garlic powder, *1 cup* cheese and macaroni. Spoon into 2-quart shallow baking dish. Bake at 400°F. for 20 minutes or until hot.

3. Stir. Sprinkle remaining cheese over beef mixture. Bake 5 minutes more or until cheese is melted.
Makes 6 servings

Variation: Substitute 4 cups hot cooked elbow macaroni (about 2 cups uncooked) for shell macaroni.

Prep Time: 15 minutes
Cook Time: 25 minutes

CHILI WAGON WHEEL CASSEROLE

8 ounces uncooked wagon wheel or other
    pasta
1 pound lean ground sirloin or ground
    turkey breast
¾ cup chopped green bell pepper
¾ cup chopped onion
1 can (14½ ounces) stewed tomatoes
1 can (8 ounces) tomato sauce
½ teaspoon black pepper
¼ teaspoon ground allspice
½ cup (2 ounces) shredded reduced-fat
    Cheddar cheese

1. Preheat oven to 350°F. Cook pasta according to package directions. Drain and rinse; set aside.

2. Spray large skillet with nonstick cooking spray. Add ground sirloin, bell pepper and onion; cook 5 minutes or until meat is no longer pink, stirring frequently. (Drain mixture if using ground sirloin.)

3. Stir in tomatoes, tomato sauce, black pepper and allspice; cook 2 minutes. Stir in pasta. Spoon mixture into 2½-quart casserole. Sprinkle with cheese.

4. Bake 20 to 25 minutes or until heated through.
Makes 6 servings

Campbell's® Beef & Mozzarella Bake

BEEF AND PARSNIP STROGANOFF

1 cube beef bouillon
¾ cup boiling water
¾ pound well-trimmed boneless top round
   beef steak, 1 inch thick
   Nonstick olive oil cooking spray
2 cups cubed peeled parsnips or potatoes*
1 medium onion, halved and thinly sliced
¾ pound mushrooms, sliced
2 teaspoons minced garlic
¼ teaspoon black pepper
¼ cup water
1 tablespoon plus 1½ teaspoons all-purpose
   flour
3 tablespoons reduced-fat sour cream
1½ teaspoons Dijon mustard
¼ teaspoon cornstarch
1 tablespoon chopped fresh parsley
4 ounces cholesterol-free wide noodles

*If using potatoes, cut into 1-inch chunks and add to slow cooker with mushroom mixture.

1. Dissolve bouillon cube in ¾ cup boiling water; cool. Meanwhile, cut steak into 2×½-inch strips. Spray large skillet with nonstick cooking spray; heat over high heat. Cook and stir beef about 4 minutes or until meat begins to brown and is barely pink. Transfer beef and juices to slow cooker.

2. Spray same skillet with cooking spray; heat over high heat. Add parsnips and onion; cook and stir until browned, about 4 minutes. Add mushrooms, garlic and pepper; cook and stir until mushrooms are tender, about 5 minutes. Transfer mushroom mixture to slow cooker; mix with beef.

3. Blend ¼ cup water and flour in small bowl until smooth. Stir flour mixture into cooled bouillon. Add to slow cooker. Cook, covered, on LOW 4½ to 5 hours or until beef and parsnips are tender.

4. Cook noodles according to package directions. Drain; set aside.

5. Turn off slow cooker. Remove beef and vegetables with slotted spoon to large bowl; reserve cooking liquid from beef. Blend sour cream, mustard and cornstarch in medium bowl. Gradually add reserved liquid to sour cream mixture; stir well to blend. Stir sour cream mixture into beef mixture. Sprinkle with parsley; serve over noodles. Garnish, if desired. *Makes 4 servings*

Beef and Parsnip Stroganoff

CHILI SPAGHETTI CASSEROLE

8 ounces uncooked spaghetti
1 pound lean ground beef
1 medium onion, chopped
¼ teaspoon salt
⅛ teaspoon black pepper
1 can (15 ounces) vegetarian chili with beans
1 can (14½ ounces) Italian-style stewed tomatoes, undrained
1½ cups (6 ounces) shredded sharp Cheddar cheese, divided
½ cup reduced-fat sour cream
1½ teaspoons chili powder
¼ teaspoon garlic powder

Preheat oven to 350°F. Spray 13×9-inch baking dish with nonstick cooking spray.

Cook pasta according to package directions. Drain and place in prepared dish.

Meanwhile, place beef and onion in large skillet; season with salt and pepper. Brown beef over medium-high heat until beef is no longer pink, stirring to separate meat. Drain fat. Stir in chili, tomatoes with juice, 1 cup cheese, sour cream, chili powder and garlic powder.

Add chili mixture to pasta; stir until pasta is well coated. Sprinkle with remaining ½ cup cheese.

Cover tightly with foil and bake 30 minutes or until hot and bubbly. Let stand 5 minutes before serving.

Makes 8 servings

SALISBURY STEAK WITH MUSHROOM & ONION TOPPING

2 pounds ground beef
2⅔ cups FRENCH'S® French Fried Onions, divided
1 teaspoon garlic salt
½ teaspoon ground black pepper
1 tablespoon butter or margarine
8 ounces mushrooms, wiped clean and sliced (3 cups)
1 jar (12 ounces) brown gravy
¼ cup water
1 tablespoon FRENCH'S® Worcestershire Sauce

Combine ground beef, *1⅓ cups* French Fried Onions, salt and pepper in large bowl. Shape into 6 oval patties.

Heat large nonstick skillet over medium-high heat. Add patties; cook about 20 minutes or until browned on both sides and juices run clear. Transfer to platter; keep warm. Pour off drippings from pan; discard.

Melt butter in same skillet over high heat. Add mushrooms; cook and stir until browned. Stir in gravy, water and Worcestershire. Return patties to skillet. Bring to a boil. Cook until heated through. Sprinkle with remaining *1⅓ cups* onions.

Makes 6 servings

Prep Time: 15 minutes
Cook Time: 25 minutes

Chili Spaghetti Casserole

BEEF TENDERLOINS IN WILD MUSHROOM SAUCE

2 boxes UNCLE BEN'S® Butter & Herb Long Grain & Wild Rice
4 bacon slices, cut into 1-inch pieces
4 beef tenderloin steaks (4 ounces each) *or* 1 pound beef top sirloin steak, cut into 4 pieces
1 package (4 ounces) sliced mixed exotic mushrooms or button mushrooms
1 cup chopped onion
⅔ cup half-and-half
2 tablespoons Dijon mustard
2 tablespoons Worcestershire sauce

1. Prepare rice according to package directions. Meanwhile, cook bacon over medium-high heat in large skillet until crisp; remove bacon from skillet, reserving 1 tablespoon drippings. Drain bacon on paper towels; set aside.

2. Add steaks to drippings in skillet; cook 2 minutes on each side or until browned. Reduce heat to medium; continue to cook steaks 3 to 4 minutes on each side for medium-rare or to desired doneness. Remove steaks from skillet, reserving drippings in skillet; cover steaks to keep warm.

3. Add mushrooms and onion to drippings in skillet; cook and stir over medium heat until tender, about 5 minutes, stirring occasionally.

4. In small bowl, combine half-and-half, mustard and Worcestershire sauce; mix well. Add to skillet with bacon; cook 3 minutes or until sauce thickens, stirring occasionally.

5. Return steaks to skillet. Continue to cook 3 minutes or until hot, turning steaks over once.

6. Season with salt and pepper to taste, if desired. Transfer steaks to serving plates; top with sauce. Serve with rice. *Makes 4 servings*

CAMPBELL'S® BEEFY MACARONI SKILLET

1 pound ground beef
1 medium onion, chopped (about ½ cup)
1 can (10¾ ounces) CAMPBELL'S® Condensed Tomato Soup
¼ cup water
1 tablespoon Worcestershire sauce
½ cup shredded Cheddar cheese (2 ounces)
2 cups cooked corkscrew macaroni (about 1½ cups uncooked)

1. In medium skillet over medium-high heat, cook beef and onion until beef is browned, stirring to separate meat. Pour off fat.

2. Add soup, water, Worcestershire, cheese and macaroni. Reduce heat to low and heat through. *Makes 4 servings*

Variation: Substitute 2 cups cooked elbow macaroni (about 1 cup uncooked) for corkscrew macaroni.

Prep Time: 10 minutes
Cook Time: 15 minutes

Campbell's® Beefy Macaroni Skillet

LASAGNA SUPREME

8 ounces lasagna noodles
½ pound ground beef
½ pound mild Italian sausage, casings removed
1 medium onion, chopped
2 cloves garlic, minced
1 can (14½ ounces) whole peeled tomatoes, undrained and chopped
1 can (6 ounces) tomato paste
2 teaspoons dried basil leaves
1 teaspoon dried marjoram leaves
1 can (4 ounces) sliced mushrooms, drained
2 eggs
1 pound cream-style cottage cheese
¾ cup Parmesan cheese, divided
2 tablespoons dried parsley flakes
½ teaspoon salt
½ teaspoon ground black pepper
2 cups (8 ounces) shredded Cheddar cheese
3 cups (12 ounces) shredded mozzarella cheese

1. Cook lasagna noodles according to package directions; drain.

2. Cook meats, onion and garlic in large skillet over medium-high heat until meat is brown, stirring to separate meat. Drain drippings. Add tomatoes with juice, tomato paste, basil and marjoram. Reduce heat to low. Cover; simmer 15 minutes, stirring often. Stir in mushrooms; set aside.

3. Preheat oven to 375°F. Beat eggs in large bowl; add cottage cheese, ½ cup Parmesan cheese, parsley, salt and pepper. Mix well.

4. Place half of noodles in bottom of 13×9-inch baking pan. Spread half of cottage cheese mixture over noodles, then half of meat mixture and half of Cheddar cheese and mozzarella cheese. Repeat layers. Sprinkle with remaining ¼ cup Parmesan cheese.

5. Bake lasagna 40 to 45 minutes or until bubbly. Let stand 10 minutes before cutting.

Makes 8 to 10 servings

YARD–O–BEEF CASSEROLE

½ cup beef broth
½ cup dry red wine
2 tablespoons olive oil
2 pounds HILLSHIRE FARM® Yard-O-Beef, cut into ½-inch-thick slices
¼ cup all-purpose flour
½ pound mushrooms, thinly sliced
2 teaspoons salt
½ teaspoon black pepper

Preheat oven to 400°F.

Combine beef broth and wine in small saucepan and heat over medium heat. Heat oil in medium skillet over medium-high heat. Dust Yard-O-Beef with flour; brown beef on both sides in skillet. Place 1 layer of beef in medium casserole; add 1 layer of mushrooms. Sprinkle with ½ of salt and pepper. Repeat layers and seasoning. Pour broth mixture over layers. Bake, covered, 35 minutes or until heated through.

Makes 6 to 8 servings

Lasagna Supreme

MEATLOAF WITH GARLIC MASHED POTATOES

4 large red potatoes, cubed
3 cloves garlic, peeled
1 pound ground sirloin
1 can (10¾ ounces) condensed cream of mushroom soup, divided
1½ cups fresh bread crumbs
2 eggs
½ cup carrot strips
½ cup zucchini strips
¼ cup minced red bell pepper
½ cup minced onion
2 tablespoons minced fresh parsley, divided
½ teaspoon dried thyme
½ teaspoon dried oregano
Nonstick cooking spray
⅓ cup cream cheese
½ teaspoon salt

Combine potatoes, garlic and enough water to cover potatoes in medium saucepan. Bring to a boil; cover and reduce heat to medium-high. Cook 20 to 25 minutes or until tender.

Meanwhile, combine beef, ⅓ cup soup, bread crumbs, eggs, carrots, zucchini, pepper, onion, 1 tablespoon parsley, thyme and oregano; mix well. Spray shallow round 2-quart baking dish with cooking spray; form beef mixture into ring around outer edge of dish, leaving center open. Bake at 400°F 20 to 25 minutes.

Drain potatoes; return potatoes to pan and mash. Add remaining soup, cream cheese, chives and salt; mash until well mixed. Remove meatloaf from oven; mound potatoes in center. Place under broiler 5 minutes or until lightly browned. Sprinkle with remaining 1 tablespoon parsley.   *Makes 6 servings*

TEXAS RANCH CHILI BEANS

1 pound lean ground beef
1 can (28 ounces) whole peeled tomatoes, undrained
2 cans (15½ ounces each) chili beans
1 cup chopped onions
1 cup water
1 package (1 ounce) HIDDEN VALLEY® Milk Recipe Original Ranch® salad dressing mix
1 teaspoon chili powder
1 bay leaf

In Dutch oven, brown beef over medium-high heat; drain off fat. Add tomatoes, breaking up with spoon. Stir in beans, onions, water, salad dressing mix, chili powder and bay leaf. Bring to boil; reduce heat and simmer, uncovered, 1 hour, stirring occasionally. Remove bay leaf just before serving.

Makes 8 servings

Meatloaf with Garlic Mashed Potatoes

LEMONY BEEF, VEGETABLES & BARLEY

1 pound lean ground beef
8 ounces mushrooms, sliced
1 medium onion, chopped
1 clove garlic, crushed
1 can (about 14 ounces) beef broth
½ cup quick-cooking barley
½ teaspoon salt
¼ teaspoon pepper
1 package (10 ounces) frozen peas and
   carrots, defrosted
1 teaspoon grated lemon peel

1. In large nonstick skillet, cook and stir ground beef, mushrooms, onion and garlic over medium heat 8 to 10 minutes or until beef is no longer pink, breaking beef up into ¾-inch crumbles. Pour off drippings.

2. Stir in broth, barley, salt and pepper. Bring to a boil; reduce heat to medium-low. Cover tightly; simmer 10 minutes.

3. Add peas and carrots; continue cooking 2 to 5 minutes or until barley is tender. Stir in lemon peel.
Makes 4 (1½-cup) servings

Prep and Cook Time: 30 minutes

Favorite recipe from **National Cattlemen's Beef Association**

OVEN–BAKED BOURGUIGNONNE

2 pounds boneless beef chuck, cut into
   1-inch cubes
¼ cup all-purpose flour
1⅓ cups sliced carrots
1 can (14½ ounces) whole peeled tomatoes,
   undrained and chopped
1 bay leaf
1 envelope LIPTON® RECIPE SECRETS®
   Onion or Beefy Onion Soup Mix
½ cup dry red wine
1 cup fresh mushrooms or canned sliced
   mushrooms, drained
1 package (8 ounces) medium or broad egg
   noodles

Preheat oven to 400°F. In 2-quart casserole, toss beef with flour. Bake uncovered 20 minutes. Add carrots, tomatoes and bay leaf, then onion soup mix blended with wine. Bake covered 1½ hours or until beef is tender. Add mushrooms and bake covered an additional 10 minutes. Remove bay leaf.

Meanwhile, cook noodles according to package directions. To serve, spoon bourguignonne over noodles. *Makes about 8 servings*

Lemony Beef, Vegetables & Barley

STUFFED BELL PEPPERS

3 large bell peppers, any color, seeded and cut in half lengthwise
1½ cups chopped fresh tomatoes
1 tablespoon chopped fresh cilantro
1 jalapeño pepper, seeded and chopped*
1 clove garlic, finely minced
½ teaspoon dried oregano leaves, divided
¼ teaspoon ground cumin
8 ounces lean ground round
1 cup cooked brown rice
¼ cup cholesterol-free egg substitute *or* 2 egg whites
2 tablespoons finely chopped onion
¼ teaspoon salt
⅛ teaspoon black pepper

Jalapeño peppers can sting and irritate the skin; wear rubber gloves when handling peppers and do not touch eyes. Wash hands after handling.

1. Preheat oven to 350°F.

2. Place steamer basket in large saucepan; add 1 inch of water, being careful not to let water touch bottom of basket. Place bell peppers in basket; cover. Bring water to a boil; reduce heat to medium. Steam peppers 8 to 10 minutes or until tender, adding additional water if necessary; drain.

3. Combine tomatoes, cilantro, jalapeño pepper, garlic, ¼ teaspoon oregano and cumin in small bowl. Set aside.

4. Thoroughly combine beef, rice, egg substitute, onion, salt and black pepper in large bowl. Stir 1 cup of tomato mixture into beef mixture.

5. Spoon filling evenly into pepper halves; place in 13×9-inch baking dish. Cover tightly with foil. Bake 45 minutes or until meat is browned and vegetables are tender. Serve with remaining tomato mixture.

Makes 6 servings

WILD RICE BEEFY VEGETABLE CASSEROLE

1 pound lean ground beef
1 cup chopped onion
1 pound frozen broccoli, carrots & cauliflower blend, thawed and drained
1 can (10¾ ounces) cream of celery soup
1 can (8 ounces) tomato sauce
3 cups cooked wild rice
2 cups shredded mild Cheddar cheese, divided
2 teaspoons dried Italian seasoning
1 teaspoon salt
½ teaspoon black pepper

Preheat oven to 350°F. In large skillet, brown beef and onion; drain. Add vegetables, soup, tomato sauce, wild rice, 1½ cups cheese and seasonings; mix lightly. Place in 3-quart casserole; top with remaining ½ cup cheese. Cover; bake 25 to 30 minutes or until heated through. Uncover; bake 5 minutes.

Makes 6 to 8 servings

Favorite recipe from **Minnesota Cultivated Wild Rice Council**

Stuffed Bell Peppers

Hearty
MEALS

STUFFED MUSHROOMS WITH TOMATO SAUCE AND PASTA

   Tomato Sauce (recipe follows)
 1 pound extra-lean (90% lean) ground beef
 ¼ cup finely chopped onion
 ¼ cup finely chopped green or red bell
    pepper
 1 large garlic clove, minced
 2 tablespoons finely chopped fresh parsley
 2 teaspoons finely chopped fresh basil *or*
    1 teaspoon dried basil leaves, crushed
 1 teaspoon finely chopped fresh oregano *or*
    ½ teaspoon dried oregano leaves,
    crushed
 ½ teaspoon salt
   Dash freshly ground black pepper
12 very large mushrooms
 ¼ cup grated Parmesan cheese
 4½ cups cooked spaghetti

Prepare Tomato Sauce; set aside.

Preheat oven to 350°F.

Combine ground beef, onion, bell pepper, garlic, parsley, basil, oregano, salt and black pepper in medium bowl; mix lightly. Remove stems from mushrooms; finely chop stems. Add to ground beef mixture. Stuff into mushroom caps, rounding tops.

Pour Tomato Sauce into shallow casserole dish large enough to hold mushrooms in single layer. Place mushrooms, stuffing side up, in sauce; cover.

Bake 20 minutes; remove cover. Sprinkle with cheese. Continue baking, uncovered, 15 minutes. Serve with spaghetti. Garnish with additional fresh basil leaves, if desired. *Makes 6 servings*

TOMATO SAUCE

 2 cans (14½ ounces) tomatoes, chopped,
    undrained
   Dash hot pepper sauce
 1 teaspoon finely chopped fresh marjoram *or*
    ½ teaspoon dried marjoram leaves,
    crushed
 1 teaspoon fennel seeds, crushed
   Salt and freshly ground black pepper

Combine all ingredients except salt and black pepper in medium saucepan. Bring to a boil. Reduce heat; simmer 5 minutes. Season to taste with salt and pepper.

Stuffed Mushrooms with Tomato Sauce and Pasta

CHILI MEATLOAF & POTATO CASSEROLE

MEATLOAF
1½ pounds lean ground beef
¾ cup finely chopped onion
⅓ cup saltine cracker crumbs
1 egg, slightly beaten
3 tablespoons milk
1 tablespoon chili powder
¾ teaspoon salt

POTATO TOPPING
3 cups prepared mashed potatoes
1 can (11 ounces) whole kernel corn with red and green peppers, drained
¼ cup thinly sliced green onions
½ to 1 cup shredded taco seasoned cheese

1. Heat oven to 375°F. In large bowl, combine meatloaf ingredients, mixing lightly but thoroughly; gently press into bottom of 9-inch square baking pan. Bake in 375°F oven 20 to 25 minutes or until no longer pink and juices show no pink color. Carefully pour off drippings.

2. Meanwhile in medium bowl, combine all topping ingredients except cheese. Spread over meatloaf to edges of pan; sprinkle with cheese. Broil 3 to 4 inches from heat 3 to 5 minutes or until top is lightly browned; cut into 6 rectangular servings.

Makes 6 servings

Favorite recipe from **National Cattlemen's Beef Association**

CORN & ZUCCHINI MEDLEY

¾ pound extra-lean (90% lean) ground beef
1 package (10-ounces) frozen corn, thawed
2 small zucchini (about ½ pound), chopped
1 large tomato, chopped
½ cup chopped onion
1 tablespoon chopped fresh basil
   or 1 teaspoon dried basil leaves
1½ teaspoons chopped fresh thyme
   or ½ teaspoon dried thyme leaves
Salt and freshly ground pepper

Brown ground beef in large skillet. Drain. Reduce heat to medium-low. Stir in corn, zucchini, tomato, onion, basil and thyme; cover. Cook 10 minutes or until zucchini is tender. Season with salt and pepper to taste.

Makes 4 servings

Food Fact

Basil, an herb, is a member of the mint family and can be used fresh, ground or dried. It is most commonly used with Italian dishes, such as pestos, sauces and salads.

Chili Meatloaf & Potato Casserole

MEXICAN STUFFED SHELLS

12 pasta stuffing shells, cooked in unsalted
    water and drained
1 pound ground beef
1 jar (12 ounces) mild or medium picante
    sauce
½ cup water
1 can (8 ounces) tomato sauce
1 can (4 ounces) chopped green chilies,
    drained
1 cup (4 ounces) shredded Monterey Jack
    cheese, divided
1⅓ cups FRENCH'S® French Fried Onions

Preheat oven to 350°F. In large skillet, brown ground
beef; drain. In small bowl, combine picante sauce,
water and tomato sauce. Stir ½ cup sauce mixture
into beef along with chilies, ½ cup cheese and ⅔ cup
French Fried Onions; mix well. Spread half the
remaining sauce mixture in bottom of 10-inch round
baking dish. Stuff cooked shells with beef mixture.
Arrange shells in baking dish; top with remaining
sauce. Bake, covered, at 350°F for 30 minutes or
until heated through. Top with remaining ⅔ cup
onions and cheese; bake, uncovered, 5 minutes or
until cheese is melted.   *Makes 6 servings*

Microwave Directions: Crumble ground beef into
medium microwave-safe bowl. Cook, covered, on
HIGH (100%) 4 to 6 minutes or until beef is cooked.
Stir beef halfway through cooking time. Drain well.
Prepare sauce mixture as above; spread ½ cup in
12×8-inch microwave-safe dish. Prepare beef
mixture as above. Stuff cooked shells with beef
mixture. Arrange shells in dish; top with remaining
sauce. Cook, covered, 10 to 12 minutes or until
heated through. Rotate dish halfway through
cooking time. Top with remaining onions and
cheese; cook, uncovered, 1 minute or until cheese
is melted. Let stand 5 minutes.

SHEPHERD'S PIE

1⅓ cups instant mashed potato buds
1⅔ cups milk
 2 tablespoons butter or margarine
 1 teaspoon salt, divided
 1 pound ground beef
¼ teaspoon black pepper
 1 jar (12 ounces) beef gravy
 1 package (10 ounces) frozen mixed
    vegetables, thawed and drained
¾ cup grated Parmesan cheese

1. Preheat broiler. Prepare 4 servings of mashed
potatoes according to package directions using milk,
butter and ½ teaspoon salt.

2. Meanwhile, brown meat in medium broilerproof
skillet over medium-high heat, stirring to separate
meat. Drain drippings. Sprinkle meat with remaining
½ teaspoon salt and pepper. Add gravy and
vegetables; mix well. Cook over medium-low heat
5 minutes or until heated through.

3. Push meat mixture to center of skillet. Spoon
prepared potatoes around outside edge of skillet.
Sprinkle cheese evenly over potatoes. Broil 4 to
5 inches from heat source 3 minutes or until cheese
melts.   *Makes 4 servings*

Shepherd's Pie

REUBEN NOODLE BAKE

8 ounces uncooked egg noodles
5 ounces thinly sliced deli-style corned beef
1 can (14½ ounces) sauerkraut with caraway seeds, drained
2 cups (8 ounces) shredded Swiss cheese
½ cup Thousand Island dressing
½ cup milk
1 tablespoon prepared mustard
2 slices pumpernickel bread
1 tablespoon margarine or butter, melted

Preheat oven to 350°F. Spray 13×9-inch baking dish with nonstick cooking spray.

Cook noodles according to package directions. Drain and set aside.

Meanwhile, cut corned beef into bite-size pieces. Combine noodles, corned beef, sauerkraut and cheese in large bowl. Pour into prepared dish.

Combine dressing, milk and mustard in small bowl. Spoon dressing mixture evenly over noodle mixture.

Tear bread into large pieces. Process in food processor or blender until crumbs form. Combine bread crumbs and margarine in small bowl; sprinkle evenly over casserole.

Bake, uncovered, 25 to 30 minutes or until heated through. *Makes 6 servings*

BAKED BEEF AND RICE MARINARA

1 pound lean ground beef
¾ cup sliced fresh mushrooms
½ cup chopped onions
½ cup chopped celery
½ cup diced green bell pepper
2 cups cooked rice
1 can (15 ounces) tomato sauce
¾ teaspoon ground oregano
½ teaspoon salt
½ teaspoon dried basil leaves
½ teaspoon garlic powder
3 slices American cheese

Conventional Directions: Cook beef and vegetables over medium-high heat in large skillet until meat is no longer pink and vegetables are crisp-tender, stirring frequently; drain. Combine meat mixture with remaining ingredients except cheese in buttered 2-quart baking dish; arrange cheese slices on top. Bake at 350°F 20 to 25 minutes.

Microwave Directions: Combine crumbled beef and vegetables in plastic colander; place colander over 2-quart microwave-safe baking dish. Cook, uncovered, on HIGH (100% power) 4 minutes; stir after 2 minutes. Drain beef mixture; return mixture to baking dish. Stir in remaining ingredients except cheese. Cook on HIGH 2 minutes. Arrange cheese slices on top; cook on HIGH 2 minutes. Let stand 5 minutes. *Makes 4 servings*

Favorite recipe from **USA Rice Federation**

Reuben Noodle Bake

MEXICAN CHILE

1 can (10¾ ounces) condensed tomato soup
¼ cup water
1 cup fat-free refried beans
   Nonstick cooking spray
10 ounces ground round
1 medium zucchini, diced
½ cup diced onion
½ cup diced green bell pepper
1 small jalapeño pepper, minced*
2 cloves garlic, minced
½ teaspoon salt
¼ teaspoon chili powder

Jalapeño peppers can sting and irritate the skin; wear rubber gloves when handling peppers and do not touch eyes. Wash hands after handling.

Combine soup, water and beans in medium bowl; mix well. Set aside. Spray large saucepan with cooking spray; cook beef until no longer pink; drain and set aside.

In same saucepan, cook and stir zuchinni, onion, bell pepper, jalapeño, garlic, salt and chili powder over medium-high heat until vegetables are tender. Add soup mixture and beef; mix well. Simmer until hot and bubbly.

Makes 4 servings

PORK–STUFFED PEPPERS

3 large green bell peppers
¼ cup raisins
1 pound ground pork
½ cup chopped onion
½ cup chopped carrot
½ cup chopped celery
¼ teaspoon salt
1 cup cooked brown rice
2 tablespoons sunflower kernels
½ cup plain yogurt

Remove tops, seeds and membranes from bell peppers. Cut in half lengthwise. Cook in boiling salted water 5 minutes; drain.

Soak raisins in water 10 to 15 minutes; drain and set aside. Combine pork, onion, carrot, celery and salt in medium skillet. Cook over low heat until pork is done and vegetables are tender, stirring occasionally. Drain thoroughly. Add rice, sunflower kernels, yogurt and raisins; mix well. Spoon mixture into peppers. Place in 12×8×2-inch baking dish. Bake at 350°F 30 to 35 minutes or until heated through.

Makes 6 servings

Prep Time: 20 minutes
Cook Time: 30 minutes

Favorite recipe from **National Pork Producers Council**

CARIBBEAN BLACK BEAN CASSEROLE WITH SPICY MANGO SALSA

2 cups chicken broth
1 cup uncooked basmati rice
2 tablespoons olive oil, divided
½ pound chorizo sausage
2 cloves garlic, minced
1 cup chopped red bell pepper
3 cups canned black beans, rinsed and
    drained
½ cup chopped fresh cilantro
2 small mangoes
1 cup chopped red onion
2 tablespoons honey
2 tablespoons white wine vinegar
1 teaspoon curry powder
½ teaspoon salt
½ teaspoon ground red pepper

1. Place chicken broth in medium saucepan. Bring to a boil over high heat; stir in rice. Reduce heat to low; simmer, covered, 20 minutes or until liquid is absorbed and rice is tender.

2. Heat 1 tablespoon oil in heavy, large skillet over medium heat. Add sausage; cook, turning occasionally, 8 to 10 minutes until browned and no longer pink in center. Remove from skillet to cutting surface. Cut into ½-inch slices; set aside. Drain fat from skillet.

3. Preheat oven to 350°F. Grease 1½-quart casserole; set aside. Add remaining tablespoon oil to skillet; heat over medium-high heat. Add garlic;

cook and stir 1 minute. Add bell pepper; cook and stir 5 minutes. Remove from heat. Stir in beans, sausage, rice and cilantro.

4. Spoon sausage mixture into prepared casserole; cover with foil. Bake 30 minutes or until heated through.

5. Peel mangoes; remove seeds. Chop enough flesh to measure 3 cups. Combine mango and remaining ingredients in large bowl. Mix thoroughly.

6. Spoon sausage mixture onto serving plates. Serve with mango salsa. *Makes 6 servings*

CAMPBELL'S® HAM & PASTA SKILLET

1 can (10¾ ounces) CAMPBELL'S®
    Condensed Broccoli Cheese Soup
1 cup milk
1 tablespoon spicy brown mustard
2 cups broccoli flowerets *or* 1 package
    (10 ounces) frozen broccoli cuts (2 cups)
1½ cups cooked ham strips
3 cups cooked medium shell macaroni
    (about 2 cups uncooked)

In medium skillet mix soup, milk, mustard and broccoli. Over medium heat, heat to a boil. Reduce heat to low. Cook 5 minutes or until broccoli is tender. Add ham and macaroni and heat through.
Makes 4 servings

Prep Time: 10 minutes
Cook Time: 15 minutes

SAUSAGE MEDLEY

1 pound **HILLSHIRE FARM**® Smoked
 Sausage
1 pound **HILLSHIRE FARM**® Polska
 Kielbasa
1 pound **HILLSHIRE FARM**® Lit'l Smokies
1 pound **HILLSHIRE FARM**® Bratwurst
1 can (15 ounces) black beans, rinsed and
 drained
1 cup chopped onion
4 cloves garlic, minced
1 jalapeño pepper, seeded and chopped
 Chili-Lemon Sauce (recipe follows)

Lightly brown Smoked Sausage, Polska Kielbasa,
Lit'l Smokies and Bratwurst in large saucepan over
medium-high heat. Add 3 cups water, beans, onion,
garlic and jalapeño pepper. Reduce heat to low;
gently simmer 40 minutes. Meanwhile, prepare
Chili-Lemon Sauce.

Remove meats. Slice as desired; arrange on serving
platter. Cover meat; keep warm. Drain liquid from
bean mixture, leaving just enough liquid so beans are
moist. Transfer to serving platter. Serve with Chili-
Lemon Sauce. *Makes 10 to 12 servings*

CHILI-LEMON SAUCE

1 onion, coarsely chopped
¾ cup lemon juice
3 jalapeño peppers, seeded and chopped
3 cloves garlic, cut into halves

Place all ingredients in food processor or blender.
Process until smooth. *Makes about 1 cup*

PORK-STUFFED EGGPLANT

1 medium eggplant
½ pound lean ground pork
1 small green bell pepper, coarsely chopped
¼ cup chopped onion
1 clove garlic, minced
¼ cup water
⅛ teaspoon dried oregano leaves, crushed
⅛ teaspoon ground black pepper
1 medium tomato, coarsely chopped

Wash eggplant and cut in half lengthwise. Remove
pulp, leaving eggplant shell about ¼ inch thick. Cut
pulp into ½-inch cubes. Set shells and pulp aside.

In large skillet cook ground pork, bell pepper, onion
and garlic until pork is browned; drain excess
drippings. Add eggplant pulp, water, oregano and
black pepper; cover and cook over low heat 10
minutes, stirring occasionally. Remove from heat
and stir in tomato. Spoon mixture into eggplant
shells. Place in 12×8×2-inch baking dish. Bake in
preheated 350°F oven 20 to 25 minutes or until
heated through. *Makes 2 servings*

Prep Time: 25 minutes
Cook Time: 25 minutes

Favorite recipe from **National Pork Producers Council**

Sausage Medley

THREE BEAN AND FRANKS BAKE

1 tablespoon vegetable oil
1 medium onion, chopped
2 cloves garlic, minced
1 red bell pepper, seeded and coarsely chopped
1 green bell pepper, seeded and coarsely chopped
1 can (16 ounces) vegetarian baked beans
1 can (16 ounces) butter or lima beans, drained
1 can (16 ounces) red or kidney beans, drained
½ cup ketchup
½ cup packed light brown sugar
2 tablespoons cider vinegar
1 tablespoon HEBREW NATIONAL® Deli Mustard
1 package (12 ounces) HEBREW NATIONAL® Beef Franks or Reduced Fat Beef Franks, cut into 1-inch pieces

Preheat oven to 350°F. Heat oil in large saucepan over medium heat; add onion and garlic and cook 8 minutes, stirring occasionally. Add red and green bell peppers; cook 5 minutes, stirring occasionally. Stir in baked, butter and red beans, ketchup, brown sugar, vinegar and mustard; bring to a boil. Stir franks into bean mixture.

Transfer mixture to 2-quart casserole or 8- or 9-inch square baking dish. Bake 40 to 45 minutes or until hot and bubbly.

Makes 6 main-dish or 10 side-dish servings

SPAM® & CREAMY NOODLE BAKE

6 ounces uncooked whole wheat noodles or egg noodles
1 cup (4 ounces) ricotta cheese
1 cup light sour cream
½ cup chopped onion
½ cup milk
2 tablespoons butter or margarine, melted
1 egg
¼ teaspoon ground nutmeg
¼ teaspoon black pepper
1 (12-ounce) can SPAM® Luncheon Meat, cubed

TOPPING
1 cup fresh torn bread cubes
⅓ cup grated Parmesan cheese
2 tablespoons butter or margarine, melted
1 tablespoon chopped fresh parsley *or* 1 teaspoon dried parsley leaves

Heat oven to 350°F. Cook noodles according to package directions; drain. In large bowl, stir together ricotta cheese, sour cream, onion, milk, 2 tablespoons butter, egg, nutmeg and pepper. Stir in SPAM® and cooked noodles. Spoon mixture into greased 2½-quart casserole. Cover. Bake, stirring halfway through baking, 35 to 40 minutes or until thoroughly heated. In small bowl, combine all topping ingredients. During last 10 minutes of baking, uncover casserole, stir noodle mixture and top with topping. *Makes 6 servings*

Three Bean and Franks Bake

FAMILY–STYLE FRANKFURTERS WITH RICE AND RED BEANS

1 tablespoon vegetable oil
1 medium onion, chopped
½ medium green bell pepper, chopped
2 cloves garlic, minced
1 can (14 ounces) red kidney beans, rinsed and drained
1 can (14 ounces) Great Northern beans, rinsed and drained
½ pound beef frankfurters, cut into ¼-inch-thick pieces
1 cup uncooked instant brown rice
1 cup vegetable broth
¼ cup ketchup
¼ cup packed brown sugar
3 tablespoons dark molasses
1 tablespoon Dijon mustard

Preheat oven to 350°F. Spray 13×9-inch baking dish with nonstick cooking spray.

Heat oil in Dutch oven over medium-high heat until hot. Add onion, bell pepper and garlic; cook and stir 2 minutes or until onion is tender.

Add beans, frankfurters, rice, broth, ketchup, sugar, molasses and mustard to vegetables; stir to combine. Pour into prepared dish.

Cover tightly with foil and bake 30 minutes or until rice is tender. *Makes 6 servings*

FRENCH FRY SPAM™ CASSEROLE

1 (20-ounce) bag frozen French-fried potatoes, thawed
2 cups (8 ounces) shredded Cheddar cheese
2 cups sour cream
1 (10¾-ounce) can condensed cream of chicken soup
1 (12-ounce) can SPAM® Luncheon Meat, cubed
½ cup chopped red bell pepper
½ cup chopped green onions
½ cup finely crushed corn flakes

Heat oven to 350°F. In large bowl, combine potatoes, cheese, sour cream and soup. Stir in SPAM®, bell pepper and green onions. Spoon into 13×9-inch baking dish. Sprinkle with corn flakes. Bake 30 to 40 minutes or until thoroughly heated.
Makes 6 to 8 servings

Family-Style Frankfurters with Rice and Red Beans

SAVORY LENTIL CASSEROLE

1¼ cups uncooked dried brown or green
     lentils, rinsed and sorted
2 tablespoons olive oil
1 large onion, chopped
3 cloves garlic, minced
8 ounces fresh shiitake or button
     mushrooms, sliced
2 tablespoons all-purpose flour
1½ cups canned beef broth
1 tablespoon Worcestershire sauce
1 tablespoon balsamic vinegar
4 ounces Canadian bacon, minced
½ teaspoon salt
½ teaspoon black pepper
½ cup grated Parmesan cheese
2 to 3 plum tomatoes, seeded and chopped

1. Preheat oven to 400°F. Place lentils in medium saucepan; cover with 1 inch water. Bring to a boil over high heat. Reduce heat to low. Simmer, covered, 20 to 25 minutes until lentils are barely tender; drain.

2. Meanwhile, heat oil in large skillet over medium heat. Add onion and garlic; cook and stir 10 minutes. Add mushrooms; cook and stir 10 minutes or until liquid is evaporated and mushrooms are tender. Sprinkle flour over mushroom mixture; stir well. Cook and stir 1 minute. Stir in beef broth, Worcestershire, vinegar, bacon, salt and pepper. Cook and stir until mixture is thick and bubbly.

3. Grease 1½-quart casserole. Stir lentils into mushroom mixture. Spread evenly into prepared casserole. Sprinkle with cheese. Bake 20 minutes.

4. Sprinkle tomatoes over casserole just before serving. *Makes 4 servings*

Cook's Tip

When cooking lentils with acidic ingredients, such as tomatoes or wine, the cooking time will increase by as much as 10 to 15 minutes.

Savory Lentil Casserole

CREAMY SPAM™ BROCCOLI CASSEROLE

Nonstick cooking spray
1 (7-ounce) package elbow macaroni
2 cups frozen cut broccoli, thawed and drained
1 (12-ounce) can SPAM® Lite Luncheon Meat, cubed
½ cup chopped red bell pepper
2 cups skim milk
2 tablespoons cornstarch
¼ teaspoon black pepper
1 cup (4 ounces) shredded fat-free Cheddar cheese
¾ cup soft bread crumbs
2 teaspoons margarine, melted

Heat oven to 350°F. Spray 2-quart casserole with nonstick cooking spray. Cook macaroni according to package directions; drain. In prepared casserole, combine macaroni, broccoli, SPAM® and bell pepper. In small saucepan, stir together milk, cornstarch and black pepper until cornstarch is dissolved. Bring to a boil, stirring constantly, until thickened. Reduce heat to low. Add cheese; stir until melted. Stir sauce into SPAM™ mixture. Combine bread crumbs and margarine; sprinkle on top of casserole. Bake 40 minutes or until thoroughly heated.

Makes 8 servings

ITALIAN SAUSAGE BAKE

1 pound mild Italian sausage, casings removed and crumbled
1 large onion, chopped
1 cup long grain rice, uncooked
1 zucchini, thinly sliced
1 yellow squash, thinly sliced
3 large Roma tomatoes, chopped
1 large green bell pepper, chopped
¾ cup LAWRY'S® Herb & Garlic Marinade with Lemon Juice
⅓ cup grated Parmesan cheese

In large skillet, brown sausage and onion over medium-high heat; drain fat. Place rice in 3-quart casserole. Top with zucchini, yellow squash, tomatoes, bell pepper and sausage mixture. Pour Herb & Garlic Marinade over layered ingredients. Cover and refrigerate 30 minutes. Bake in 400°F oven 40 minutes. Sprinkle Parmesan on top. Bake additional 5 minutes or until golden brown.

Makes 6 to 8 servings

Serving Suggestion: Serve with a mixed green salad.

Hint: Substitute other sausages, such as sliced or chopped kielbasa, for Italian sausage.

Creamy Spam™ Broccoli Casserole

CREAMY HAM AND GARDEN ROTINI

8 ounces uncooked rotini pasta
1 bag (16 ounces) frozen vegetable blend
    (broccoli, cauliflower, red bell peppers
    and corn)
4 ounces turkey ham, chopped
1½ cups skim milk
2 tablespoons all-purpose flour
1¼ cups (5 ounces) shredded reduced-fat
    Monterey Jack cheese
    Black pepper

1. Preheat oven to 325°F. Spray 11×8-inch baking pan with nonstick cooking spray; set aside. Cook pasta according to package directions; drain. Place in bottom of prepared pan; set aside.

2. Meanwhile, add ½ cup water to large nonstick skillet. Bring to a boil over high heat. Add vegetables; return to a boil. Reduce heat to low; simmer, covered, 4 minutes. Drain. Toss vegetables and ham with pasta; set aside.

3. Combine milk and flour in small bowl; whisk until smooth. Pour milk mixture into same skillet; cook over medium-high heat, stirring constantly, until slightly thickened. Remove from heat. Pour over pasta mixture. Top with cheese; sprinkle with pepper. Cover loosely with foil. Bake 25 to 30 minutes or until heated through.

Makes 4 servings

CORNMEAL AND SAUSAGE LAYERED DINNER

1½ pounds BOB EVANS® Italian Roll Sausage
1 cup chopped onion
1 clove garlic, minced
1 (16-ounce) can diced tomatoes, undrained
1 (8-ounce) can tomato sauce
1 tablespoon chopped fresh basil *or*
    1 teaspoon dried basil leaves
½ teaspoon ground black pepper
1½ cups yellow cornmeal
¾ teaspoon salt
3 cups water
1 cup grated Romano cheese

Crumble and cook sausage in large skillet until browned. Remove sausage from skillet and reserve. Pour off all but 1 tablespoon drippings. Add onion and garlic to skillet; cook until tender. Stir in tomatoes, tomato sauce, basil, pepper and sausage. Bring to a boil; reduce heat to low and simmer, uncovered, 25 minutes. Preheat oven to 375°F.

While sausage mixture is cooking, combine cornmeal, salt and water in medium saucepan. Bring to a boil, stirring constantly; cook and stir until thickened. Remove from heat; let cool slightly. Pour half of cornmeal mixture into greased 2½-quart casserole dish. Top with half of sausage mixture and sprinkle with half of cheese. Repeat with remaining cornmeal mixture, sausage mixture and cheese. Bake, uncovered, 30 minutes. Refrigerate leftovers.

Makes 6 servings

Creamy Ham and Garden Rotini

SMOKED SAUSAGE AND SAUERKRAUT CASSEROLE

6 fully-cooked smoked sausage links, such as German or Polish sausage (about 1½ pounds)
¼ cup packed brown sugar
2 tablespoons Dijon mustard, country-style Dijon mustard or German-style mustard
1 teaspoon caraway seed
½ teaspoon dill weed
1 jar (32 ounces) sauerkraut, drained
1 small green bell pepper, stemmed, seeded and diced
½ cup (2 ounces) shredded Swiss cheese

1. Place sausage in large skillet with ⅓ cup water. Cover; bring to a boil over medium heat. Reduce heat to low; simmer, covered, 10 minutes. Uncover and simmer until water evaporates and sausages brown lightly.

2. While sausage is cooking, combine sugar, mustard, caraway and dill in medium saucepan; stir until blended. Add sauerkraut and bell pepper; stir until well mixed. Cook, covered, over medium heat 10 minutes or until very hot.

3. Spoon sauerkraut into microwavable 2- to 3-quart casserole; sprinkle with cheese. Place sausage into sauerkraut; cover. Microwave on HIGH 30 seconds or until cheese melts.

Makes 6 servings

Prep and Cook Time: 20 minutes

SPAM™ VEGETABLE CASSEROLE

2 (10¾-ounce) cans cream of mushroom soup
½ cup milk
½ cup pasteurized processed cheese spread
1 (16-ounce) package mixed frozen vegetables, thawed
1 (12-ounce) can SPAM® Luncheon Meat, cubed
1¼ cups uncooked instant rice
1 cup (4 ounces) shredded Cheddar cheese
1 (2.8-ounce) can French-fried onions
2 cups crushed butter crackers
⅓ cup butter or margarine, melted

Heat oven to 350°F. In medium bowl, combine soup, milk and cheese spread. In large bowl, combine vegetables, SPAM®, rice, cheese and onions; stir in soup mixture. Pour into 13×9-inch baking pan. Combine crackers and melted butter; sprinkle over casserole. Bake 50 to 55 minutes or until hot.

Makes 8 servings

Smoked Sausage and Sauerkraut Casserole

BAYOU–STYLE POT PIE

1 tablespoon olive oil
1 large onion, chopped
1 green bell pepper, chopped
1½ teaspoons minced garlic
8 ounces boneless skinless chicken thighs,
    cut into 1-inch pieces
1 can (14½ ounces) stewed tomatoes,
    undrained
8 ounces fully cooked smoked sausage or
    kielbasa, thinly sliced
¾ teaspoon hot pepper sauce or to taste
2¼ cups buttermilk baking mix
¾ teaspoon dried thyme leaves
⅛ teaspoon black pepper
⅔ cup milk

1. Preheat oven to 450°F. Heat oil in medium ovenproof skillet over medium-high heat until hot. Add onion, bell pepper and garlic. Cook 3 minutes, stirring occasionally.

2. Add chicken and cook 1 minute. Add tomatoes with juice, sausage and hot pepper sauce. Cook, uncovered, over medium-low heat 5 minutes.

3. While chicken is cooking, combine baking mix, thyme and black pepper. Stir in milk. Drop batter by heaping tablespoonfuls in mounds over chicken mixture. Bake 14 minutes or until biscuits are golden brown and cooked through and chicken mixture is bubbly. *Makes 4 servings*

Prep and Cook Time: 28 minutes

Food Fact

Salmonella is a bacteria common to raw eggs and poultry. A good way to prevent the spread of this bacteria is to use a separate cutting board for cutting whole chicken or chicken pieces. When finished working, discard any scraps and thoroughly clean the board in hot soapy water. Always wash your hands after handling raw chicken.

Bayou-Style Pot Pie

COUNTRY SAUSAGE MACARONI AND CHEESE

1 pound **BOB EVANS**® Special Seasonings
   Roll Sausage
1½ cups milk
12 ounces pasteurized processed Cheddar
   cheese, cut into cubes
½ cup Dijon mustard
1 cup diced fresh or drained canned
   tomatoes
1 cup sliced mushrooms
⅓ cup sliced green onions
⅛ teaspoon cayenne pepper
12 ounces uncooked elbow macaroni
2 tablespoons Parmesan cheese

Preheat oven to 350°F. Crumble and cook sausage in medium skillet until browned. Drain on paper towels. Combine milk, cheese and mustard in medium saucepan; cook and stir over low heat until cheese melts and mixture is smooth. Stir in sausage, tomatoes, mushrooms, green onions and cayenne pepper. Remove from heat.

Cook macaroni according to package directions; drain. Combine hot macaroni and cheese mixture in large bowl; toss until well coated. Spoon into greased 2-quart casserole dish. Cover and bake 15 to 20 minutes. Stir; sprinkle with Parmesan cheese. Bake, uncovered, 5 minutes more. Let stand 10 minutes before serving. Refrigerate leftovers.

Makes 6 to 8 servings

SPRING LAMB SKILLET

2 teaspoons olive oil
1 pound boneless lamb, cut into
   1-inch cubes
2 cups thinly sliced yellow squash
2 cups (about 8 ounces) sliced fresh
   mushrooms
2 medium tomatoes, seeded and chopped
½ cup sliced green onions
3 cups cooked brown rice
½ teaspoon dried rosemary
½ teaspoon salt
½ teaspoon cracked black pepper

Heat oil in large skillet over medium heat until hot. Add lamb and cook 3 to 5 minutes or until lamb is browned. Remove from skillet; reserve. Add squash, mushrooms, tomatoes and onions to skillet; cook 2 to 3 minutes or until vegetables are tender. Stir in rice, rosemary, salt, pepper and reserved lamb. Cook until heated through. *Makes 6 servings*

Favorite recipe from **USA Rice Federation**

Country Sausage Macaroni and Cheese

Ethnic FLAVORS

CHICKEN ENCHILADA SKILLET CASSEROLE

1 bag (16 ounces) BIRDS EYE® frozen Farm Fresh
   Mixtures Broccoli, Corn & Red Peppers
1 package (1¼ ounces) taco seasoning mix
1 can (16 ounces) diced tomatoes, undrained
3 cups shredded cooked chicken
1 cup shredded Monterey Jack cheese
8 ounces tortilla chips

• In large skillet, combine vegetables, seasoning mix, tomatoes and chicken; bring to boil over medium-high heat.

• Cover; cook 4 minutes or until vegetables are cooked and mixture is heated through.

• Sprinkle with cheese; cover and cook 2 minutes more or until cheese is melted.

• Serve with chips. *Makes 4 servings*

Birds Eye Idea: Here's a quick lunch item for kids. Cut up 4 cooked hot dogs; stir into 1 bag of prepared Birds Eye® frozen Pasta Secrets White Cheddar.

Prep Time: 5 minutes
Cook Time: 10 minutes

Left: *Chicken Enchilada Skillet Casserole*

Top: *Sweet & Sour Chicken and Rice (page 174)*

PLUM CHICKEN

6 ounces fresh uncooked Chinese egg
   noodles
¼ cup plum preserves or jam
3 tablespoons rice wine vinegar
3 tablespoons reduced sodium soy sauce
1 tablespoon cornstarch
3 teaspoons oil, divided
1 small red onion, thinly sliced
2 cups fresh snow peas, diagonally sliced
12 ounces boneless skinless chicken breasts,
   cut into thin strips
4 medium plums or apricots, pitted and
   sliced

1. Cook noodles according to package directions.
Drain and keep warm.

2. Stir together plum preserves, rice wine vinegar,
soy sauce and cornstarch; set aside.

3. Heat 2 teaspoons oil in large nonstick skillet. Add
onion and cook 2 minutes or until slightly softened.
Add pea pods and cook 3 minutes. Remove
vegetables to medium bowl.

4. Heat remaining 1 teaspoon oil in skillet. Add
chicken and cook over medium-high heat 2 to
3 minutes or until no longer pink. Push chicken to
one side of skillet.

5. Stir sauce; add to skillet. Cook and stir until thick
and bubbly. Stir in vegetables and plums; coat
evenly. Cook 3 minutes or until heated through.
Toss with noodles and serve immediately.

Makes 4 servings

CHEESY CHICKEN TETRAZZINI

2 whole chicken breasts, boned, skinned
   and cut into 1-inch pieces (about
   1½ pounds)
2 tablespoons butter or margarine
1½ cups sliced mushrooms
1 red bell pepper, cut into julienne strips
½ cup sliced green onions
¼ cup all-purpose flour
1¾ cups chicken broth
1 cup light cream or half-and-half
2 tablespoons dry sherry
½ teaspoon salt
¼ teaspoon black pepper
¼ teaspoon dried thyme leaves, crushed
1 package (8 ounces) tri-color rotelle pasta,
   cooked until just tender and drained
¼ cup freshly grated Parmesan cheese
2 tablespoons chopped fresh parsley
1 cup shredded NOKKELOST or
   JARLSBERG Cheese

In skillet, brown chicken in butter. Add mushrooms
and brown. Add red pepper and green onions; cook
several minutes, stirring occasionally. Stir in flour
and cook several minutes until blended. Gradually
blend in chicken broth, cream and sherry. Cook,
stirring, until thickened and smooth. Season with
salt, pepper and thyme. Toss sauce with pasta,
Parmesan cheese and parsley. Spoon into 1½-quart
baking dish. Bake at 350°F. for 30 minutes. Top with
shredded cheese. Bake until cheese is melted.

Makes 6 servings

Plum Chicken

CURRIED CHICKEN, VEGETABLES AND COUSCOUS SKILLET

1 package (16 ounces) frozen vegetable medley, such as broccoli, carrots and cauliflower or bell pepper and onion strips
1 pound chicken tenders
2 teaspoons curry powder, divided
¾ teaspoon garlic salt
⅛ teaspoon ground red pepper
4½ teaspoons vegetable oil
1 can (about 14 ounces) chicken broth
1 cup uncooked couscous

1. Thaw vegetables according to package directions.

2. While vegetables are thawing, place chicken in medium bowl. Sprinkle with 1 teaspoon curry powder, garlic salt and red pepper; toss to coat.

3. Heat oil in large deep skillet over medium-high heat until hot. Add chicken mixture, spreading in one layer. Cook 5 to 6 minutes or until chicken is no longer pink in center, turning occasionally.

4. Transfer chicken to plate; set aside. Add broth and remaining 1 teaspoon curry powder to skillet; bring to a boil over high heat, scraping up browned bits on bottom of skillet.

5. Stir thawed vegetables into skillet; return to a boil. Stir in couscous; top with chicken. Cover and remove from heat. Let stand 5 minutes or until liquid is absorbed. *Makes 4 servings*

Prep and Cook Time: 19 minutes

PORTUGUESE CHICKEN WITH PEPPERS AND OLIVES

6 boneless skinless chicken breast halves
1 teaspoon salt
½ teaspoon red pepper flakes
¼ teaspoon black pepper
1 tablespoon olive oil
2 large onions, halved and sliced
2 red bell peppers, sliced
2 cloves garlic, minced
½ cup sliced black olives

1. Preheat oven to 475°F. Sprinkle chicken with salt, red pepper and black pepper. Heat oil in a large nonstick skillet over medium-high heat. Add chicken; cook 3 to 4 minutes. Turn chicken; cook 4 minutes more. Remove chicken to casserole with cover.

2. Add onion to same skillet and cook 2 to 3 minutes, stirring often, adding a little water if onion starts to brown too much. Add bell pepper and garlic and cook, covered, 2 to 3 minutes longer, adding additional water if needed to prevent burning. Stir in olives.

3. Pour onion mixture over chicken and cover. Bake 15 minutes or until chicken is no longer pink in center. *Makes 6 servings*

Prep Time: 5 minutes
Cook Time: 25 minutes

Curried Chicken, Vegetables and Couscous Skillet

ITALIAN-STYLE CHICKEN STIR-FRY

1 can (14½ ounces) **CONTADINA**® Stewed
    Tomatoes
3 tablespoons olive oil, divided
2 tablespoons chopped fresh basil *or*
    1 teaspoon dried basil leaves, crushed
2 large cloves garlic, finely chopped
½ teaspoon salt
¼ teaspoon ground black pepper
¼ teaspoon crushed red pepper flakes
    (optional)
1 pound boneless, skinless chicken breast
    halves, cut into 3-inch strips
1 small green bell pepper, thinly sliced
1 small onion, thinly sliced
1 can (2¼ ounces) sliced ripe olives, drained
3 to 4 pita breads, warmed

1. Drain tomatoes reserving ¼ cup juice. Combine reserved tomato juice, 2 tablespoons oil, basil, garlic, salt, black pepper and red pepper flakes in medium bowl.

2. Add chicken; stir to coat. Cover; chill for at least 1 hour.

3. Heat remaining 1 tablespoon oil in large skillet over high heat. Add chicken mixture, bell pepper and onion; cook, stirring constantly, for 5 to 6 minutes or until chicken is no longer pink in center. Add tomatoes and olives; heat through.

4. Cut pitas in half; stuff mixture into pockets.

Makes 3 to 4 servings

MEXICAN LASAGNA

4 boneless skinless chicken breast halves
2 tablespoons vegetable oil
2 teaspoons chili powder
1 teaspoon ground cumin
1 can (14½ ounces) diced tomatoes with
    garlic, drained
1 can (8 ounces) tomato sauce
1 teaspoon hot pepper sauce (optional)
1 cup part-skim ricotta cheese
1 can (4 ounces) diced green chilies
¼ cup chopped fresh cilantro, divided
12 (6-inch) corn tortillas
1 cup (4 ounces) shredded Cheddar cheese

Preheat oven to 375°F. Cut chicken into ½-inch pieces.

Heat oil in large skillet over medium heat. Add chicken, chili powder and cumin. Cook 4 minutes or until tender, stirring occasionally. Stir in diced tomatoes, tomato sauce and hot pepper sauce; bring to a boil. Reduce heat; simmer 2 minutes.

Combine ricotta cheese, chilies and 2 tablespoons cilantro in small bowl; mix until well blended.

Spoon half of chicken mixture in bottom of 12×8-inch baking dish. Top with 6 tortillas, ricotta cheese mixture, remaining tortillas, remaining chicken mixture, Cheddar cheese and remaining cilantro. Bake 25 minutes or until heated through.

Makes 6 to 8 servings

Mexican Lasagna

CHICKEN ENCHILADAS

1 whole broiler-fryer chicken (about
   3 pounds), cut into 8 pieces
3 fresh poblano chilies*, roasted, peeled,
   seeded, deveined and diced
1 large tomato, peeled, seeded, and
   chopped
½ cup finely chopped white onion
1 clove garlic, minced
½ teaspoon ground cumin
¼ teaspoon salt
½ cup chicken broth
1½ cups heavy cream
12 corn tortillas (6-inch diameter)
2 cups (8 ounces) shredded queso
   Chihuahua or Monterey Jack cheese
   Green onions and slivered red bell peppers
   for garnish

Chili peppers can sting and irritate the skin; wear rubber gloves when handling peppers and do not touch eyes. Wash hands after handling.

1. Place chicken in single layer in 12-inch skillet. Sprinkle with chilies, tomato, white onion, garlic, cumin and salt; add broth. Bring to a boil over medium-high heat. Reduce heat. Cover; simmer 1 hour or until chicken is tender.

2. Remove chicken from skillet with tongs, shaking off vegetable pieces. Let stand until cool enough to handle.

3. Skim and discard fat from skillet. Bring remaining broth mixture to a boil over medium-high heat. Boil 4 to 8 minutes until mixture is reduced to 2 cups. Pour reduced broth mixture into 13×9-inch baking dish.

4. Remove and discard skin and bones from chicken. Using fingers, pull chicken into coarse shreds.

5. Preheat oven to 375°F. Heat cream in medium skillet over medium heat until hot but not boiling; remove from heat.

6. Dip 1 tortilla in cream with tongs a few seconds or until limp. Remove, draining off excess cream. Spread about 3 tablespoons chicken down center of tortilla.

7. Roll up; place on sauce in baking dish. Repeat with remaining tortillas, cream and chicken. Pour any remaining cream over enchiladas.

8. Sprinkle cheese over enchiladas. Bake 25 to 30 minutes until sauce is bubbly and cheese is melted. Garnish, if desired.   *Makes 4 to 6 servings*

Chicken Enchiladas

CHICKEN CACCIATORE

4 pounds chicken pieces with bone (breasts, legs, thighs)
¾ teaspoon salt
¾ teaspoon freshly ground black pepper
⅓ cup all-purpose flour
1 tablespoon fresh oregano leaves or
**   1 teaspoon dried oregano**
3 tablespoons olive oil, divided
2 teaspoons minced garlic
1 cup chopped yellow onion
3 cups (8 ounces) sliced mushrooms
2 cups red bell pepper strips
3 cups fresh ripe tomato wedges
⅔ cup red wine (with or without alcohol)
⅓ cup low-salt tomato juice
1 tablespoon fresh rosemary leaves or
**   1 teaspoon dried rosemary**
2 cups (8 ounces) shredded ALPINE LACE®
**   Fat Free Pasteurized Process Skim Milk**
**   Cheese Product—For Mozzarella Lovers**
¼ cup minced fresh parsley

1. Rinse the chicken and pat dry with paper towels. Sprinkle with the salt and black pepper. In a large self-sealing plastic bag, combine the flour and oregano. Add the chicken and shake well.

2. In a large deep nonstick skillet, heat 2 tablespoons of the oil over medium-high heat. Add the chicken pieces in batches and cook, turning occasionally, for 8 minutes or until golden brown. Transfer to a plate.

3. Add the remaining tablespoon of oil to the skillet with the garlic and onion. Sauté for 5 minutes or until soft. Add the mushrooms and bell pepper and sauté 5 minutes longer. Stir in the tomatoes, wine, tomato juice and rosemary. Return the chicken to the skillet and bring to a boil. Reduce the heat. Cover; simmer, turning the chicken occasionally, for 30 minutes or until juices run clear.

4. Preheat the broiler. Sprinkle the chicken with the cheese and broil for 3 minutes or just until melted. Garnish with the parsley.   *Makes 6 servings*

CHILAQUILES

1 can (10¾ ounces) condensed cream of
**   chicken soup**
½ cup mild green chili salsa
1 can (4 ounces) diced green chilies,
**   undrained**
8 cups tortilla chips
2 to 3 cups shredded cooked chicken or
**   turkey**
2 cups (8 ounces) shredded Cheddar cheese
**   Sliced pitted black olives for garnish**
**   Cilantro sprigs for garnish**

Preheat oven to 350°F. Combine soup and salsa in medium bowl; stir in green chilies. Place ⅓ of chips in 2- to 2½-quart casserole; top with ⅓ of chicken. Spread ⅓ of soup mixture over chicken; sprinkle with ⅓ of cheese. Repeat layering. Bake, uncovered, 15 minutes or until casserole is heated through and cheese is melted. Garnish with olives and cilantro.

Makes 6 servings

Chicken Cacciatore

ITALIAN ANTIPASTO BAKE

2 cups rotini or elbow macaroni, cooked in
  unsalted water and drained
1 bag (16 ounces) frozen vegetable
  combination (broccoli, water chestnuts,
  red pepper), thawed and drained
2 chicken breast halves, skinned, boned and
  cut into strips
⅔ cup bottled Italian salad dressing
½ cup drained garbanzo beans (optional)
¼ cup sliced pitted ripe olives (optional)
¼ cup (1 ounce) grated Parmesan cheese
½ teaspoon Italian seasoning
1 cup (4 ounces) shredded mozzarella
  cheese, divided
1⅓ cups FRENCH'S® French Fried Onions,
  divided

Preheat oven to 350°F. In 13×9-inch baking dish,
combine hot pasta, vegetables, chicken, salad
dressing, garbanzo beans, olives, Parmesan cheese
and Italian seasoning. Stir in ½ cup mozzarella
cheese and ⅔ cup French Fried Onions. Bake,
covered, at 350°F for 35 minutes or until chicken
is done. Top with remaining mozzarella cheese and
⅔ cup onions; bake, uncovered, 5 minutes or until
onions are golden brown.   *Makes 4 to 6 servings*

Microwave Directions: In 8×12-inch microwave-
safe dish, combine ingredients, except chicken
strips, as above. Arrange uncooked chicken strips
around edges of dish. Cook, covered, on HIGH 6
minutes. Stir center of casserole; rearrange chicken
and rotate dish. Cook, covered, 5 to 6

minutes or until chicken is done. Stir casserole to
combine chicken and pasta mixture. Top with
remaining mozzarella cheese and onions; cook,
uncovered, 1 minute or until cheese melts. Let stand
5 minutes.

ORANGE GINGER CHICKEN & RICE

1 package (6.9 ounces) RICE-A-RONI®
  With ⅓ Less Salt Chicken Flavor
1 tablespoon margarine or butter
1 cup orange juice
¾ pound skinless boneless chicken breasts,
  cut into thin strips
2 cloves garlic, minced
¼ teaspoon ground ginger
  Dash red pepper flakes (optional)
1½ cups carrots, cut into short thin strips *or*
  3 cups broccoli flowerets

1. In large skillet, sauté Rice-A-Roni® mix and
margarine over medium heat, stirring frequently
until vermicelli is golden brown.

2. Stir in 1½ cups water, orange juice, chicken,
garlic, ginger, red pepper flakes and contents of
seasoning packet; bring to a boil over high heat.

3. Cover; reduce heat. Simmer 10 minutes.

4. Stir in carrots.

5. Cover; continue to simmer 5 to 10 minutes or
until liquid is absorbed and rice is tender.

Makes 4 servings

Orange Ginger Chicken & Rice

MEXICAN CHICKEN CASSEROLE

8 ounces elbow noodles or small shell pasta
2 teaspoons olive oil
1 large carrot, grated
1 medium green bell pepper, finely chopped
1 tablespoon garlic
¾ pound chicken tenders, cut in ¾-inch pieces
2 teaspoons cumin
1½ teaspoons dried oregano leaves
½ teaspoon salt
¼ teaspoon ground red pepper
2 cups (8 ounces) shredded Monterey Jack cheese, divided
1 bottle (16 ounces) tomato salsa, divided

1. Cook pasta according to package directions. While pasta is cooking, heat oil in large nonstick skillet over medium heat. Add carrot, bell pepper and garlic; cook and stir 3 minutes until vegetables are tender. Add chicken, increase heat to medium-high; cook and stir 3 to 4 minutes or until chicken is no longer pink in center. Add cumin, oregano, salt and ground red pepper; cook and stir 1 minute. Remove from heat; set aside.

2. Grease 13×9-inch microwavable dish. Drain and rinse pasta under cold running water; place in large bowl. Add chicken mixture, 1 cup cheese and 1 cup salsa. Mix well; pour into prepared dish. Top with remaining 1 cup salsa and 1 cup cheese. Cover with vented plastic wrap; microwave on HIGH 4 to 6 minutes, turning dish halfway through cooking time. Serve immediately. *Makes 4 to 6 servings*

CHICKEN ENCHILADA CASSEROLE

2 tablespoons vegetable oil
1 medium onion, chopped
4 cups shredded, cooked chicken or turkey
1 can (14½ ounces) whole tomatoes, undrained and cut up
1 can (15 ounces) tomato sauce
1 package (1.25 ounces) LAWRY'S® Taco Spices & Seasonings
½ teaspoon LAWRY'S® Garlic Powder with Parsley
1 dozen corn tortillas
2 cans (2¼ ounces each) sliced ripe olives, drained
3 cups (12 ounces) shredded Monterey Jack cheese

In large skillet, heat oil and sauté onion. Add chicken, tomatoes, tomato sauce, Taco Spices & Seasonings and Garlic Powder with Parsley; mix well. Bring to a boil over medium-high heat; reduce heat to low and simmer, uncovered, 15 minutes. In 13×9×2-inch baking dish, place 4 corn tortillas. Pour ⅓ of chicken mixture on tortillas, spreading evenly. Layer with ⅓ of olives and cheese. Repeat layers 2 times, ending with cheese. Bake, uncovered, in 350°F oven 30 to 40 minutes.
Makes 6 to 8 servings

Presentation: Serve with Mexican rice and a green salad.

Mexican Chicken Casserole

SWEET & SOUR CHICKEN AND RICE

1 pound chicken tenders
1 can (8 ounces) pineapple chunks, drained and juice reserved
1 cup uncooked rice
2 carrots, thinly sliced
1 green bell pepper, cut into 1-inch pieces
1 large onion, chopped
3 cloves garlic, minced
1 can (14½ ounces) reduced-sodium chicken broth
⅓ cup soy sauce
3 tablespoons sugar
3 tablespoons apple cider vinegar
1 tablespoon dark sesame oil
1½ teaspoons ground ginger
¼ cup chopped peanuts (optional)
Chopped fresh cilantro (optional)

Preheat oven to 350°F. Spray 13×9-inch baking dish with nonstick cooking spray.

Combine chicken, pineapple, rice, carrots, pepper, onion and garlic in prepared dish.

Place broth, reserved pineapple juice, soy sauce, sugar, vinegar, sesame oil and ginger in small saucepan; bring to a boil over high heat. Remove from heat and pour over chicken mixture.

Cover tightly with foil and bake 40 to 50 minutes or until chicken is no longer pink in center and rice is tender. Sprinkle with peanuts and cilantro, if desired.

Makes 6 servings

CHICKEN ENCHILADAS

2 cups chopped cooked chicken
2 cups shredded Wisconsin Cheddar cheese, divided
2 cups shredded Wisconsin Monterey Jack cheese, divided
1 cup Wisconsin dairy sour cream
1 teaspoon chili powder
¼ teaspoon salt
⅛ teaspoon ground red pepper
10 (6-inch) flour tortillas
1½ cups enchilada sauce
½ cup sliced black olives
¼ cup minced green onion

Combine chicken, 1 cup Cheddar cheese, 1 cup Monterey Jack cheese, sour cream and seasonings; mix well. Spread ¼ cup chicken mixture on each tortilla; roll up tightly. Pour ½ cup enchilada sauce on bottom of 12×8-inch baking dish. Place tortillas in baking dish, seam side down; top with remaining sauce. Sprinkle with remaining 1 cup Cheddar cheese and 1 cup Monterey Jack cheese. Bake at 350°F, 20 minutes or until thoroughly heated. Top with olives and green onion. *Makes 5 servings*

Favorite recipe from **Wisconsin Milk Marketing Board**

Sweet & Sour Chicken and Rice

EASY TEX–MEX BAKE

8 ounces uncooked thin mostaccioli
1 pound ground turkey breast
⅔ cup bottled medium or mild salsa
1 package (10 ounces) frozen corn, thawed and drained
1 container (16 ounces) low-fat cottage cheese
1 egg
1 tablespoon minced fresh cilantro
½ teaspoon ground white pepper
¼ teaspoon ground cumin
½ cup (2 ounces) shredded Monterey Jack cheese

1. Cook pasta according to package directions. Drain and rinse well; set aside.

2. Spray large nonstick skillet with nonstick cooking spray. Add turkey; cook until no longer pink, about 5 minutes. Stir in salsa and corn. Remove from heat.

3. Preheat oven to 350°F. Combine cottage cheese, egg, cilantro, white pepper and cumin in small bowl.

4. Spoon ½ of turkey mixture in bottom of 11×7-inch baking dish. Top with pasta. Spoon cottage cheese mixture over pasta. Top with remaining turkey mixture. Sprinkle Monterey Jack cheese over casserole.

5. Bake 25 to 30 minutes or until heated through.

Makes 6 servings

TURKEY CAZUELA

8 ounces uncooked linguini*, broken in half
1⅓ cups FRENCH'S® French Fried Onions, divided
2 cups (10 ounces) cubed cooked turkey
1 can (10¾ ounces) condensed cream of chicken soup
1 jar (8 ounces) picante sauce
½ cup sour cream
1 cup (4 ounces) shredded Cheddar cheese

*Or, substitute 4 cups cooked pasta for uncooked linguini.

Preheat oven to 350°F. Grease 2-quart shallow baking dish. Cook linguini according to package directions, using shortest cooking time. Layer linguini, ⅔ cup French Fried Onions and turkey in prepared baking dish.

Combine soup, picante sauce and sour cream in large bowl. Pour over turkey.

Cover; bake 40 minutes or until hot and bubbling. Stir gently. Sprinkle with cheese and remaining ⅔ cup onions. Bake 5 minutes or until onions are golden. *Makes 4 to 6 servings*

Prep Time: 20 minutes
Cook Time: 45 minutes

Easy Tex-Mex Bake

SOBA STIR-FRY

8 ounces uncooked soba noodles (Japanese buckwheat pasta)
1 tablespoon light olive oil
2 cups sliced fresh shiitake mushrooms
1 medium red bell pepper, cut into thin strips
2 whole dried red peppers *or* ¼ teaspoon red pepper flakes
1 clove garlic, minced
2 cups shredded napa cabbage
½ cup reduced-sodium chicken broth
2 tablespoons reduced-sodium tamari or soy sauce
1 tablespoon rice wine or dry sherry
2 teaspoons cornstarch
1 package (14 ounces) firm tofu, drained and cut into 1-inch cubes
2 green onions, thinly sliced

1. Cook noodles according to package directions. Drain and set aside.

2. Heat oil in large nonstick skillet or wok over medium heat. Add mushrooms, bell pepper, dried peppers and garlic. Cook 3 minutes or until mushrooms are tender. Add cabbage. Cover. Cook 2 minutes or until cabbage is wilted.

3. Combine chicken broth, tamari, rice wine and cornstarch in small bowl. Stir sauce into vegetable mixture. Cook 2 minutes or until sauce is bubbly. Stir in tofu and noodles; toss gently until heated through. Sprinkle with green onions. Serve immediately. *Makes 4 (2-cup) servings*

BRAZILIAN CORN AND SHRIMP MOQUECA CASSEROLE

2 tablespoons olive oil
½ cup chopped onion
¼ cup chopped green bell pepper
¼ cup tomato sauce
2 tablespoons chopped parsley
½ teaspoon TABASCO® brand Pepper Sauce
1 pound medium cooked shrimp
   Salt to taste
2 tablespoons all-purpose flour
1 cup milk
1 can (16 ounces) cream-style corn
   Grated Parmesan cheese

Heat oil in large oven-proof skillet over medium-high heat. Add onion, bell pepper, tomato sauce, parsley and TABASCO® Sauce and cook, stirring occasionally, for 5 minutes. Add shrimp and salt. Cover and reduce heat to low, and simmer for 2 to 3 minutes. Preheat oven to 375°F. Sprinkle flour over shrimp mixture; stir. Add milk gradually, stirring after each addition. Cook over medium heat until mixture thickens. Remove from heat. Pour corn over mixture; do not stir. Sprinkle with Parmesan cheese. Bake for 30 minutes or until browned. *Makes 4 servings*

Soba Stir-Fry

Ethnic
FLAVORS

MID-EASTERN SKILLET DINNER

½ pound ground lamb
½ pound ground raw turkey
1 teaspoon garlic powder
1 teaspoon Italian seasoning, crushed, *or*
  ½ teaspoon each dried oregano and basil leaves, crushed
2 cups cooked garbanzo beans (chick-peas) or cooked white beans*
2 medium tomatoes, chopped
  Juice of 1 SUNKIST® Lemon
2 tablespoons tomato paste mixed with
  ¼ cup water
2 teaspoons sugar
1 teaspoon dried mint leaves, crushed
  Grated peel of ½ SUNKIST® Lemon

To cook dry beans: For every 1 cup dry beans/peas, bring to boil in 6 to 8 cups water. Boil 2 minutes. Cover; remove from heat and let stand 1 hour. Drain beans and replace water. Bring to boil; cover and cook over low heat 1½ to 2 hours or until beans are tender. One cup dry beans yields about 2¾ cups cooked beans.

Thoroughly combine lamb, turkey, garlic powder and Italian seasoning. Shape into 8 small patties. In large, lightly oiled nonstick skillet, brown patties on both sides over medium-high heat (10 to 12 minutes). Pour off fat. Add remaining ingredients except lemon peel. Bring to boil; cover and cook over low heat 25 minutes, stirring occasionally. Uncover last 5 minutes to slightly thicken sauce. Add lemon peel.   *Makes 4 servings*

PASTITSO

8 ounces uncooked elbow macaroni
½ cup cholesterol-free egg substitute
¼ teaspoon ground nutmeg
¾ pound lean ground lamb, beef or turkey
½ cup chopped onion
1 clove garlic, minced
1 can (8 ounces) tomato sauce
¾ teaspoon dried mint leaves
½ teaspoon dried oregano leaves
½ teaspoon ground black pepper
⅛ teaspoon ground cinnamon
2 teaspoons reduced-calorie margarine
3 tablespoons all-purpose flour
1½ cups skim milk
2 tablespoons grated Parmesan cheese

Cook pasta according to package directions. Drain and transfer to medium bowl; stir in egg substitute and nutmeg. Lightly spray bottom of 9-inch square baking dish with nonstick cooking spray. Spread pasta mixture in bottom of baking dish. Set aside.

Preheat oven to 350°F. Cook ground lamb, onion and garlic in large nonstick skillet over medium heat until lamb is no longer pink. Stir in tomato sauce, mint, oregano, black pepper and cinnamon. Reduce heat and simmer 10 minutes; spread over pasta.

Melt margarine in small nonstick saucepan. Add flour. Stir constantly for 1 minute. Whisk in milk. Cook, stirring constantly, until thickened, about 6 minutes; spread over meat mixture. Sprinkle with Parmesan cheese. Bake 30 to 40 minutes or until set.   *Makes 6 servings*

Ethnic
FLAVORS

LAMB ENCHILADAS WITH GREEN SAUCE

1 can (13 ounces) tomatillos, drained and rinsed
1 can (4 ounces) chopped green chilies, drained
¼ cup chopped onion
2 sprigs cilantro or parsley
2 cloves garlic, minced, divided
½ cup chicken broth
1 teaspoon sugar
   Dash black pepper
½ pound lean American Ground Lamb
½ cup chopped green bell pepper
¼ cup chopped celery
8 (6-inch) flour tortillas
½ cup shredded mozzarella or Monterey Jack cheese (2 ounces)
   Light sour cream or plain yogurt
   Sliced green onion

For Green Sauce, combine tomatillos, chilies, onion, cilantro and 1 clove garlic in blender or food processor. Blend or process till smooth. Pour into small saucepan. Add broth, sugar and black pepper. Bring to a boil; reduce heat. Simmer, covered, 10 minutes.

In skillet cook lamb, 1 clove garlic, green pepper and celery until lamb is no longer pink and vegetables are crisp-tender. Drain fat. To soften tortillas, alternately stack tortillas with paper towels. Microwave on HIGH (100% power) 1 to 2 minutes or until tortillas are pliable. (Or, if desired, wrap tortillas in foil. Heat in 350°F oven about 10 minutes or until pliable). Spoon meat mixture onto each tortilla, then roll up. Place filled tortillas, seam side down, in 11×7-inch baking dish. Top with Green Sauce. Cover with foil. Bake in 350°F oven for 20 minutes. Uncover; sprinkle with cheese. Return to oven for 5 minutes. Serve garnished with sour cream and green onion. *Makes 4 servings*

Note: Substitute salsa or taco sauce for the Green Sauce above. Prepare and serve as above.

Favorite recipe from **American Lamb Council**

MOROCCAN LAMB OR BEEF

¾ pound ground lamb or beef
1 cup chopped onion
1 can (14½ ounces) DEL MONTE® Original Recipe Stewed Tomatoes
⅓ cup chopped dried apricots
¼ cup seedless raisins
1 teaspoon ground cinnamon
¼ teaspoon ground cloves
1 banana, sliced
2 cups hot cooked rice, brown rice or bulgur

1. Brown meat in large skillet over medium-high heat.

2. Add onion and cook until tender; drain. Add tomatoes, apricots, raisins, cinnamon and cloves.

3. Cover and simmer 10 minutes. Season with salt and pepper, if desired. Add banana. Heat through. Serve over rice. Top with plain yogurt and chopped peanuts, if desired. *Makes 4 to 5 servings*

WOK SUKIYAKI

1 package (3¾ ounces) bean thread noodles
½ cup beef broth
½ cup teriyaki sauce
¼ cup sake, rice wine or dry sherry
1 tablespoon sugar
2 tablespoons vegetable oil, divided
1 pound beef tenderloin or sirloin, cut into
   ¼-inch strips
12 fresh shiitake or button mushrooms (about
   6 ounces), stems removed
½ pound firm tofu, drained and cut into
   1-inch cubes
6 green onions with tops, cut into 2-inch
   pieces
½ pound fresh spinach, stems removed

1. Place noodles in bowl; cover with cold water. Let stand 30 minutes or until softened; drain. Cut into 4-inch lengths; set aside.

2. Combine beef broth, teriyaki sauce, sake and sugar in small bowl; mix well. Set aside.

3. Heat wok over high heat 1 minute or until hot. Drizzle 1 tablespoon oil into wok and heat 30 seconds. Add ½ of beef; stir-fry 3 minutes or until browned. Remove from wok to bowl; set aside. Repeat with remaining 1 tablespoon oil and beef.

4. Reduce heat to medium. Add mushrooms to wok; stir-fry 1 minute and move to one side of wok. Add tofu to bottom of wok; fry 1 minute, stirring gently. Move to another side of wok. Add green onions to bottom of wok. Add broth mixture and bring to a boil. Move onions up side of wok.

5. Add noodles and spinach, keeping each in separate piles and stirring gently to soften in teriyaki sauce. Push up side of wok. Add beef and any juices; heat through. *Makes 4 servings*

BEEF FRIED RICE

¾ pound extra-lean (90% lean) ground beef
6 green onions, chopped
3 large stalks celery, chopped
8 ounces bean sprouts
½ cup sliced fresh mushrooms
½ cup finely chopped red bell pepper
1 teaspoon grated fresh ginger
3 cups cooked rice
2 tablespoons soy sauce
   Salt and freshly ground black pepper

Brown ground beef in large skillet. Drain. Stir in onions, celery, bean sprouts, mushrooms, red bell pepper and ginger. Cook over medium-high heat 5 minutes or until vegetables are crisp-tender, stirring frequently. Stir in rice and soy sauce. Season with salt and black pepper to taste. Heat through, stirring occasionally. *Makes 4 servings*

Wok Sukiyaki

BEEF MOLE TAMALE PIE

1½ pounds ground chuck
 1 medium onion, chopped
 1 green bell pepper, chopped
 2 cloves garlic, minced
1¼ cups medium-hot salsa
 1 package (10 ounces) frozen corn, partially
    thawed
 1 tablespoon unsweetened cocoa powder
 2 teaspoons ground cumin
 1 teaspoon dried oregano leaves
1½ teaspoons salt, divided
 ¼ teaspoon ground cinnamon
 2 cups (8 ounces) shredded Monterey Jack
    or Cheddar cheese
 ⅓ cup chopped fresh cilantro
 1 cup all-purpose flour
 ¾ cup yellow cornmeal
 3 tablespoons sugar
 2 teaspoons baking powder
 ⅔ cup milk
 3 tablespoons butter, melted
 1 egg, beaten
    Cilantro leaves, chili pepper and sour
    cream for garnish (optional)

Preheat oven to 400°F. Spray 11×7-inch baking dish with nonstick cooking spray. Brown ground chuck with onion, bell pepper and garlic in large deep skillet or Dutch oven over medium heat until meat just loses its pink color. Pour off drippings. Stir in salsa, corn, cocoa, cumin, oregano, 1 teaspoon salt and cinnamon. Bring to a boil. Reduce heat to medium-low; simmer, uncovered, 8 minutes, stirring occasionally. Remove from heat; stir in cheese and cilantro. Spread in prepared dish.

Combine flour, cornmeal, sugar, baking powder and remaining ½ teaspoon salt in large bowl. Add milk, butter and egg; stir just until dry ingredients are moistened. Spread batter evenly over meat mixture with spatula.

Bake 15 minutes. *Reduce oven temperature to 350°F.* Bake 20 minutes or until topping is light brown and filling is bubbly. Let stand 5 minutes before serving. Garnish, if desired.   *Makes 6 servings*

Food Fact

Monterey Jack cheese gets its name from Monterey, California. It is a mild buttery, semisoft cheese from cow's milk. This cheese is sometimes flavored with peppers and garlic and is often used in Tex-Mex cooking.

Beef Mole Tamale Pie

Ethnic
FLAVORS

CURRY BEEF

12 ounces uncooked wide egg noodles *or*
    1⅓ cups uncooked long-grain rice
1 tablespoon olive oil
1 medium onion, thinly sliced
1 tablespoon curry powder
1 teaspoon ground cumin
2 cloves garlic, minced
1 pound lean ground beef
1 cup (8 ounces) sour cream
½ cup reduced-fat (2%) milk
½ cup raisins, divided
1 teaspoon sugar
¼ cup chopped walnuts, almonds or pecans

1. Cook noodles or rice according to package directions. Meanwhile, heat oil in large skillet over medium-high heat until hot. Add onion; cook and stir 3 to 4 minutes. Add curry powder, cumin and garlic; cook 2 to 3 minutes longer or until onion is tender. Add meat; cook 6 to 8 minutes or until meat is no longer pink, breaking meat apart with wooden spoon.

2. Stir in sour cream, milk, ¼ cup raisins and sugar. Reduce heat to medium, stirring constantly, until heated through. Spoon over drained noodles or rice. Sprinkle with remaining ¼ cup raisins and nuts.

Makes 4 servings

Prep and Cook Time: 30 minutes

FIESTA CORN CASSEROLE

1 tablespoon butter
3 cups cornflakes, divided
1 pound ground beef
1 can (8 ounces) tomato sauce
1 package (1.0 ounce) LAWRY'S® Taco
    Spices & Seasonings
½ teaspoon LAWRY'S® Seasoned Salt
1 can (17 ounces) whole kernel corn,
    drained (reserve ¼ cup liquid)
2 cups (8 ounces) shredded cheddar cheese

MICROWAVE DIRECTIONS

In large skillet, heat butter; add 2 cups cornflakes; mix well. Remove buttered cornflakes and set aside. Wipe skillet clean. In same skillet, cook ground beef over medium-high heat until brown and crumbly; drain fat. Add tomato sauce, Taco Spices & Seasonings, Seasoned Salt and ¼ cup corn liquid; mix well. In 1½-quart casserole, layer half buttered cornflakes, corn, meat mixture and cheese; repeat layers. Sprinkle remaining 1 cup crushed cornflakes over top in diagonal strips. Bake in 350°F oven 15 to 20 minutes until heated through.

Makes 4 to 6 servings

Serving Suggestion: Serve with sliced tomatoes, cucumbers and fresh fruit.

Hint: May use 2 cups broken taco shell pieces and 1 cup crushed taco shells.

Curry Beef

FAJITA STUFFED SHELLS

¼ cup fresh lime juice
1 clove garlic, minced
½ teaspoon dried oregano leaves
¼ teaspoon ground cumin
1 (6-ounce) boneless lean round or flank steak
1 medium green bell pepper, halved and seeded
1 medium onion, cut in half
12 uncooked jumbo pasta shells (about 6 ounces)
½ cup reduced-fat sour cream
2 tablespoons shredded reduced-fat Cheddar cheese
1 tablespoon minced fresh cilantro
⅔ cup chunky salsa
2 cups shredded leaf lettuce

1. Combine lime juice, garlic, oregano and cumin in shallow nonmetallic dish. Add steak, bell pepper and onion. Cover and refrigerate 8 hours or overnight.

2. Preheat oven to 350°F. Cook pasta shells according to package directions. Drain and rinse well under cold water; set aside.

3. Grill steak and vegetables over medium-hot coals 3 to 4 minutes per side or until desired doneness; cool slightly. Cut steak into thin slices. Chop vegetables. Place steak slices and vegetables in medium bowl. Stir in sour cream, Cheddar cheese and cilantro. Stuff shells evenly with meat mixture, mounding slightly.

4. Arrange shells in 8-inch baking dish. Pour salsa over filled shells. Cover with foil and bake 15 minutes or until heated through. Divide lettuce evenly among 4 plates; arrange 3 shells on each plate. *Makes 4 servings*

Food Fact

Cilantro, an herb, is best used fresh.
The leaves of this plant can be used whole
or chopped and add an exciting flavor to many
Latin and Asian dishes.

Fajita Stuffed Shells

MALAYSIAN CURRIED BEEF

2 tablespoons vegetable oil
2 large yellow onions, chopped
1 piece fresh ginger (about 1 inch square), minced
2 cloves garlic, minced
2 tablespoons curry powder
1 teaspoon salt
2 large baking potatoes (1 pound), peeled and cut into chunks
1 cup beef broth
1 pound ground beef chuck
2 ripe tomatoes (12 ounces), peeled and cut into chunks
  Hot cooked rice
  Purple kale and watercress sprigs for garnish (optional)

1. Heat large skillet or wok over medium-high heat 1 minute or until hot. Add oil and heat 30 seconds. Add onions and stir-fry 2 minutes. Add ginger, garlic, curry and salt. Cook and stir 1 minute. Add potatoes; cook and stir 2 to 3 minutes.

2. Add beef broth to potato mixture. Cover and bring to a boil. Reduce heat to low; simmer about 20 minutes or until potatoes are fork-tender.

3. Stir ground beef into potato mixture. Cook and stir about 5 minutes or until beef is browned and no longer pink; drain fat.

4. Add tomato chunks and stir gently until thoroughly heated. Spoon beef mixture into serving dish. Top center with rice. Garnish, if desired.

Makes 4 servings

LASAGNA ITALIANO

1½ pounds ground beef
½ cup chopped onion
1 (14½-ounce) can tomatoes, cut up
1 (6-ounce) can tomato paste
⅓ cup water
1 garlic clove, minced
1 teaspoon dried oregano leaves, crushed
¼ teaspoon pepper
6 ounces lasagna noodles, cooked, drained
2 (6-ounce) packages KRAFT® Low-Moisture Part-Skim Mozzarella Cheese Slices
½ pound (8 ounces) VELVEETA® Pasteurized Prepared Cheese Product, thinly sliced
½ cup (2 ounces) KRAFT® 100% Grated Parmesan Cheese

In large skillet, brown meat; drain. Add onion; cook until tender. Stir in tomatoes, tomato paste, water, garlic and seasonings. Cover; simmer 30 minutes. In 12×8-inch baking dish, layer half of noodles, meat sauce, mozzarella cheese, prepared cheese product and Parmesan cheese; repeat layers. Bake at 350°F, 30 minutes. Let stand 10 minutes before serving.

Makes 6 to 8 servings

Prep Time: 40 minutes
Bake Time: 30 minutes plus standing

Malaysian Curried Beef

Ethnic
FLAVORS

SPETZQUE

9 lasagna noodles
2 pounds ground beef
1 can (4½ ounces) chopped ripe olives, drained
1 can (4 ounces) mushroom stems and pieces, drained
1 small onion, finely chopped
1 jar (16 ounces) spaghetti sauce
   Dash pepper
   Dash dried oregano leaves
   Dash Italian seasoning
1¼ cups frozen corn, thawed
1¼ cups frozen peas, thawed
2 cups (8 ounces) shredded mozzarella cheese

1. Cook lasagna noodles according to package directions; drain.

2. Cook beef in large skillet over medium-high heat until meat is brown, stirring to separate meat; drain drippings. Add olives, mushrooms and onion. Cook, stirring occasionally, until vegetables are tender. Add spaghetti sauce, pepper, oregano and Italian seasoning. Heat through, stirring occasionally.

3. Preheat oven to 350°F.

4. Place 3 noodles in bottom of 13×9-inch baking pan. Spread half the beef mixture over noodles, then half the corn and peas. Repeat layers ending with noodles. Bake lasagna 25 minutes. Sprinkle with cheese; bake 5 minutes more or until bubbly. Let stand 10 minutes before cutting.

Makes 6 servings

BEEF & VEGETABLE FRIED RICE

1 pound lean ground beef
2 cloves garlic, crushed
1 teaspoon grated fresh ginger *or* ¼ teaspoon ground ginger
2 tablespoons water
1 red bell pepper, cut into ½-inch pieces
1 package (6 ounces) frozen pea pods
3 cups cold cooked rice
3 tablespoons soy sauce
2 teaspoons dark sesame oil
¼ cup thinly sliced green onions

1. In large nonstick skillet, brown ground beef, garlic and ginger over medium heat 8 to 10 minutes or until beef is no longer pink, breaking up into ¾-inch crumbles. Remove with slotted spoon; pour off drippings.

2. In same skillet, heat water over medium-high heat until hot. Add bell pepper and pea pods; cook 3 minutes or until bell pepper is crisp-tender, stirring occasionally. Add rice, soy sauce and sesame oil; mix well. Return beef to skillet; heat through, about 5 minutes. Stir in green onions before serving.

Makes 4 (1½-cup) servings

Prep and Cook Time: 25 minutes

Favorite recipe from **National Cattlemen's Beef Association**

Spetzque

BEEF SPAGHETTI PIE OLÉ

PASTA SHELL

  1 package (7 ounces) uncooked spaghetti
  ⅓ cup shredded Monterey Jack or Cheddar
    cheese
  1 egg
  ½ teaspoon salt
  ¼ teaspoon garlic powder

FILLING

  1 pound lean ground beef
  1 teaspoon garlic powder
  ½ teaspoon salt
  ½ teaspoon ground cumin
  1 can (10 ounces) diced tomatoes with green
    chilies, undrained
  ¾ cup light dairy sour cream
  1 cup shredded Monterey Jack or Cheddar
    cheese

1. Heat oven to 350°F. Cook pasta according to package directions; drain well. In large bowl, whisk together remaining pasta shell ingredients. Add pasta; toss to coat. Arrange pasta in 9-inch pie dish, pressing down and up side to form shell; set aside.

2. Meanwhile, heat large nonstick skillet over medium heat until hot. Add ground beef; brown 4 to 5 minutes, breaking up into ¾-inch crumbles. Pour off drippings. Season beef with 1 teaspoon garlic powder, ½ teaspoon salt and cumin; stir in tomatoes. Bring to a boil; cook 3 to 5 minutes or until liquid is almost evaporated, stirring occasionally.

3. Reserve 2 tablespoons beef mixture for garnish. Stir sour cream into remaining beef; spoon into pasta shell. Place 1 cup cheese in center, leaving 2-inch border around edge. Spoon reserved beef mixture onto center of cheese; bake in 350°F oven 15 minutes or until heated through.

4. To serve, cut into wedges.   *Makes 4 servings*

Prep and Cook Time: 40 minutes

Favorite recipe from **National Cattlemen's Beef Association**

Food Fact

Italian pasta is made from durum wheat, water and sometimes eggs. Durum wheat is high in gluten and is used only for pasta. Coarsely ground durum wheat is called semolina.

Beef Spaghetti Pie Olé

MIXED VEGETABLES WITH NOODLES AND BEEF

2 tablespoons dried Asian mushrooms
5 ounces fresh spinach, washed and stemmed
4 ounces Chinese-style egg vermicelli or mung bean noodles
2 tablespoons soy sauce, divided
1 teaspoon sesame oil
2 tablespoons vegetable oil, divided
1 cup julienned carrots
1 medium onion, cut into halves and thinly sliced
1 piece fresh ginger (about 1 inch square), finely chopped
1 teaspoon minced garlic
8 ounces flank steak, cut into 2-inch-long pieces
2 tablespoons Sesame Salt (recipe follows)
1 teaspoon sugar
⅛ teaspoon black pepper
Chives and chive blossom for garnish

1. Place mushrooms in bowl; cover with hot water. Let stand 30 minutes or until caps are soft. Drain mushrooms; squeeze out excess water. Remove and discard stems. Cut caps into thin slices.

2. Meanwhile, prepare Sesame Salt; set aside. Bring 1 quart lightly salted water to a boil in medium saucepan. Add spinach; return to a boil. Cook 2 to 3 minutes or until crisp-tender. Drain spinach; plunge into cold water to stop cooking. Drain; cool. Squeeze spinach to remove excess moisture. Finely chop.

3. Bring 2 quarts water to a boil in large saucepan over high heat. Add noodles; cook 2 minutes or according to package directions. Drain and immediately run cold water over noodles to stop cooking. Cut noodles into short strands.

4. Return noodles to saucepan. Stir in 1 tablespoon soy sauce and sesame oil; toss to coat. Set aside and keep warm.

5. Heat 1 tablespoon vegetable oil in wok or large skillet over medium-high heat. Add carrots; stir-fry 5 minutes or until crisp-tender. Add mushrooms and onion; stir-fry 2 minutes or just until wilted. Remove vegetables from wok.

6. Heat wok over high heat 1 minute or until hot. Drizzle remaining 1 tablespoon vegetable oil into wok; heat 30 seconds. Add ginger and garlic; stir-fry 30 seconds or until fragrant.

7. Add beef to wok; stir-fry 3 to 5 minutes or until lightly browned. Remove wok from heat; stir in Sesame Salt, sugar, pepper and remaining 1 tablespoon soy sauce. Return vegetables and noodles to wok; cook and stir until heated through. Garnish, if desired. *Makes 4 servings*

SESAME SALT

½ cup white sesame seeds
¼ teaspoon salt

To toast sesame seeds, heat small skillet over medium heat. Add sesame seeds; cook and stir about 5 minutes or until seeds are golden. Cool. Process sesame seeds and salt in clean coffee or spice grinder. Refrigerate in covered glass jar.

Mixed Vegetables with Noodles and Beef

CORN BREAD TACO BAKE

1½ **pounds ground beef**
1 **package (about 1⅛ ounces) taco seasoning
   mix**
½ **cup water**
1 **can (12 ounces) whole kernel corn,
   drained**
½ **cup chopped green bell pepper**
1 **can (8 ounces) tomato sauce**
1 **package (8½ ounces) corn muffin mix, plus
   ingredients to prepare mix**
1⅓ **cups FRENCH'S® French Fried Onions,
   divided**
½ **cup (2 ounces) shredded Cheddar cheese**

Preheat oven to 400°F. In large skillet, brown ground beef; drain. Stir in taco seasoning, water, corn, bell pepper and tomato sauce; pour mixture into 2-quart casserole. In small bowl, prepare corn muffin mix according to package directions; stir in ⅔ cup French Fried Onions. Spoon corn muffin batter around edge of beef mixture. Bake, uncovered, at 400°F for 20 minutes or until corn bread is done. Top corn bread with cheese and remaining ⅔ *cup* onions; bake, uncovered, 1 to 3 minutes or until onions are golden brown. *Makes 6 servings*

Microwave Directions: Crumble ground beef into 8×12-inch microwave-safe dish. Cook, covered, on HIGH 4 to 6 minutes or until beef is cooked. Stir beef halfway through cooking time. Drain well. Prepare beef mixture and top with corn muffin batter as above. Cook, uncovered, on MEDIUM (50-60%) 7 to 9 minutes or until corn bread is nearly done. Rotate dish halfway through cooking time. Top corn bread with cheese and remaining ⅔ cup onions; cook, uncovered, on HIGH 1 minute or until cheese melts. Cover casserole and let stand 10 minutes. (Corn bread will finish baking during standing time.)

SKILLET ITALIANO

1 **pound ground beef**
½ **medium onion, chopped**
1 **package (1.5 ounces) LAWRY'S® Original
   Style Spaghetti Sauce Spices &
   Seasonings**
1 **can (14½ ounces) whole tomatoes, cut up,
   undrained**
1 **package (10 ounces) frozen Italian-cut
   green beans, thawed**
  LAWRY'S® Seasoned Salt to taste
1 **cup (4 ounces) grated cheddar cheese**

In large skillet, cook ground beef and onion until beef is browned and crumbly; drain fat. Add Spaghetti Sauce Spices & Seasonings, tomatoes and beans; mix well. Bring to a boil over medium-high heat; reduce heat to low, cover and simmer 20 minutes. Add Seasoned Salt to taste. Top with cheese; cover and heat until cheese melts.
Makes 4 to 6 servings

Serving Suggestion: Serve with warm bread and a tossed fruit salad.

STUFFED BEEF & BLACK BEAN TAMALE PIE

1 pound lean ground beef
1 packet (1¼ ounces) taco seasoning mix
1 can (15 to 16 ounces) black beans, rinsed, drained
½ cup water
1 can (8¾ ounces) whole kernel corn, very well drained
¾ cup light dairy sour cream
¾ cup shredded Co-Jack or Cheddar cheese
⅓ cup thinly sliced green onions

CRUST

1 package (8½ ounces) corn muffin mix
¾ cup shredded Co-Jack or Cheddar cheese
¾ cup light dairy sour cream
½ cup thinly sliced green onions

1. Heat oven to 400°F. Heat large nonstick skillet over medium heat until hot. Add ground beef; brown 5 to 7 minutes, stirring occasionally. Pour off drippings. Stir in seasoning mix, beans and water. Bring to a boil; reduce heat. Simmer 5 minutes, stirring occasionally; set aside.

2. Meanwhile in medium bowl, combine crust ingredients, mixing just until dry ingredients are moistened. (Batter will be stiff.) Using spoon dipped in water, spread slightly more than ½ of batter onto bottom and up side of 9-inch pie pan.

3. Arrange corn over batter; top with beef mixture. Spoon remaining batter over beef, along outer edge of pie. Carefully spread batter toward center, leaving a 3-inch circle uncovered. Bake in 400°F oven 23 to 25 minutes or until top is golden brown.

4. To serve, dollop ¾ cup sour cream over top; sprinkle with ¾ cup cheese and ⅓ cup green onions. Cut into wedges. *Makes 4 servings*

Prep and Cook Time: 50 minutes

Favorite recipe from **National Cattlemen's Beef Association**

Cook's Tip

Cooking dried beans uncovered will result in a firmer texture. To achieve a softer texture, cover beans while cooking. For best results, always cook dried beans at a gentle simmer.

MOUSSAKA

1 large eggplant
2½ teaspoons salt, divided
2 large zucchini
2 large russet potatoes, peeled
½ to ¾ cup olive oil, divided
5 tablespoons butter or margarine, divided
1 large onion, chopped
1½ pounds ground beef or lamb
2 cloves garlic, minced
1 cup chopped tomatoes
½ cup dry red or white wine
¼ cup chopped fresh parsley
¼ teaspoon ground cinnamon
⅛ teaspoon black pepper
1 cup grated Parmesan cheese, divided
⅓ cup all-purpose flour
¼ teaspoon ground nutmeg
2 cups milk

Cut eggplant lengthwise into ½-inch-thick slices. Place in large colander set over bowl; sprinkle with 1 teaspoon salt. Drain 30 minutes. Cut zucchini lengthwise into ⅜-inch-thick slices. Cut potatoes lengthwise into ¼-inch-thick slices.

Heat ¼ cup oil in large skillet over medium heat until hot. Add potatoes in single layer. Cook 5 minutes per side or until tender and lightly browned. Remove potatoes from skillet; drain on paper towels. Add more oil to skillet, if needed. Cook zucchini 2 minutes per side or until tender. Drain on paper towels. Add more oil to skillet. Cook eggplant 5 minutes per side or until tender. Drain on paper towels. Drain oil from skillet; discard.

Melt 1 tablespoon butter in same skillet over medium heat. Add onion. Cook and stir 5 minutes. Add beef and garlic to skillet. Cook and stir 10 minutes or until meat is no longer pink. Pour off drippings. Stir in tomatoes, wine, parsley, 1 teaspoon salt, cinnamon and pepper. Bring to a boil over high heat. Reduce heat to low. Simmer 10 minutes or until liquid is evaporated.

Preheat oven to 325°F. Grease 13×9-inch baking dish. Arrange potatoes in bottom; sprinkle with ¼ cup cheese. Top with zucchini and ¼ cup cheese, then eggplant and ¼ cup cheese. Spoon meat mixture over top.

To prepare sauce, melt remaining 4 tablespoons butter in medium saucepan over low heat. Blend in flour, remaining ½ teaspoon salt and nutmeg with wire whisk. Cook 1 minute, whisking constantly. Gradually whisk in milk. Cook over medium heat, until mixture boils and thickens, whisking constantly. Pour sauce evenly over meat mixture in dish; sprinkle with remaining ¼ cup cheese. Bake 30 to 40 minutes or until hot and bubbly. Garnish as desired. *Makes 6 to 8 servings*

Moussaka

QUICK TAMALE CASSEROLE

1½ pounds ground beef
¾ cup sliced green onions
1 can (4 ounces) chopped green chilies,
   drained and divided
1 can (10¾ ounces) condensed tomato soup
¾ cup salsa
1 can (16 ounces) whole kernel corn, drained
1 can (2¼ ounces) chopped pitted ripe olives
   (optional)
1 tablespoon Worcestershire sauce
1 teaspoon chili powder
¼ teaspoon garlic powder
4 slices (¾ ounce each) American cheese,
   halved
4 corn muffins, cut into ½-inch cubes
   Mexican Sour Cream Topping (recipe
   follows, optional)

In medium skillet, brown ground beef with green onions. Reserve 2 tablespoons chilies for Mexican Sour Cream Topping, if desired. Stir in remaining chilies, tomato soup, salsa, corn, olives, Worcestershire sauce, chili powder and garlic powder until well blended. Place in 2-quart casserole. Top with cheese, then evenly spread muffin cubes over cheese. Bake at 350°F for 5 to 10 minutes or until cheese is melted. Serve with Mexican Sour Cream Topping, if desired.   *Makes 6 servings*

MEXICAN SOUR CREAM TOPPING

1 cup sour cream
2 tablespoons chopped green chilies,
   reserved from above
2 teaspoons chopped jalapeño peppers
   (optional)
2 teaspoons lime juice

Combine all ingredients in small bowl; mix until well blended.   *Makes about 1 cup*

Food Fact

Chili Peppers make up 90 percent of the capsicum family (any plant bearing fruit called peppers). There are over 100 varieties of chili peppers in Mexico alone, each with its own distinct flavor. Smaller chilies tend to be hotter, but this not always guaranteed. Heat can vary even within the same variety.

Quick Tamale Casserole

TACO POT PIE

1 pound ground beef
1 package (1¼ ounces) taco seasoning mix
¼ cup water
1 can (8 ounces) kidney beans, rinsed and drained
1 cup chopped tomato
¾ cup frozen corn, thawed
¾ cup frozen peas, thawed
1½ cups (6 ounces) shredded Cheddar cheese
1 package (11.5 ounces) refrigerated corn breadsticks

1. Preheat oven to 400°F. Brown meat in medium ovenproof skillet over medium-high heat, stirring to separate meat. Drain drippings. Add seasoning mix and water to skillet. Cook over medium-low heat 3 minutes or until most of liquid is absorbed, stirring occasionally.

2. Stir in beans, tomato, corn and peas. Cook 3 minutes or until mixture is hot. Remove from heat; stir in cheese.

3. Unwrap corn bread dough; separate into 16 strips. Twist strips, cutting to fit skillet. Arrange attractively over meat mixture. Press ends of dough lightly to edges of skillet to secure. Bake 15 minutes or until corn bread is golden brown and meat mixture is bubbly. *Makes 4 to 6 servings*

Prep and Cook Time: 30 minutes

ZESTY ITALIAN STUFFED PEPPERS

3 bell peppers (green, red or yellow)
1 pound ground beef
1 jar (14 ounces) spaghetti sauce
1⅓ cups FRENCH'S® French Fried Onions, divided
2 tablespoons FRANK'S® REDHOT® Hot Sauce
½ cup uncooked instant rice
¼ cup sliced ripe olives
1 cup (4 ounces) shredded mozzarella cheese

Preheat oven to 400°F. Cut bell peppers in half lengthwise through stems; discard seeds. Place pepper halves, cut side up, in 2-quart shallow baking dish; set aside.

Place beef in large microwavable bowl. Microwave on HIGH 5 minutes or until meat is browned, stirring once. Drain. Stir in spaghetti sauce, ⅔ cup French Fried Onions, REDHOT® sauce, rice and olives. Spoon evenly into bell pepper halves.

Cover; bake 35 minutes or until bell peppers are tender. Uncover; sprinkle with cheese and remaining ⅔ cup onions. Bake 1 minute or until onions are golden. *Makes 6 servings*

Prep Time: 10 minutes
Cook Time: 36 minutes

Taco Pot Pie

SPANISH–STYLE COUSCOUS

1 cup uncooked couscous
1 pound ground round
½ medium onion, chopped
2 cloves garlic, minced
1 teaspoon ground cumin
½ teaspoon dried thyme leaves
1 can (about 14 ounces) beef broth
½ cup pimiento-stuffed green olives, sliced
1 small green bell pepper, cut into ½-inch pieces

1. Bring 1⅓ cups water to a boil over high heat in 1-quart saucepan. Stir in couscous. Cover; remove from heat.

2. Place meat in large skillet; cook over high heat 6 to 8 minutes or until meat is no longer pink, breaking meat apart with wooden spoon. Pour off drippings.

3. Add onion, garlic, cumin and thyme; cook and stir 30 seconds or until onion and garlic are tender. Add beef broth and olives; bring to a boil. Boil, uncovered, 5 minutes. Add pepper; cover and simmer 5 minutes more or until broth is reduced by half.

4. Fluff couscous with fork. Spoon couscous onto plates or into serving bowls. Spoon meat mixture and broth over couscous.   *Makes 4 servings*

Serving Suggestion: Serve with carrot sticks.

Prep and Cook Time: 20 minutes

BAKED CHEESEY ROTINI

¾ pound lean ground beef
½ cup chopped onion
2 cups cooked rotini, prepared according to package directions and drained
1 (15-ounce) can HUNT'S® Ready Tomato Sauces Chunky Italian
¼ cup chopped green bell pepper
¾ teaspoon garlic salt
¼ teaspoon pepper
1½ cups cubed processed American cheese

In large skillet, brown beef with onion; drain fat. Stir in remaining ingredients except cheese. Pour beef mixture into 1½-quart casserole. Top with cheese. Bake, covered, at 350°F for 20 minutes.

Makes 6 servings

Food Fact

Because of its texture and flavor, couscous is often mistaken for a type of rice. It is actually a pasta made from durum wheat. Couscous is a staple in North African cuisines. Most of the couscous found in the United States cooks very quickly, as it is either precooked or instant.

Spanish-Style Couscous

Ethnic
FLAVORS

VEAL PICCATA

1 pound veal leg cutlets, cut ⅛ to ¼ inch
    thick
2 tablespoons all-purpose flour
½ teaspoon salt
⅛ teaspoon paprika
⅛ teaspoon ground white pepper
1 tablespoon olive oil

LEMON-CAPER SAUCE
⅔ cup dry white wine
2 tablespoons fresh lemon juice
2 teaspoons drained capers
1 teaspoon butter

1. Pound veal cutlets to ⅛-inch thickness, if necessary. Combine flour, salt, paprika and pepper. Lightly coat both sides of veal with flour mixture.

2. In large skillet, heat half of oil over medium heat until hot. Place half of veal in skillet and cook 2 minutes on each side or until cooked through. Remove to serving platter; keep warm. Repeat procedure with remaining veal and oil.

3. In same skillet, add wine and lemon juice; bring to a boil, stirring to dissolve any browned bits attached to skillet. Cook and stir 1 to 2 minutes or until slightly thickened. Remove from heat; stir in capers and butter. Spoon sauce over veal.

Makes 4 servings

Favorite recipe from **National Cattlemen's Beef Association**

PASTA PAPRIKASH

Nonstick cooking spray
12 ounces boneless beef eye of round steak,
    cut into 1-inch cubes
4 tablespoons all-purpose flour, divided
2 cans (14½ ounces each) beef broth, divided
2 green bell peppers, sliced
1 onion, sliced
2 cloves garlic, minced
2 tablespoons sweet Hungarian paprika
¼ teaspoon black pepper
⅛ teaspoon ground red pepper
1 can (6 ounces) reduced-sodium tomato
    paste
1 cup reduced-fat sour cream
8 ounces fettucine, cooked and kept warm

1. Spray large skillet with cooking spray. Heat over medium heat until hot. Coat beef with 2 tablespoons flour; cook 5 to 8 minutes or until browned. Add 1 cup beef broth and bring to a boil. Reduce heat and simmer, covered, 15 to 20 minutes or until beef is tender. Remove meat from skillet.

2. Add bell peppers, onion and garlic to skillet; cook and stir about 5 minutes or until tender. Stir in remaining 2 tablespoons flour, paprika, black pepper and red pepper; cook, stirring constantly, 1 minute. Stir in tomato paste and ½ cup broth. Add beef and remaining broth and bring to a boil. Reduce heat and simmer, uncovered, 5 to 7 minutes or until sauce is thickened.

3. Stir in sour cream; cook over low heat 1 to 2 minutes, stirring frequently. Serve over fettucine.

Makes 4 servings (about 1½ cups each)

BEAN THREADS
WITH MINCED PORK

4 ounces bean threads or Chinese rice vermicelli
3 dried mushrooms
1 small red or green hot chili pepper*
3 green onions, divided
2 tablespoons minced fresh ginger
2 tablespoons hot bean sauce
1½ cups chicken broth
1 tablespoon soy sauce
1 tablespoon dry sherry
2 tablespoons vegetable oil
6 ounces lean ground pork
2 cilantro sprigs for garnish

*Chili peppers can sting and irritate the skin; wear rubber gloves when handling peppers and do not touch eyes. Wash hands after handling.

Place bean threads and dried mushrooms in separate bowls. Cover each with hot water. Let stand 30 minutes; drain. Cut bean threads into 4-inch pieces. Squeeze out excess water from mushrooms. Cut off and discard stems; cut caps into thin slices.

Cut chili pepper in half and scrape out seeds. Mince chili pepper. Thinly slice 2 onions. Cut remaining onion into 1½-inch slivers and reserve for garnish. Combine ginger and hot bean sauce in small bowl. Combine chicken broth, soy sauce and sherry in medium bowl.

Heat oil in wok or large skillet over high heat. Add pork and stir-fry until meat is no longer pink, about 2 minutes. Add chili pepper, sliced onions and ginger-bean sauce mixture. Stir-fry until meat absorbs color from bean sauce, about 1 minute.

Add chicken broth mixture, bean threads and mushrooms. Simmer, uncovered, until most of the liquid is absorbed, about 5 minutes. Garnish with onion slivers and cilantro sprigs.

Makes 4 servings

Cook's Tip

A safe and easy way to peel the skin from fresh ginger is to scrape it off with a metal tableware spoon. Care should be taken when scraping, since the most flavorful flesh is just below the skin.

Dinner in
MINUTES

BY–THE–SEA CASSEROLE

**1 bag (16 ounces) BIRDS EYE® frozen Mixed
    Vegetables**
2 cans (6½ ounces each) tuna in water, drained
1 cup uncooked instant rice
1 can (10¾ ounces) cream of celery soup
1 cup 1% milk
1 cup cheese-flavored fish-shaped crackers

• In medium bowl, combine vegetables and tuna.

• Stir in rice, soup and milk.

• Place tuna mixture in 1½-quart microwave-safe casserole
dish; cover and microwave on HIGH 6 minutes. Stir;
microwave, covered, 6 to 8 minutes more or until rice is
tender.

• Stir casserole and sprinkle with crackers.

Makes 6 servings

Prep Time: 10 minutes
Cook Time: 15 minutes

Left: *By-the Sea
Casserole*

Top: *Tuscan Pot
Pie (page 242)*

211

EASY TUNA & PASTA POT PIE

1 tablespoon butter or margarine
1 large onion, chopped
1½ cups cooked small shell pasta or elbow
    macaroni
1 can (10¾ ounces) condensed cream of
    celery or mushroom soup
1 cup frozen peas, thawed
1 can (6 ounces) tuna in water, drained and
    flaked
½ cup sour cream
½ teaspoon dried dill weed
¼ teaspoon salt
1 package (7½ ounces) refrigerated
    buttermilk or country biscuits

1. Preheat oven to 400°F. Melt butter in medium ovenproof skillet over medium heat. Add onion; cook 5 minutes, stirring occasionally.

2. Stir in pasta, soup, peas, tuna, sour cream, dill and salt; mix well. Cook 3 minutes or until hot. Press mixture down in skillet to form even layer.

3. Unwrap biscuit dough; arrange individual biscuits over tuna mixture. Bake 15 minutes or until biscuits are golden brown and tuna mixture is bubbly.

Makes 5 servings

Prep and Cook Time: 28 minutes

SO–EASY FISH DIVAN

1 package (about 1⅛ ounces) cheese sauce
    mix
1⅓ cups milk
1 bag (16 ounces) frozen vegetable
    combination (brussels sprouts, carrots,
    cauliflower), thawed and drained
1⅓ cups FRENCH'S® French Fried Onions,
    divided
1 pound unbreaded fish fillets, thawed if
    frozen
½ cup (2 ounces) shredded Cheddar cheese

Preheat oven to 375°F. In small saucepan, prepare cheese sauce mix according to package directions using 1⅓ cups milk. In 12×8-inch baking dish, combine vegetables and ⅔ cup French Fried Onions; top with fish fillets. Pour cheese sauce over fish and vegetables. Bake, covered, at 375°F for 25 minutes or until fish flakes easily with fork. Top fish with Cheddar cheese and remaining ⅔ cup onions; bake, uncovered, 3 minutes or until onions are golden brown.

Makes 3 to 4 servings

Easy Tuna & Pasta Pot Pie

TUNA PESTO & PASTA

1 box (9 ounces) **BIRDS EYE**® **frozen Peas and Pearl Onions**
3 cups cooked rotini pasta or other shaped pasta
1 can (6 ounces) tuna packed in water, drained
¼ cup mayonnaise
2 to 4 tablespoons prepared pesto
    Grated Parmesan cheese

• Prepare vegetables in medium saucepan according to package directions.

• Stir in pasta, tuna, mayonnaise and pesto; heat through.

• Serve with cheese.   *Makes about 2 servings*

Serving Suggestion: Chill Tuna Pesto & Pasta and serve as a cold pasta salad.

Prep Time: 5 minutes
Cook Time: 12 minutes

SUPERB STROGANOFF

1 pound sirloin steak, cut into thin strips
2 tablespoons vegetable oil
½ cup chopped onion
1 can (4 ounces) mushrooms, drained
1 bag (16 ounces) **BIRDS EYE**® **frozen Pasta Secrets Creamy Peppercorn**
⅔ cup sour cream

• In large skillet, brown steak in oil over medium heat, stirring frequently.

• Stir in onion and mushrooms; cook 5 minutes or until onion is tender.

• Stir in Pasta Secrets and ¼ cup water; cover and cook over medium heat 5 minutes or until pasta is tender. Reduce heat to low; stir in sour cream. Cook until heated through.   *Makes 4 servings*

Prep Time: 5 minutes
Cook Time: 20 minutes

Food Fact

Traditional pesto sauce is made from fresh basil, pine nuts, garlic, Parmesan cheese and olive oil. The ingredients can be mashed together in a blender or food processor. Today there are many variations to the classic pesto recipe, substituting various herbs for traditional basil.

Tuna Pesto & Pasta

ZUCCHINI MEAT SAUCE WITH PASTA

1 package (12 ounces) shell macaroni or corkscrew pasta
2 pounds ground beef
2 onions, chopped
2 cans (26½ ounces each) DEL MONTE® Chunky Spaghetti Sauce with Garlic & Herb
1 can (14½ ounces) DEL MONTE® Diced Tomatoes, undrained
2 small zucchini, thinly sliced

1. Cook pasta in 8-quart pot according to package directions; drain. Keep pasta hot.

2. Brown meat in 6-quart pot over medium-high heat. Season with salt and pepper, if desired; drain. Add onions; cook until tender. Stir in spaghetti sauce and tomatoes; cook 5 minutes, stirring occasionally. (Pour half of sauce into freezer container; cool, cover and freeze for another meal.)

3. Add zucchini to remaining sauce; cover and cook over medium heat 7 to 10 minutes or until zucchini is tender. Serve sauce over hot pasta. Sprinkle with grated Parmesan cheese and garnish, if desired.

Makes 4 servings

Prep and Cook Time: 30 minutes

CANTONESE BEEF & BROCCOLI

¾ pound cooked steak or deli roast beef, cut into thin strips
1½ tablespoons reduced-sodium or regular soy sauce
1 package (6.8 ounces) RICE-A-RONI® Beef Flavor
2 tablespoons margarine or butter
½ cup chopped onion
2 cups broccoli flowerets
½ teaspoon ground ginger

1. Toss meat with soy sauce; set aside.

2. In round 3-quart microwaveable glass casserole, combine rice-vermicelli mix, margarine and onion. Microwave, uncovered, on HIGH 4 to 5 minutes or until vermicelli is golden brown, stirring after 2 minutes.

3. Stir in 2¾ cups water and contents of seasoning packet. Cover; microwave on HIGH 11 minutes.

4. Stir in meat mixture, broccoli and ginger. Cover; microwave on HIGH 8 to 10 minutes or until most of liquid is absorbed and rice is tender.

5. Let stand 3 minutes. Stir before serving.

Makes 4 servings

Zucchini Meat Sauce with Pasta

FIX-IT-FAST CORNED BEEF & CABBAGE

**1 small head cabbage (about 1½ pounds),
   cored and cut into 6 wedges
1 can (12 ounces) corned beef, sliced, *or*
   ½ pound sliced deli corned beef
1 can (14 ounces) sliced carrots, drained
1 can (16 ounces) sliced potatoes, drained
1⅓ cups FRENCH'S® French Fried Onions,
   divided
1 can (10¾ ounces) condensed cream of
   celery soup
¾ cup water**

Preheat oven to 375°F. Arrange cabbage wedges and corned beef slices alternately down center of 13×9-inch baking dish. Place carrots, potatoes and ⅔ cup French Fried Onions along sides of dish. In small bowl, combine soup and water; pour over meat and vegetables. Bake, covered, at 375°F for 40 minutes or until cabbage is tender. Top with remaining ⅔ cup onions; bake, uncovered, 3 minutes or until onions are golden brown.

Makes 4 to 6 servings

Microwave Directions: Arrange cabbage wedges down center of 12×8-inch microwave-safe dish; add 2 tablespoons water. Cook, covered, on HIGH 10 to 12 minutes or until fork-tender. Rotate the dish halfway through cooking time. Drain. Arrange cabbage, corned beef, carrots, potatoes and ⅔ cup onions in dish as above.

Reduce water to ¼ cup. In small bowl, combine soup and water; pour over meat and vegetables. Cook, covered, 8 to 10 minutes or until vegetables are heated through. Rotate the dish halfway through cooking time. Top with remaining ⅔ cup onions; cook, uncovered, 1 minute. Let stand 5 minutes.

ALL-IN-ONE BURGER STEW

**1 pound lean ground beef
2 cups frozen Italian vegetables
1 can (14½ ounces) chopped tomatoes with
   basil and garlic
1 can (about 14 ounces) beef broth
2½ cups uncooked medium egg noodles
   Salt**

1. Cook meat in Dutch oven or large skillet over medium-high heat until no longer pink, breaking meat apart with wooden spoon. Drain drippings.

2. Add vegetables, tomatoes and broth; bring to a boil over high heat.

3. Add noodles; reduce heat to medium. Cover and cook 12 to 15 minutes or until noodles have absorbed liquid and vegetables are tender. Add salt and pepper to taste.   *Makes 6 servings*

Prep and Cook Time: 25 minutes

All-in-One Burger Stew

CHILI-STUFFED POBLANO PEPPERS

1 pound lean ground beef
4 large poblano peppers*
1 can (15 ounces) chili-seasoned beans
1 can (14½ ounces) chili-style chunky tomatoes, undrained
1 tablespoon Mexican (adobo) seasoning
⅔ cup shredded Mexican cheese blend or Monterey Jack cheese

Chili peppers can sting and irritate the skin; wear rubber gloves when handling peppers and do not touch eyes. Wash hands after handling.

1. Preheat broiler. Bring 2 quarts water to a boil in 3-quart saucepan. Cook ground beef in large nonstick skillet over medium-high heat 5 to 6 minutes or until no longer pink. Drain drippings.

2. While meat is cooking, cut peppers in half lengthwise; remove stems and seeds. Add 4 pepper halves to boiling water; cook 3 minutes or until bright green and slightly softened. Remove; drain upside down on plate. Repeat with remaining 4 halves. Set aside.

3. Add beans, tomatoes and Mexican seasoning to ground beef. Cook and stir over medium heat 5 minutes or until mixture thickens slightly.

4. Arrange peppers, cut side up, in 13×9-inch baking dish. Divide chili mixture evenly among each pepper; top with cheese. Broil 6 inches from heat 1 minute or until cheese is melted. Serve immediately.   *Makes 4 servings*

CREAMY BEEF AND VEGETABLE CASSEROLE

1 pound lean ground beef
1 small onion, chopped
1 bag (16 ounces) BIRDS EYE® frozen Farm Fresh Mixtures Broccoli, Corn & Red Peppers
1 can (10¾ ounces) cream of mushroom soup

• In medium skillet, brown beef and onion; drain excess fat.

• Meanwhile, in large saucepan, cook vegetables according to package directions; drain.

• Stir in beef mixture and soup. Cook over medium heat until heated through.   *Makes 4 servings*

Serving Suggestion: Serve over rice and sprinkle with ½ cup shredded Cheddar cheese.

Prep Time: 5 minutes
Cook Time: 10 to 15 minutes

Chili-Stuffed Poblano Pepper

BEEFY BEAN SKILLET

1 box (9 ounces) BIRDS EYE® frozen Cut Green Beans
½ pound lean ground beef
½ cup chopped onion
1 cup instant rice
1 can (10 ounces) au jus gravy*
¾ cup ketchup

*Or, substitute 1 can (10 ounces) beef broth.

• In medium saucepan, cook green beans according to package directions; drain and set aside.

• Meanwhile, in large skillet, brown beef; drain excess fat. Add onion; cook and stir until onion is tender.

• Add rice, gravy and ketchup. Bring to boil over medium-high heat; cover and reduce heat to medium-low. Simmer 5 to 10 minutes or until rice is cooked, stirring occasionally.

• Stir in beans. Simmer until heated through.

Makes 4 servings

Prep Time: 10 minutes
Cook Time: 20 minutes

PREGO® EASY SPAGHETTI & MEATBALLS

1 pound ground beef
2 tablespoons water
⅓ cup seasoned dry bread crumbs
1 egg, beaten
1 jar (28 ounces) PREGO® Traditional Pasta Sauce *or* Pasta Sauce Flavored with Meat
4 cups hot cooked spaghetti

1. Mix beef, water, bread crumbs and egg. Shape meat mixture into 12 (2-inch) meatballs. Arrange in 2-quart shallow microwave-safe baking dish.

2. Microwave on HIGH 5 minutes or until meatballs are no longer pink (160°F). Pour off fat. Pour pasta sauce over meatballs. Cover and microwave 3 minutes more or until sauce is hot. Serve over spaghetti. *Makes 4 servings*

Prep Time: 15 minutes
Cook Time: 10 minutes

Beefy Bean Skillet

NO-FUSS BEEF & SPINACH LASAGNA

1 pound lean ground beef
¼ teaspoon salt
1 jar or can (26 to 30 ounces) prepared low-fat spaghetti sauce
1 can (14½ ounces) Italian-style diced tomatoes, undrained
¼ teaspoon ground red pepper
1 carton (15 ounces) part-skim ricotta cheese
1 package (10 ounces) frozen chopped spinach, defrosted, well drained
¼ cup grated Parmesan cheese
1 egg, beaten
10 uncooked lasagna noodles
1½ cups shredded part-skim mozzarella cheese

1. Heat oven to 375°F. In large nonstick skillet, brown ground beef over medium heat 8 to 10 minutes or until no longer pink. Pour off drippings. Season beef with salt; add spaghetti sauce, tomatoes and red pepper, stirring to combine. Set aside.

2. Meanwhile in medium bowl, combine ricotta cheese, spinach, Parmesan cheese and egg. Spread 2 cups beef sauce over bottom of 13×9-inch baking dish. Arrange 5 lasagna noodles in single layer, completely covering bottom of dish; press noodles into sauce. Spread entire ricotta cheese mixture on top of noodles; sprinkle with 1 cup mozzarella cheese and top with 2 cups beef sauce. Arrange remaining noodles in single layer; press lightly into sauce. Top with remaining beef sauce.

3. Bake in 375°F oven 45 minutes or until noodles are tender. Sprinkle remaining mozzarella cheese on top; tent lightly with foil. Let stand 15 minutes before cutting into 12 squares.   *Makes 12 servings*

Note: There's no need to precook the noodles for this no-fuss lasagna—the noodles cook during baking.

Prep and Cook Time: 65 minutes

Favorite recipe from **National Cattlemen's Beef Association**

Food Fact

Spinach is an excellent source of fiber and beta-carotene. If eaten raw, it supplies a good amount of vitamin C.

No-Fuss Beef & Spinach Lasagna

PREGO® BAKED ZITI SUPREME

1 pound ground beef
1 medium onion, chopped (about ½ cup)
1 jar (28 ounces) PREGO® Pasta Sauce with
   Fresh Mushrooms
1½ cups shredded mozzarella cheese
   (6 ounces), divided
5 cups hot cooked medium tube-shaped
   macaroni (about 3 cups uncooked)
¼ cup grated Parmesan cheese

1. In large saucepan over medium-high heat, cook beef and onion until beef is browned, stirring to separate meat. Pour off fat.

2. Stir in pasta sauce, *1 cup* mozzarella cheese and macaroni. Spoon into 3-quart shallow baking dish. Sprinkle with remaining mozzarella cheese and Parmesan cheese. Bake at 350°F. for 30 minutes.

Makes 6 servings

Tip: A salad of mixed greens and hot toasted garlic bread team perfectly with this quick and easy casserole.

Prep Time: 25 minutes
Cook Time: 30 minutes

FRENCH–AMERICAN WALNUT RICE

½ pound lean ground beef or ground turkey
1 box (10 ounces) BIRDS EYE® frozen White
   and Wild Rice
1½ teaspoons soy sauce
½ cup walnuts

• In large skillet, cook beef over medium-high heat 5 minutes or until well browned.

• Stir in rice; cook 5 minutes more or until rice is tender, stirring occasionally.

• Stir in soy sauce and walnuts; cook 1 minute or until heated.

Makes 4 servings

Prep Time: 5 minutes
Cook Time: 10 to 12 minutes

Food Fact

Rice was considered the symbol of life and fertility in ancient China. This explains the custom of showering bridal couples with grains of rice.

Prego® Baked Ziti Supreme

Dinner in MINUTES

SKILLET PASTA DINNER

1 pound ground beef
1 jar (28 ounces) RAGÚ® Hearty Robust
    Blend Pasta Sauce
8 ounces rotini pasta, cooked and drained
1 cup shredded cheddar cheese, divided
2 teaspoons chili powder (optional)

In 12-inch skillet, brown ground beef over medium-high heat; drain. Stir in Ragú® Hearty Robust Blend Pasta Sauce, hot pasta, ¾ cup cheese and chili powder. Simmer uncovered, stirring occasionally, 5 minutes or until heated through. Sprinkle with remaining ¼ cup cheese.   *Makes 4 servings*

15 MINUTE CHEESEBURGER RICE

1 pound ground beef
1¾ cups water
⅔ cup catsup
1 tablespoon Kraft® Pure Prepared Mustard
2 cups MINUTE® White Rice, uncooked
1 cup KRAFT® Shredded Cheddar Cheese

BROWN meat in large skillet; drain.

ADD water, catsup and mustard. Bring to boil.

STIR in rice. Sprinkle with cheese; cover. Cook on low heat 5 minutes.   *Makes 4 servings*

Prep Time: 5 minutes
Cook Time: 15 minutes

BEEF WITH CABBAGE AND CARROTS

¾ pound extra-lean (90% lean) ground beef
4 cups shredded cabbage
1½ cups shredded carrot (1 large carrot)
½ teaspoon caraway seeds
2 tablespoons seasoned rice vinegar
Salt and freshly ground pepper

Brown ground beef in large skillet. Drain. Reduce heat to low. Stir in cabbage, carrot and caraway seeds; cover. Cook 10 minutes or until vegetables are tender, stirring occasionally. Stir in vinegar. (Add 1 tablespoon water for extra moistness, if desired.) Season with salt and pepper to taste.

Makes 4 servings

Variation: Substitute 1 teaspoon sugar and 1 tablespoon white wine vinegar for 2 tablespoons seasoned rice vinegar.

RICE–STUFFED PEPPERS

**1 package LIPTON® Rice & Sauce—
Cheddar Broccoli**
2 cups water
1 tablespoon margarine or butter
1 pound ground beef
**4 large red or green bell peppers, halved
lengthwise and seeded**

Preheat oven to 350°F.

Prepare rice & sauce—cheddar broccoli with water and margarine according to package directions.

Meanwhile, in 10-inch skillet, brown ground beef over medium-high heat; drain. Stir into rice & sauce. Fill each pepper half with rice mixture. In 13×9-inch baking dish, arrange stuffed peppers. Bake covered 20 minutes. Remove cover and continue baking 10 minutes or until peppers are tender. Sprinkle, if desired, with shredded cheddar cheese.   *Makes about 4 main-dish servings*

CAMPBELL'S® SHORTCUT BEEF STEW

1 tablespoon vegetable oil
**1 pound boneless beef sirloin steak, cut into
1-inch cubes**
**1 can (10¾ ounces) CAMPBELL'S®
Condensed Tomato Soup**
**1 can (10¾ ounces) CAMPBELL'S®
Condensed Beefy Mushroom Soup**
1 tablespoon Worcestershire sauce
**1 bag (24 ounces) frozen vegetables for stew
(potatoes, carrots, celery)**

1. In Dutch oven over medium-high heat, heat oil. Add beef and cook until browned, stirring often. Set beef aside.

2. Add soups, Worcestershire and vegetables. Heat to a boil. Return beef to pan. Reduce heat to low. Cover and cook 10 minutes or until vegetables are tender, stirring occasionally.   *Makes 4 servings*

Prep Time: 5 minutes
Cook Time: 25 minutes

HAMBURGER CASSEROLE OLÉ

1 pound lean ground beef or ground turkey
1 package (1¼ ounces) taco seasoning mix
1 cup water
1 box (9 ounces) BIRDS EYE® frozen Cut Green Beans
½ cup shredded sharp Cheddar cheese
½ cup shredded mozzarella cheese

• Preheat oven to 325°F.

• Brown beef; drain excess fat. Add taco mix and water; cook over low heat 8 to 10 minutes or until liquid has been absorbed.

• Meanwhile, cook green beans according to package directions; drain.

• Spread meat in greased 13×9-inch baking pan. Spread beans over meat. Sprinkle with cheeses.

• Bake 15 to 20 minutes or until hot and cheese is melted.
Makes 4 servings

Serving Suggestion: Serve over tortillas or corn chips and top with sour cream, chopped avocado, chopped lettuce and/or chopped tomatoes.

Birds Eye Idea: Try substituting plain low-fat yogurt for sour cream in your recipes for a lighter version.

Prep Time: 15 minutes
Cook Time: 20 minutes

WESTERN WAGON WHEELS

1 pound lean ground beef or ground turkey
2 cups wagon wheel pasta, uncooked
1 can (14½ ounces) stewed tomatoes
1½ cups water
1 box (10 ounces) BIRDS EYE® frozen Sweet Corn
½ cup barbecue sauce
Salt and pepper to taste

• In large skillet, cook beef over medium heat 5 minutes or until well browned.

• Stir in pasta, tomatoes, water, corn and barbecue sauce; bring to boil.

• Reduce heat to low; cover and simmer 15 to 20 minutes or until pasta is tender, stirring occasionally. Season with salt and pepper.
Makes 4 servings

Serving Suggestion: Serve with corn bread or corn muffins.

Prep Time: 5 minutes
Cook Time: 25 minutes

Western Wagon Wheels

Dinner in
MINUTES

CURRIED TURKEY DINNER

1 package (10 ounces) frozen broccoli
 spears, cooked and drained
2 cups cubed cooked turkey
1 can (10½ ounces) reduced-sodium cream
 of mushroom soup
¼ cup reduced-calorie mayonnaise
1½ teaspoons lemon juice
1 teaspoon curry powder
1 cup seasoned croutons

1. Preheat oven to 350°F.

2. In 8-inch square baking dish arrange broccoli; top with turkey.

3. In small bowl combine soup, mayonnaise, lemon juice and curry powder. Pour over turkey and top with croutons.

4. Bake 20 to 25 minutes or until bubbly.

Makes 4 servings

Favorite recipe from **National Turkey Federation**

SWANSON® 25–MINUTE CHICKEN & NOODLES

1 can (14½ ounces) SWANSON® Chicken
 Broth (1¾ cups)
½ teaspoon dried basil leaves, crushed
⅛ teaspoon pepper
2 cups frozen vegetable combination
 (broccoli, cauliflower, carrots)
2 cups *uncooked* medium egg noodles
2 cups cubed cooked chicken

1. In medium skillet mix broth, basil, pepper and vegetables. Over medium-high heat, heat to a boil. Reduce heat to medium. Cover and cook 5 minutes.

2. Stir in noodles. Cover and cook 5 minutes, stirring often. Add chicken and heat through.

Makes 4 servings

Tip: For 2 cups cubed cooked chicken: In medium saucepan over medium heat, in 4 cups boiling water, cook 1 pound skinless, boneless chicken breasts **or** thighs, cubed, 5 minutes or until chicken is no longer pink. Chicken should be cooked to a minimum internal temperature of 165°F.

Prep Time: 10 minutes
Cook Time: 15 minutes

Swanson® 25-Minute Chicken & Noodles

CHICKEN À LA KING EXPRESS

3 boneless, skinless chicken breasts, cooked and diced
1 can (10¾ ounces) condensed cream of celery soup
½ cup sliced green onions
½ cup sliced mushrooms
1 clove garlic, minced
2 tablespoons reduced-fat (2%) milk
½ teaspoon salt
¼ teaspoon white pepper
2 English muffins, halved

Combine chicken, soup, green onions, mushrooms, pepper, garlic, milk, pepper and salt in medium bowl; mix well. Spray 4 (6-ounce) custard cups with nonstick cooking spray; place equal portions of chicken mixture. Top with English muffin halves, split sides down.

Place cups on cookie sheet; bake at 450°F 13 to 15 minutes or until muffins are golden brown and chicken mixture is hot and bubbly. Invert cups onto serving dish. *Makes 4 servings*

FLORENTINE CHICKEN

2 boxes (10 ounces each) BIRDS EYE® frozen Chopped Spinach
1 package (1¼ ounces) hollandaise sauce mix
½ teaspoon TABASCO® Pepper Sauce or to taste
⅓ cup shredded Cheddar cheese, divided
1½ cups cooked cubed chicken

Preheat oven to 350°F.

Cook spinach according to package directions; drain. Prepare hollandaise sauce according to package directions.

Blend spinach, hollandaise sauce, Tabasco sauce and half of cheese. Pour into 9×9-inch baking dish; top with chicken.

Sprinkle remaining cheese on top. Bake 10 to 12 minutes or until heated through.

Makes 4 servings

Prep Time: 2 minutes
Cook Time: 10 to 12 minutes

Chicken à la King Express

PREGO® QUICK CHICKEN PARMIGIANA

1 package (about 10 ounces) frozen fully cooked breaded chicken patties *or* 1 package (about 14 ounces) refrigerated fully cooked breaded chicken cutlets
1 jar (28 ounces) PREGO® Traditional Pasta Sauce, divided
2 tablespoons grated Parmesan cheese
½ cup shredded mozzarella cheese (2 ounces)
4 cups hot cooked spaghetti (about 8 ounces uncooked)

1. In 2-quart shallow baking dish arrange patties. Top each with ¼ *cup* pasta sauce. Sprinkle with Parmesan cheese and mozzarella cheese.

2. Bake at 400°F. for 15 minutes or until chicken is hot and cheese is melted.

3. Heat remaining sauce until hot. Serve sauce with chicken and spaghetti.   *Makes 4 servings*

Microwave Directions: In 2-quart shallow microwave-safe baking dish arrange patties. Microwave on HIGH 4 minutes (3 minutes for refrigerated cutlets). Top each patty with ¼ *cup* pasta sauce, *1 teaspoon* Parmesan cheese and *2 tablespoons* mozzarella cheese. Microwave 2 minutes more or until sauce is hot and cheese is melted.

Prep Time: 5 minutes
Cook Time: 15 minutes

CAMPBELL'S® HEALTHY REQUEST® CHICKEN MOZZARELLA

4 skinless, boneless chicken breast halves (about 1 pound)
1 can (10¾ ounces) CAMPBELL'S® HEALTHY REQUEST® Condensed Tomato Soup
½ teaspoon Italian seasoning *or* dried oregano leaves, crushed
½ teaspoon garlic powder
¼ cup shredded mozzarella cheese (1 ounce)
4 cups hot cooked corkscrew macaroni (about 3 cups uncooked), cooked without salt

1. Place chicken in 2-quart shallow baking dish. Mix soup, Italian seasoning and garlic powder. Spoon over chicken and bake at 400°F. for 20 minutes or until chicken is no longer pink.

2. Sprinkle cheese over chicken. Remove chicken. Stir sauce. Serve with macaroni.

Makes 4 servings

Prep Time: 10 minutes
Cook Time: 20 minutes

Campbell's® Healthy Request® Chicken Mozzarella

HERBED CHICKEN AND POTATOES

1 pound all-purpose potatoes, thinly sliced
**4 bone-in chicken breast halves (about
   2 pounds)***
**1 envelope LIPTON® RECIPE SECRETS®
   Savory Herb with Garlic Soup Mix**
⅓ cup water
1 tablespoon olive or vegetable oil

Preheat oven to 375°F. In 13×9-inch baking or roasting pan, add potatoes; arrange chicken on top. Pour savory herb with garlic soup mix blended with water and oil over chicken and potatoes.

Bake uncovered 50 minutes or until chicken is no longer pink and potatoes are tender. Garnish, if desired, with lemon slices.

Makes about 4 servings

Variation: Also delicious if 1 chicken (2½ to 3 pounds) cut into serving pieces, is substituted for chicken breast halves.

Also terrific with LIPTON® RECIPE SECRETS® Golden Herb with Lemon Soup Mix.

BROCCOLI, CHICKEN AND RICE CASSEROLE

**1 box UNCLE BEN'S® Broccoli Rice
   au Gratin**
2 cups boiling water
**4 boneless, skinless chicken breasts (about
   1 pound)**
¼ teaspoon garlic powder
2 cups frozen broccoli
**1 cup (4 ounces) reduced-fat shredded
   Cheddar cheese**

1. Heat oven to 425°F. In 13×9-inch baking pan, combine rice and contents of seasoning packet. Add boiling water; mix well. Add chicken; sprinkle with garlic powder. Cover and bake 30 minutes.

2. Add broccoli and cheese; continue to bake, covered, 8 to 10 minutes or until chicken is no longer pink in center.

Makes 4 servings

Broccoli, Chicken and Rice Casserole

CAMPBELL'S® 15–MINUTE CHICKEN & RICE DINNER

1 tablespoon vegetable oil
4 skinless, boneless chicken breast halves
(about 1 pound)
1 can (10¾ ounces) CAMPBELL'S®
Condensed Cream of Chicken Soup *or*
98% Fat Free Cream of Chicken Soup
1½ cups water
¼ teaspoon paprika
¼ teaspoon pepper
1½ cups uncooked Minute® Original Rice
2 cups fresh *or* **thawed frozen broccoli**
flowerets

1. In medium skillet over medium-high heat, heat oil. Add chicken and cook 8 minutes or until browned. Set chicken aside. Pour off fat.

2. Add soup, water, paprika and pepper. Heat to a boil.

3. Stir in rice and broccoli. Place chicken on rice mixture. Reduce heat to low. Cover and cook 5 minutes or until chicken is no longer pink.

Makes 4 servings

Chicken & Rice Dinner with Green Beans:
Substitute 2 cups fresh *or* thawed frozen cut green beans for broccoli.

Tip: For creamier rice, increase water to 1⅔ cups.

Prep/Cook Time: 15 minutes

MEDITERRANEAN CHICKEN

1 teaspoon oil
4 boneless skinless chicken breasts, cubed
2 (10.75-ounce) jars LOST ACRES® Country
Sides Mediterranean Relish
¼ cup SMUCKER'S® Sweet Orange
Marmalade
¼ cup water
½ cup grated Parmesan cheese
Pasta or rice, cooked

Brown chicken in oil; drain.

Combine chicken, relish, orange marmalade and water; mix well. Place in 2-quart casserole dish; top with cheese.

Bake at 350°F for 30 minutes or until hot and bubbly. Serve over hot cooked pasta or rice.

Makes 6 servings

Note: A packaged rice pilaf mix would be a quick, delicious choice to accompany this recipe.

Campbell's® 15-Minute Chicken & Rice Dinner

TUSCAN POT PIE

¾ **pound sweet or hot Italian sausage**
1 **jar (26 to 28 ounces) prepared chunky vegetable or mushroom spaghetti sauce**
1 **can (19 ounces) cannellini beans, rinsed and drained**
½ **teaspoon dried thyme leaves**
1½ **cups (6 ounces) shredded mozzarella cheese**
1 **package (8 ounces) refrigerated crescent dinner rolls**

1. Preheat oven to 425°F. Remove sausage from casings. Brown sausage in medium ovenproof skillet, stirring to separate meat. Drain drippings.

2. Add spaghetti sauce, beans and thyme to skillet. Simmer uncovered over medium heat 5 minutes. Remove from heat; stir in cheese.

3. Unroll crescent dough; divide into triangles. Arrange spiral fashion with points of dough towards center, covering sausage mixture completely. Bake 12 minutes or until crust is golden brown and meat mixture is bubbly. *Makes 4 to 6 servings*

Prep and Cook Time: 27 minutes

PIZZA CASSEROLE

1 **pound BOB EVANS® Italian Roll Sausage**
12 **ounces wide noodles, cooked according to package directions**
2 **(14-ounce) jars pepperoni pizza sauce**
2 **cups (8 ounces) shredded Cheddar cheese**
2 **cups (8 ounces) shredded mozzarella cheese**
6 **ounces sliced pepperoni**

Preheat oven to 350°F. Crumble and cook sausage in medium skillet over medium heat until browned. Drain sausage on paper towels. Layer half of noodles in lightly greased 13×9-inch casserole dish. Top with half of sausage, half of pizza sauce, half of cheeses and half of pepperoni. Repeat layers with remaining ingredients, reserving several pepperoni slices for garnish on top of casserole. Bake 35 to 40 minutes. Refrigerate leftovers.

Makes 6 to 8 servings

Tuscan Pot Pie

PREGO® MIRACLE LASAGNA

1 jar (28 ounces) PREGO® Traditional Pasta Sauce
6 uncooked lasagna noodles
1 container (15 ounces) ricotta cheese
8 ounces shredded mozzarella cheese (2 cups)
¼ cup grated Parmesan cheese

1. In 2-quart shallow baking dish (11- by 7-inch) spread **1 cup** pasta sauce. Top with **3 uncooked** lasagna noodles, ricotta cheese, **1 cup** mozzarella cheese, Parmesan cheese and 1 cup pasta sauce. Top with remaining **3 uncooked** lasagna noodles and remaining pasta sauce. **Cover.**

2. Bake at 375°F. for 1 hour. Uncover and top with remaining mozzarella cheese. Let stand 5 minutes.
Makes 6 servings

Meat or Mushroom Miracle Lasagna: Use 3-quart shallow baking dish (13- by 9-inch). Proceed as in Step 1. Top Parmesan cheese with 1 pound ground beef **or** sausage, cooked and drained, **or** 2 cups sliced fresh mushrooms **or** 2 jars (4½ ounces *each*) sliced mushrooms, drained.

Tip: For a variation, substitute PREGO® Pasta Sauce with Fresh Mushrooms *or* PREGO® Italian Sausage & Garlic Pasta Sauce.

Prep Time: 5 minutes
Cook Time: 1 hour
Stand Time: 5 minutes

SPEEDY MAC & CHEESE

1 can (10¾ ounces) condensed Cheddar cheese soup
1 cup milk
4 cups hot cooked medium shell macaroni (3 cups uncooked)
1⅓ cups FRENCH'S® French Fried Onions, divided
1 cup (4 ounces) shredded Cheddar cheese

Combine soup and milk in 2-quart microwavable casserole. Stir in macaroni, ⅔ cup French Fried Onions and cheese. Cover; microwave on HIGH 10 minutes* or until heated through, stirring halfway through cooking time. Top with remaining ⅔ cup onions. Microwave 1 minute or until onions are golden.
Makes 6 servings

*Or, bake, covered, in 350°F oven 25 to 30 minutes.

Prep Time: 10 minutes
Cook Time: 11 minutes

Prego® Miracle Lasagna

WISCONSIN CHEESE PASTA CASSEROLE

1 pound spaghetti or fettuccine, broken into 3-inch pieces
1 quart prepared spaghetti sauce
½ cup plus ⅓ cup grated Wisconsin Romano cheese, divided
1¾ cups (7 ounces) sliced or shredded Wisconsin Colby cheese
1½ cups (6 ounces) shredded Wisconsin Mozzarella cheese

Prepare pasta according to package directions; drain. Toss warm pasta with prepared spaghetti sauce to coat. Add ½ cup Romano cheese to mixture and mix well. Spread half of sauced pasta into bottom of 13×9×2-inch baking dish. Cover with 1 cup Colby cheese. Spread remaining pasta over cheese. Top with remaining ¾ cup Colby cheese. Sprinkle with remaining ⅓ cup Romano cheese and Mozzarella cheese. Bake at 350°F for 35 to 40 minutes or until top is lightly browned and casserole is bubbly. Remove from heat and let stand at least 10 minutes before serving.

Makes 6 to 8 servings

Favorite recipe from **Wisconsin Milk Marketing Board**

THREE CHEESE BAKED ZITI

1 container (15 ounces) part-skim ricotta cheese
2 eggs, beaten
¼ cup grated Parmesan cheese
1 box (16 ounces) ziti pasta, cooked and drained
1 jar (28 ounces) RAGÚ® Chunky Gardenstyle Pasta Sauce
1 cup shredded mozzarella cheese (about 4 ounces)

Preheat oven to 350°F. In large bowl, combine ricotta cheese, eggs and Parmesan cheese; set aside.

In another bowl, thoroughly combine pasta and Ragú® Chunky Gardenstyle Pasta Sauce.

In 13×9-inch baking dish, spoon ½ of the pasta mixture; evenly top with ricotta cheese mixture, then remaining pasta mixture. Sprinkle with mozzarella cheese. Bake 30 minutes or until heated through. Serve, if desired, with additional heated pasta sauce.

Makes 8 servings

Three Cheese Baked Ziti

Meatless
MAIN DISHES

CAMPBELL'S® ONE–DISH PASTA & VEGETABLES

1½ cups *uncooked* corkscrew macaroni
2 medium carrots, sliced (about 1 cup)
1 cup broccoli flowerets
1 can (10¾ ounces) CAMPBELL'S® Condensed
   Cheddar Cheese Soup
½ cup milk
1 tablespoon prepared mustard

1. In large saucepan prepare macaroni according to package directions. Add carrots and broccoli for last 5 minutes of cooking time. Drain.

2. In same pan mix soup, milk, mustard and macaroni mixture. Over medium heat, heat through, stirring often.

Makes 5 servings

Prep Time: 15 minutes
Cook Time: 15 minutes

*Left:
Campbell's®
One-Dish Pasta
& Vegetables*

Above: *Miami
Rice and Bean
Burritos (page
282)*

249

BAKED PROVENÇAL ZITI PROVOLONE

10 ounces uncooked ziti pasta
1 cup evaporated skimmed milk
½ cup fat-free (skim) milk
4 egg whites
1 tablespoon Dijon mustard
½ teaspoon salt
½ cup finely chopped green onions, with tops
   Black pepper
4 ounces sliced provolone cheese
2 tablespoons grated Parmesan cheese

1. Preheat oven to 325°F. Spray 9-inch square baking pan with nonstick cooking spray; set aside. Cook pasta according to package directions; drain. Place in prepared pan.

2. Meanwhile, combine evaporated milk, skim milk, egg whites, mustard and salt in food processor or blender; process until smooth.

3. Sprinkle green onions over pasta. Pour milk mixture over green onions. Sprinkle with pepper and top with provolone cheese.

4. Bake 35 minutes or until heated through. Remove from oven. Sprinkle with Parmesan cheese. Let stand 5 minutes before serving. *Makes 4 servings*

THREE–CHEESE MACARONI

3 cups uncooked elbow macaroni or rotini pasta
1 can (11 ounces) condensed Cheddar cheese soup
1 cup milk
2 teaspoons FRENCH'S® Classic Yellow® Mustard
½ cup (2 ounces) shredded Swiss cheese
½ cup (2 ounces) shredded Cheddar cheese
½ cup grated Parmesan cheese
1⅓ cups FRENCH'S® French Fried Onions, divided

Preheat oven to 350°F. Cook pasta according to package directions using shortest cooking time. Drain.

Combine soup, milk and mustard in 1½-quart casserole. Stir in cooked pasta, cheeses and ⅔ cup French Fried Onions; mix well.

Cover; bake 25 minutes or until heated through. Stir; sprinkle with remaining ⅔ cup onions. Bake, uncovered, 5 minutes or until onions are golden.

Makes 6 servings

Prep Time: 10 minutes
Cook Time: 30 minutes

Baked Provençal Ziti Provolone

CANNELLINI PARMESAN CASSEROLE

2 tablespoons olive oil
1 cup chopped onion
2 teaspoons bottled minced garlic
1 teaspoon dried oregano leaves
¼ teaspoon black pepper
2 cans (14½ ounces each) onion- and garlic-flavored diced tomatoes, undrained
1 jar (14 ounces) roasted red peppers, drained and cut into ½-inch squares
2 cans (19 ounces each) white cannellini beans, rinsed and drained
1 teaspoon dried basil leaves *or* 2 tablespoons chopped fresh basil
¾ cup (3 ounces) grated Parmesan cheese

1. Heat oil in Dutch oven over medium heat until hot. Add onion, garlic, oregano and pepper; cook and stir 5 minutes or until onion is tender.

2. Increase heat to high. Add tomatoes with juice and red peppers; cover and bring to a boil.

3. Reduce heat to medium. Stir in beans; cover and simmer 5 minutes, stirring occasionally. Stir in basil and sprinkle with cheese.   *Makes 6 servings*

Prep and Cook Time: 20 minutes

V8® HEARTY VEGETARIAN CHILI

2 tablespoons vegetable oil
1 large onion, chopped (about 1 cup)
1 small green pepper, chopped (about ½ cup)
1 tablespoon chili powder
½ teaspoon ground cumin
¼ teaspoon garlic powder *or* 2 cloves garlic, minced
2½ cups V8® 100% Vegetable Juice
1 can (16 ounces) black beans, rinsed and drained
1 can (15 ounces) pinto beans, rinsed and drained

1. In large saucepan over medium heat, heat oil. Add onion, pepper, chili powder, cumin and garlic powder and cook until tender.

2. Add vegetable juice. Heat to a boil. Reduce heat to low. Cook 5 minutes. Add beans and heat through.   *Makes 4 servings*

Prep Time: 10 minutes
Cook Time: 20 minutes

Cannellini Parmesan Casserole

MAIN DISHES

PREGO® BROCCOLI–CHEESE STUFFED SHELLS

1 container (15 ounces) ricotta cheese
1 package (10 ounces) frozen chopped broccoli (2 cups), thawed and well drained
1 cup shredded mozzarella cheese (4 ounces)
⅓ cup grated Parmesan cheese
¼ teaspoon black pepper
18 cooked jumbo pasta shells (about 8 ounces uncooked)
1 jar (27.75 ounces) PREGO® Extra Chunky® Garden Combination Pasta Sauce

1. In medium bowl mix ricotta cheese, broccoli, *½ cup* mozzarella cheese, Parmesan cheese and pepper. Spoon about *2 tablespoons* into each shell.

2. In 3-quart shallow baking dish spread *1 cup* pasta sauce. Arrange stuffed shells in single layer in sauce. Pour remaining sauce over shells. Sprinkle with remaining mozzarella cheese.

3. Bake at 400°F. for 25 minutes or until hot.

Makes 6 servings

Tip: To thaw broccoli, microwave on HIGH 4 minutes.

Prep Time: 25 minutes
Cook Time: 25 minutes

CHEESE–SAUCED MANICOTTI

8 manicotti shells
1 cup chopped onion
¼ cup water
2 cloves garlic, minced
3 tablespoons all-purpose flour
1⅔ cups fat-free (skim) milk, divided
¾ cup (3 ounces) shredded part-skim mozzarella cheese
1 teaspoon dried Italian seasoning
¼ teaspoon ground black pepper
1 package (10 ounces) frozen chopped spinach, thawed and well drained
1 cup nonfat ricotta cheese
½ cup 1% low-fat cottage cheese
½ teaspoon dried marjoram leaves
1 medium tomato, sliced

Prepare manicotti according to package directions; drain. Rinse under cold water; drain.

Meanwhile, preheat oven to 350°F. Coat 13×9-inch baking dish with nonstick cooking spray.

To make sauce, combine onion, water and garlic in medium saucepan. Bring to a boil over high heat. Reduce heat to medium-low. Cover; simmer 3 to 4 minutes or until onion is tender. Blend flour and ⅓ cup milk in small bowl until smooth. Stir into onion mixture. Stir in remaining 1⅓ cups milk. Cook and stir over medium heat until mixture boils and thickens. Cook and stir 1 minute. Add mozzarella cheese, Italian seasoning and pepper. Cook and stir until cheese melts.

Meatless
MAIN DISHES

Combine spinach, ricotta cheese, cottage cheese, marjoram and ⅓ cup sauce in medium bowl. Spoon ⅓ cup spinach mixture into each manicotti shell. Place in prepared baking dish. Pour remaining sauce over top. Cover; bake 30 to 35 minutes or until heated through. Arrange tomato slices on top. Bake, uncovered, 4 to 5 minutes or until tomato is heated through.

Makes 4 servings

INDONESIAN HONEY–BAKED BEANS

- **2 cans (15 ounces each) white beans, drained**
- **2 apples, peeled and diced**
- **1 small onion, diced**
- **⅔ cup honey**
- **½ cup golden raisins**
- **⅓ cup sweet pickle relish**
- **1 tablespoon prepared mustard**
- **1 teaspoon curry powder or to taste**
- **Salt to taste**

Combine all ingredients in 2½-quart casserole. Add enough water just to cover. Bake at 300°F about 1½ hours, adding more water if needed.

Makes 8 servings

Favorite recipe from **National Honey Board**

MONTEREY SPAGHETTI CASSEROLE

- **4 ounces uncooked spaghetti**
- **1 cup sour cream**
- **1 egg, beaten**
- **2 cups (8 ounces) shredded Monterey Jack cheese**
- **¼ cup grated Parmesan cheese**
- **1 package (10 ounces) frozen chopped spinach, thawed and drained**
- **1⅓ cups FRENCH'S® French Fried Onions, divided**

Preheat oven to 350°F. Cook spaghetti according to package directions using shortest cooking time. Drain.

Combine sour cream and egg in 8-inch square baking dish. Stir in spaghetti, cheeses, spinach and ⅔ cup French Fried Onions.

Cover; bake 30 minutes or until heated through. Stir. Top with remaining ⅔ cup onions. Bake, uncovered, 5 minutes or until onions are golden.

Makes 4 servings

Prep Time: 10 minutes
Cook Time: 35 minutes

MAIN DISHES

CANNELLONI WITH TOMATO–EGGPLANT SAUCE

1 package (10 ounces) fresh spinach
1 cup nonfat ricotta cheese
4 egg whites, beaten
¼ cup grated Parmesan cheese
2 tablespoons finely chopped fresh parsley
½ teaspoon salt (optional)
8 manicotti noodles (about 4 ounces),
    cooked and cooled
    Tomato-Eggplant Sauce (recipe follows)
1 cup (4 ounces) shredded reduced-fat
    mozzarella cheese

1. Preheat oven to 350°F.

2. Wash spinach; do not pat dry. Place spinach in saucepan; cook, covered, over medium-high heat 3 to 5 minutes or until spinach is wilted. Cool slightly and drain; chop finely.

3. Combine ricotta cheese, spinach, egg whites, Parmesan cheese, parsley and salt in large bowl; mix well. Spoon mixture into manicotti shells; arrange in 13×9-inch baking pan. Spoon Tomato-Eggplant Sauce over manicotti; sprinkle with mozzarella cheese.

4. Bake manicotti, uncovered, 25 to 30 minutes or until hot and bubbly.

Makes 4 servings (2 manicotti each)

TOMATO–EGGPLANT SAUCE

Olive oil-flavored nonstick cooking spray
1 small eggplant, coarsely chopped
½ cup chopped onion
2 cloves garlic, minced
½ teaspoon dried tarragon leaves
¼ teaspoon dried thyme leaves
1 can (16 ounces) no-salt-added whole
    tomatoes, undrained and coarsely
    chopped
Salt and black pepper

1. Spray large skillet with cooking spray; heat over medium heat until hot. Add eggplant, onion, garlic, tarragon and thyme; cook and stir about 5 minutes or until vegetables are tender.

2. Stir in tomatoes; bring to a boil. Reduce heat and simmer, uncovered, 3 to 4 minutes. Season to taste with salt and pepper. *Makes about 2½ cups*

Cannelloni with Tomato-Eggplant Sauce

MAIN DISHES

EGGPLANT CRÊPES WITH ROASTED TOMATO SAUCE

Roasted Tomato Sauce (recipe follows)
2 eggplants (about 8 to 9 inches long)
Nonstick cooking spray
1 package (10 ounces) frozen chopped
    spinach, thawed and pressed dry
1 cup ricotta cheese
½ cup grated Parmesan cheese
1¼ cups (5 ounces) shredded Gruyère* cheese
Fresh oregano leaves for garnish

*Gruyère cheese is a Swiss cheese that has been aged for 10 to 12 months. Any Swiss cheese may be substituted.

1. Prepare Roasted Tomato Sauce.

2. *Reduce oven temperature to 425°F.* Cut eggplants lengthwise into ¼-inch-thick slices. Arrange 18 of largest slices on nonstick baking sheets in single layer. Spray both sides of eggplant slices with cooking spray. (Reserve any remaining slices for other uses.)

3. Bake eggplant 10 minutes; turn and bake 5 to 10 minutes more or until tender. Cool. *Reduce oven temperature to 350°F.*

4. Combine spinach, ricotta and Parmesan cheese; mix well. Spray 12×8-inch baking pan with cooking spray. Spread spinach mixture evenly on eggplant slices; roll up slices, beginning at short ends. Place rolls, seam-side down, in baking dish. Cover dish with foil. Bake 25 minutes. Uncover; sprinkle rolls with Gruyère cheese. Bake, uncovered, 5 minutes more or until cheese is melted.

5. Serve with Roasted Tomato Sauce. Garnish, if desired.   *Makes 4 to 6 servings*

ROASTED TOMATO SAUCE

20 ripe plum tomatoes (about 2⅔ pounds),
    cut in half and seeded
 3 tablespoons olive oil, divided
 ½ teaspoon salt
 ⅓ cup minced fresh basil
 ½ teaspoon ground black pepper

Preheat oven to 450°F. Toss tomatoes with 1 tablespoon oil and salt. Place, cut sides down, on nonstick baking sheet. Bake 20 to 25 minutes or until skins are blistered. Cool. Process tomatoes, remaining 2 tablespoons oil, basil and pepper in food processor until smooth.   *Makes about 1 cup*

Eggplant Crêpes with Roasted Tomato Sauce

MAIN DISHES

FRESH VEGETABLE LASAGNA

8 ounces uncooked lasagna noodles
1 package (10 ounces) frozen chopped
    spinach, thawed, well drained
1 cup shredded carrots
½ cup sliced green onions
½ cup sliced red bell pepper
¼ cup chopped fresh parsley
½ teaspoon black pepper
1½ cups low-fat cottage cheese
1 cup buttermilk
½ cup plain nonfat yogurt
2 egg whites
1 cup sliced mushrooms
1 can (14 ounces) artichoke hearts, drained
    and chopped
2 cups (8 ounces) shredded part-skim
    mozzarella cheese
¼ cup freshly grated Parmesan cheese

1. Cook pasta according to package directions. Drain. Rinse under cold water; drain well. Set aside.

2. Preheat oven to 375°F. Pat spinach with paper towels to remove excess moisture. Combine spinach, carrots, green onions, bell pepper, parsley and black pepper in large bowl. Set aside.

3. Combine cottage cheese, buttermilk, yogurt and egg whites in food processor or blender; process until smooth.

4. Spray 13×9-inch baking pan with nonstick cooking spray. Arrange half of lasagna noodles in bottom of pan. Spread with half each of cottage cheese mixture, vegetable mixture, mushrooms, artichokes and mozzarella. Repeat layers, ending with noodles. Sprinkle with Parmesan cheese.

5. Cover and bake 30 minutes. Remove cover; continue baking 20 minutes or until bubbly and heated through. Let stand 10 minutes before serving.
Makes 8 servings

Food Fact

Green bell peppers are picked before they ripen. When they are ripe, bell peppers can be red, yellow, orange, white or purple, depending on the variety. Ripe peppers are sweeter and crisper than green peppers.

Fresh Vegetable Lasagna

MEDITERRANEAN STEW

1 medium butternut or acorn squash,
   peeled and cut into 1-inch cubes
2 cups unpeeled eggplant, cut into 1-inch
   cubes
2 cups sliced zucchini
1 can (15½ ounces) chick-peas, rinsed and
   drained
1 package (10 ounces) frozen cut okra
1 can (8 ounces) tomato sauce
1 cup chopped onion
1 medium tomato, chopped
1 medium carrot, thinly sliced
½ cup reduced-sodium vegetable broth
⅓ cup raisins
1 clove garlic, minced
½ teaspoon ground cumin
½ teaspoon ground turmeric
¼ to ½ teaspoon ground red pepper
¼ teaspoon ground cinnamon
¼ teaspoon paprika
6 to 8 cups hot cooked couscous or rice
   Fresh parsley (optional)

SLOW COOKER DIRECTIONS

Combine all ingredients except couscous and parsley in slow cooker; mix well. Cover and cook on LOW 8 to 10 hours or until vegetables are crisp-tender. Serve over couscous. Garnish with parsley, if desired.

Makes 6 servings

BAKED EGGPLANT PARMESAN

2 cups seasoned dry bread crumbs
1½ cups grated Parmesan cheese, divided
2 medium eggplants (about 2 pounds),
   peeled and cut into ¼-inch round slices
4 eggs, beaten with 3 tablespoons water
1 jar (28 ounces) RAGÚ® Hearty Robust
   Blend Pasta Sauce
1½ cups shredded mozzarella cheese (about
   6 ounces)

Preheat oven to 350°F. In medium bowl, combine bread crumbs and ½ cup Parmesan cheese. Dip eggplant slices in egg mixture, then bread crumb mixture. On lightly oiled baking sheets, arrange eggplant slices in single layer; bake 25 minutes or until golden.

In 13×9-inch baking dish, evenly spread 1 cup Ragú® Hearty Robust Blend Pasta Sauce. Layer ½ of the baked eggplant slices, then 1 cup sauce and ½ cup Parmesan cheese; repeat. Cover with aluminum foil and bake 45 minutes. Remove foil and sprinkle with mozzarella cheese. Bake uncovered an additional 10 minutes or until cheese is melted.

Makes 6 servings

Mediterranean Stew

TRIPLE PEPPER TOMATO PROVOLONE LASAGNA

1 red bell pepper, chopped
1 yellow bell pepper, chopped
1 green bell pepper, chopped
1 package (8 ounces) sliced fresh mushrooms
1 cup thinly sliced zucchini
½ cup chopped onion
4 cloves garlic, minced
1½ cups vegetable juice cocktail
1 can (16 ounces) diced tomatoes, undrained
1½ to 1¾ teaspoons Italian seasoning blend
1 tablespoon olive oil
9 uncooked lasagna noodles
1 cup nonfat cottage cheese
⅓ cup grated Parmesan cheese
4 ounces sliced provolone cheese

1. Preheat oven to 350°F. Combine first 10 ingredients in Dutch oven. Bring to a boil over high heat. Reduce heat to low; simmer, uncovered, 15 minutes. Remove from heat; stir in oil.

2. Spray 12×8-inch baking pan with nonstick cooking spray. Place 3 lasagna noodles on bottom of pan. Spread ⅓ of the sauce over noodles. Spread ½ cup cottage cheese evenly over sauce; sprinkle with 2 tablespoons Parmesan cheese. Repeat layers, ending with sauce.

3. Bake, uncovered, 1 hour or until bubbly. Place provolone slices on top of lasagna. Sprinkle with remaining Parmesan cheese. Bake 5 minutes longer or until cheese is melted. Let stand 15 minutes before serving. *Makes 6 servings*

GARDEN VEGETABLE TABBOULEH STEW

1 large onion, chopped
2 medium carrots, cut lengthwise into halves, then cut into 1-inch pieces
1 cup green beans, cut into 1-inch pieces
2 medium green onions, thinly sliced
1 small zucchini (4 ounces), sliced
1 can (15½ ounces) chick-peas, rinsed and drained
2 cans (14½ ounces each) diced tomatoes, undrained
¼ teaspoon salt
⅛ teaspoon black pepper
1 box (6 to 7 ounces) tabbouleh mix
1½ cups water
¼ cup olive oil
Sour cream (optional)
Fresh mint (optional)

SLOW COOKER DIRECTIONS

Layer ingredients in slow cooker in the following order: onion, carrots, green beans, green onions, zucchini, chick-peas, tomatoes with juice, salt and pepper. Sprinkle tabbouleh mix over vegetables. Pour water and olive oil evenly over top. Cover and cook on LOW 6 to 8 hours or until vegetables are crisp-tender. Serve in bowls and garnish with sour cream and fresh mint, if desired.

Makes 4 servings

Garden Vegetable Tabbouleh Stew

ITALIAN LASAGNA ROLLS

8 ounces lasagna noodles (about 12 noodles)
2 (10-ounce) packages frozen spinach, thawed and well drained
16 ounces nonfat cottage cheese
2½ cups (10 ounces) shredded mozzarella cheese, divided
1½ cups grated Parmesan cheese, divided
8 ounces nonfat cream cheese, softened
½ teaspoon dried basil leaves
¼ teaspoon salt
¼ teaspoon dried oregano leaves
¼ teaspoon black pepper
Light Tomato Sauce (recipe follows)

Cook lasagna noodles according to package directions; drain and cool slightly.

Combine spinach, cottage cheese, 2 cups mozzarella cheese, 1 cup Parmesan cheese, cream cheese, basil, salt, oregano and pepper in large bowl; stir well.

Spread scant ½ cup spinach mixture on each lasagna noodle; roll up jelly-roll fashion, starting at narrow end. Place lasagna rolls, seam side down, in 13×9×2-inch baking dish. Pour Light Tomato Sauce evenly over rolls; sprinkle with ½ cup Parmesan cheese and ½ cup mozzarella cheese.

Bake at 350°F for 50 to 60 minutes, covering baking dish with foil for first 30 minutes. (To prevent mozzarella cheese from sticking, coat foil with cooking spray.) *Makes 5 to 6 servings*

LIGHT TOMATO SAUCE

1 large onion, chopped
¼ cup finely chopped green pepper
3 cloves garlic, minced
3 tablespoons low-fat margarine
2 (28-ounce) cans crushed tomatoes in tomato puree
1 (15-ounce) can tomato sauce
2 tablespoons sugar
2 teaspoons dried basil leaves
2 teaspoons dried Italian seasoning
¼ teaspoon salt
¼ teaspoon black pepper

Sauté onion, green pepper and garlic in margarine in large skillet until tender. Add remaining ingredients; simmer 30 minutes.

Favorite recipe from **North Dakota Wheat Commission**

MAIN DISHES

CHEESY PASTA SWIRLS

1 bag (16 ounces) frozen vegetable
    combination (peas, carrots,
    cauliflower), thawed and drained
1 cup (4 ounces) shredded mozzarella cheese
½ cup (2 ounces) cubed provolone cheese
1⅓ cups FRENCH'S® French Fried Onions,
    divided
4 ounces fettuccine, cooked in unsalted
    water and undrained
1 can (10¾ ounces) condensed cream of
    mushroom soup
¾ cup milk
½ teaspoon garlic salt
⅓ cup (about 1½ ounces) grated Parmesan
    cheese

Preheat oven to 350°F. In 12×8-inch baking dish, combine vegetables, mozzarella, provolone and ⅔ cup French Fried Onions. Twirl a few strands of hot fettuccine around long-tined fork to form a pasta swirl. Remove pasta swirl from fork; stand upright on top of vegetable mixture. Repeat process to form 5 more swirls.

In medium bowl, stir together soup, milk and garlic salt; pour over pasta swirls and vegetable mixture. Bake, loosely covered, at 350°F for 30 minutes or until vegetables are done. Top pasta swirls with Parmesan cheese; sprinkle remaining ⅔ cup onions around swirls. Bake, uncovered, 5 minutes or until onions are golden brown. *Makes 6 servings*

Microwave Directions: In 12×8-inch microwave-safe dish, prepare vegetable mixture as above. Form pasta swirls and place on vegetables as above. Prepare soup mixture as above; pour over pasta and vegetables. Cook, loosely covered, on HIGH 14 to 16 minutes or until vegetables are done. Rotate dish halfway through cooking time. Top pasta swirls with Parmesan cheese and remaining onions as above; cook, uncovered, 1 minute. Let stand 5 minutes.

Food Fact

A sauce is generally defined as a thickened, seasoned liquid that is served with food to add flavor, moisture and to enhance its appearance. The most common ways to thicken sauces are with flour, butter, cornstarch or eggs.

TURTLE SHELLS

24 jumbo pasta shells, uncooked
1 (10-ounce) package frozen chopped spinach, thawed and squeezed dry
8 ounces shredded part-skim mozzarella cheese (about 1¾ cup)
1½ cups low-fat, part-skim ricotta cheese
3 medium carrots, peeled and grated
3 egg whites
¼ teaspoon freshly ground black pepper
  Large pinch ground nutmeg
2 cups low-sodium canned tomato sauce
¼ cup Parmesan cheese (optional)

Cook pasta according to package directions; drain and rinse under cold water until completely cool. Drain thoroughly.

Preheat oven to 350°F. In large bowl, stir together spinach, mozzarella cheese, ricotta cheese, carrots, egg whites, pepper and nutmeg until thoroughly blended.

Line bottom of 11×7-inch baking dish with ½ cup tomato sauce. Divide ricotta mixture among pasta shells, pressing filling into shells with spoon to completely fill each shell. Arrange shells side by side in baking dish. Coat shells with even layer of remaining tomato sauce. Sprinkle with Parmesan cheese, if desired.

Bake until center of shells are heated through and sauce is bubbling, about 40 minutes. Let stand 10 minutes before serving.   *Makes 6 servings*

Favorite recipe from **National Pasta Association**

CAMPBELL'S® BAKED MACARONI & CHEESE

1 can (10¾ ounces) CAMPBELL'S® Condensed Cheddar Cheese Soup
½ soup can milk
⅛ teaspoon pepper
2 cups hot cooked corkscrew *or* medium shell macaroni (about 1½ cups uncooked)
1 tablespoon dry bread crumbs
2 teaspoons margarine *or* butter, melted

1. In 1-quart casserole mix soup, milk, pepper and macaroni.

2. Mix bread crumbs with margarine and sprinkle over macaroni mixture.

3. Bake at 400°F. for 20 minutes or until hot.
    Makes 4 servings

To Double Recipe: Double all ingredients, except increase margarine to 1 tablespoon, use 2-quart casserole and increase baking time to 25 minutes.

Variation: Substitute 2 cups hot cooked elbow macaroni (about 1 cup uncooked) for corkscrew *or* shell macaroni.

Prep Time: 20 minutes
Cook Time: 20 minutes

Campbell's® Baked Macaroni & Cheese

MAIN DISHES

DOUBLE SPINACH BAKE

8 ounces uncooked spinach fettuccine
   noodles
1 cup fresh mushroom slices
1 green onion with top, finely chopped
1 clove garlic, minced
4 to 5 cups fresh spinach, coarsely chopped
1 tablespoon water
1 container (15 ounces) nonfat ricotta
   cheese
¼ cup fat-free (skim) milk
1 egg, beaten
½ teaspoon ground nutmeg
½ teaspoon ground black pepper
¼ cup (1 ounce) shredded reduced-fat Swiss
   cheese

1. Preheat oven to 350°F. Cook pasta according to package directions. Drain; set aside.

2. Spray medium skillet with nonstick cooking spray. Add mushrooms, green onion and garlic. Cook and stir over medium heat until mushrooms are softened. Add spinach and water. Cover; cook until spinach is wilted, about 3 minutes.

3. Combine ricotta cheese, milk, egg, nutmeg and black pepper in large bowl. Gently stir in noodles and vegetables; toss to coat evenly.

4. Coat shallow 1½-quart casserole with cooking spray. Spread noodle mixture in casserole. Sprinkle with Swiss cheese. Bake 25 to 30 minutes or until knife inserted into center comes out clean.

Makes 6 (1-cup) servings

VEGETABLE MANICOTTI ALFREDO

1 can (10¾ ounces) condensed cream of
   celery soup
¼ cup reduced-fat (2%) milk
2 tablespoons shredded Parmesan cheese
½ teaspoon dried dill weed
2 medium zucchini, diced
1 medium yellow squash, diced
1 cup diced red bell pepper
½ cup sliced green onions
1 clove garlic, minced
½ teaspoon salt
⅛ teaspoon black pepper
¾ cup ricotta cheese
10 cooked manicotti shells

In medium bowl, combine soup, milk, Parmesan cheese and dill; mix well. Set aside. In another medium bowl, combine zucchini, squash, bell pepper, green onions, garlic, salt, black pepper and ricotta cheese; blend well.

Spray 13×9-inch baking dish with nonstick cooking spray. Spread half of soup mixture over bottom of dish. Fill manicotti shells with vegetable mixture; place filled shells over soup mixture. Pour remaining soup mixture over manicotti. Cover and bake at 350°F 30 to 35 minutes or until hot and bubbly.

Makes 5 servings

Double Spinach Bake

MAIN DISHES

HOT THREE–BEAN CASSEROLE

2 tablespoons olive oil
1 cup coarsely chopped onion
1 cup chopped celery
2 cloves garlic, minced
1 can (15 ounces) chick-peas, drained and rinsed
1 can (15 ounces) kidney beans, drained and rinsed
1 cup coarsely chopped tomato
1 can (8 ounces) tomato sauce
1 cup water
1 to 2 jalapeño peppers*, minced
1 tablespoon chili powder
2 teaspoons sugar
1½ teaspoons ground cumin
1 teaspoon salt
1 teaspoon dried oregano
¼ teaspoon ground black pepper
2½ cups (10 ounces) frozen cut green beans

*Jalapeño peppers can sting and irritate the skin; wear rubber gloves when handling peppers and do not touch your eyes. Wash hands after handling jalapeño peppers.

1. Heat olive oil in large skillet over medium heat until hot. Add onion, celery and garlic. Cook and stir 5 minutes or until onion is tender.

2. Add remaining ingredients except green beans. Bring to a boil; reduce heat to low. Simmer, uncovered, 20 minutes. Add green beans. Simmer, uncovered, 10 minutes or until green beans are just tender.   *Makes 12 (½-cup) servings*

SWANSON® VEGETABLE STIR–FRY

1 can (14½ ounces) SWANSON® Vegetable Broth
2 tablespoons cornstarch
1 tablespoon soy sauce
¼ teaspoon ground ginger
1 tablespoon vegetable oil
5 cups cut-up vegetables*
⅛ teaspoon garlic powder *or* 1 clove garlic, minced

*Use a combination of broccoli flowerets, sliced mushrooms, sliced carrots, sliced celery, red or green pepper strips and sliced green onions.

1. In bowl mix broth, cornstarch, soy sauce and ginger until smooth. Set aside.

2. In medium skillet over medium-high heat, heat oil. Add vegetables and garlic powder and stir-fry until tender-crisp.

3. Stir cornstarch mixture and add to vegetable mixture. Cook until mixture boils and thickens, stirring constantly.
Makes 4 main-dish servings or 8 side-dish servings

Prep Time: 15 minutes
Cook Time: 10 minutes

Hot Three-Bean Casserole

MAIN DISHES

GOURMET BEAN & SPINACH BURRITOS

Avocado Relish (recipe follows)
1 pound spinach leaves, divided
2 teaspoons olive oil
1 cup finely chopped onion
2 cloves garlic, minced
2 cans (15 ounces each) black beans, drained
1 can (10 ounces) whole tomatoes with
   green chilies, undrained
2 teaspoons ground cumin
½ teaspoon ground oregano
8 flour tortillas (8-inch diameter)
2 cups (8 ounces) shredded Monterey Jack
   cheese

1. Prepare Avocado Relish. Set aside.

2. Wash and dry spinach. Remove and discard stems from spinach leaves. Set aside 24 to 30 large leaves. Coarsely shred remaining leaves. Set aside.

3. Heat olive oil in large nonstick skillet over medium heat until hot. Add onion and garlic; cook and stir 5 minutes or until tender. Add beans, tomatoes, cumin and oregano. Simmer, uncovered, until all liquid has evaporated. Remove from heat; mash bean mixture with potato masher.

4. Preheat oven to 350°F. Arrange 3 to 4 whole spinach leaves on each tortilla. Spoon bean mixture onto bottom half of tortillas; sprinkle cheese evenly over bean mixture. Roll up tortillas to enclose filling.

5. Arrange tortillas, seam side down, in 12×8-inch baking dish. Cover with foil. Bake 20 minutes or until heated through.

6. Serve burritos on shredded spinach. Top with Avocado Relish.   *Makes 4 servings*

AVOCADO RELISH

1 large, firm, ripe avocado, finely diced
2 tablespoons fresh lime juice
¾ cup finely chopped, seeded tomato
½ cup minced green onions
⅓ cup minced fresh cilantro
½ to 1 teaspoon hot pepper sauce

Combine avocado and lime juice in bowl; toss. Add tomato, onions, cilantro and hot sauce; toss gently. Cover and refrigerate 1 hour. Serve at room temperature.   *Makes about 2¼ cups*

Gourmet Bean & Spinach Burritos

LUSCIOUS VEGETARIAN LASAGNA

8 ounces lasagna noodles
1 can (14½ ounces) whole peeled tomatoes, undrained and coarsely chopped
1 can (12 ounces) tomato sauce
1 teaspoon dried oregano leaves
1 teaspoon dried basil leaves
   Dash black pepper
2 tablespoons olive oil
1 large onion, chopped
1½ teaspoons minced garlic
2 small zucchini, diced
1 large carrot, diced
1 green bell pepper, diced
8 ounces mushrooms, sliced
2 cups 1% low-fat cottage cheese
1 cup (4 ounces) shredded mozzarella cheese
1 cup grated Parmesan or Romano cheese
   Parsley sprigs for garnish

1. Cook lasagna noodles according to package directions; drain.

2. Place tomatoes with juice, tomato sauce, oregano, basil and black pepper in medium saucepan. Bring to a boil over high heat. Reduce heat to low. Simmer, uncovered, 6 to 10 minutes.

3. Heat oil in large skillet over medium-high heat. Cook and stir onion and garlic until onion is golden. Add zucchini, carrot, bell pepper and mushrooms. Cook and stir 5 to 10 minutes or until vegetables are tender. Stir vegetables into tomato mixture; bring to a boil. Reduce heat to low. Simmer, uncovered, 15 minutes.

4. Preheat oven to 350°F. Combine mozzarella, cottage cheese and Parmesan cheese in large bowl; blend well.

5. Spoon about 1 cup sauce in bottom of 12×8-inch baking pan. Place a layer of noodles over sauce, then half the cheese mixture and half the remaining sauce. Repeat layers of noodles, cheese mixture and sauce.

6. Bake lasagna 30 to 45 minutes or until bubbly. Let stand 10 minutes. Garnish with parsley.

Makes 6 to 8 servings

Luscious Vegetarian Lasagna

MAIN DISHES

LENTIL STEW OVER COUSCOUS

3 cups lentils (1 pound), rinsed
3 cups water
1 can (14½ ounces) diced tomatoes, undrained
1 can (14½ ounces) reduced-sodium vegetable broth
4 ribs celery, chopped
1 large onion, chopped
1 green bell pepper, chopped
1 medium carrot, cut lengthwise into halves, then cut into 1-inch pieces
2 cloves garlic, chopped
1 teaspoon dried marjoram leaves
¼ teaspoon black pepper
1 tablespoon cider vinegar
1 tablespoon olive oil
4½ to 5 cups hot cooked couscous

SLOW COOKER DIRECTIONS

Combine onion, bell pepper, celery, carrot, garlic, lentils, tomatoes, broth, water, black pepper and marjoram in slow cooker. Stir; cover and cook on LOW 8 to 9 hours.

Stir in vinegar and olive oil. Serve over couscous. Garnish with carrot curls and celery leaves, if desired. *Makes 12 servings*

VEGGIE JACK BURRITO

1 tablespoon vegetable oil
2 cups broccoli flowerettes
2 cups mushrooms, sliced
1 red onion, sliced
1 medium carrot, shredded
1 medium zucchini, shredded
¼ cup sliced green onion
1 clove garlic, minced
1 cup green salsa
3 cups (12 ounces) shredded Wisconsin Monterey Jack cheese or Mexican cheese blend, divided
8 flour tortillas
   Additional green or red salsa

In 10-inch skillet heat oil until hot; add vegetables and garlic. Cook over medium-high heat until slightly tender, 5 to 7 minutes. Stir in 1 cup salsa. Place vegetable mixture and 2 cups cheese on tortillas. Fold burrito- or taco-style; place in 12×8-inch baking dish. Cover with foil. Bake at 400°F for 15 to 20 minutes or until heated through. Top with salsa and remaining 1 cup cheese. Continue baking 5 to 7 minutes or until cheese is melted.

Makes 8 burritos

Favorite recipe from **Wisconsin Milk Marketing Board**

Lentil Stew over Couscous

WILD MUSHROOM LASAGNE

    Olive oil-flavored nonstick cooking spray
1 cup chopped red bell pepper, divided
¾ cup chopped onion
4 cloves garlic, minced
16 ounces shiitaki, portobello and white
    mushrooms, sliced
2 zucchini, sliced
1½ teaspoons dried oregano leaves
½ teaspoon dried thyme leaves
    Salt and black pepper
1 container (15 ounces) nonfat ricotta
    cheese
1 cup reduced-fat ricotta cheese
2 cups (8 ounces) shredded reduced-fat
    mozzarella cheese
¾ cup fat-free (skim) milk
    Parmesan White Sauce (recipe follows)
12 lasagne noodles, cooked

1. Preheat oven to 350°F. Spray large saucepan with cooking spray. Heat over medium heat until hot. Add ¾ cup bell pepper; cook and stir until tender. Remove from skillet.

2. Add onion and garlic; cook and stir 2 to 3 minutes or until tender. Add mushrooms; cook, covered, until mushrooms wilt and release liquid. Add zucchini, oregano and thyme; cook, uncovered, 8 to 10 minutes or until vegetables are tender and excess liquid evaporates. Season to taste with salt and pepper.

3. Mix ricotta cheeses, mozzarella cheese and milk in medium bowl. Spread about ⅔ cup Parmesan White Sauce in bottom of 13×9-inch baking pan; top with 4 lasagne noodles, overlapping slightly. Spoon ⅓ of the mushroom mixture over noodles; spread with ⅓ of the cheese mixture. Pour 1⅓ cups Parmesan White Sauce over cheese mixture. Repeat layers 2 more times, ending with remaining 1⅓ cups Parmesan White Sauce. Sprinkle with remaining ¼ cup bell pepper.

4. Bake lasagne, loosely covered with foil, 50 minutes. Uncover and bake about 10 minutes longer or until sauce is bubbly.

Makes 8 main-dish servings

PARMESAN WHITE SAUCE

4 tablespoons margarine
¼ cup plus 3 tablespoons all-purpose flour
1 can (14½ ounces) fat-free reduced-sodium
    chicken broth
2⅔ cups skim milk
⅓ cup grated Parmesan cheese
2 teaspoons dried oregano leaves
1½ teaspoons dried sage leaves
¼ teaspoon ground nutmeg
    Salt and black pepper

Melt margarine in large saucepan over medium heat. Stir in flour; cook and stir 1 to 2 minutes. Whisk in chicken broth and milk; bring to a boil. Boil, whisking constantly, 1 to 2 minutes or until thickened. Remove from heat; stir in cheese, oregano, sage and nutmeg. Season to taste with salt and pepper.

Makes about 4⅔ cups

MAIN DISHES

EASY CHEESY LASAGNA

2 tablespoons olive oil
3 small zucchini, quartered and thinly sliced
1 package (8 ounces) mushrooms, thinly sliced
1 medium onion, chopped
5 cloves garlic, minced
2 containers (15 ounces each) reduced-fat ricotta cheese
¼ cup grated Parmesan cheese
2 eggs, beaten
½ teaspoon dried Italian seasoning
¼ teaspoon garlic salt
⅛ teaspoon black pepper
1 can (28 ounces) crushed tomatoes in purée, undrained
1 jar (26 ounces) spaghetti sauce
1 package (16 ounces) lasagna noodles, uncooked
4 cups (16 ounces) shredded mozzarella cheese, divided

Preheat oven to 375°F. Spray 13×9-inch baking dish or lasagna pan with nonstick cooking spray.

Heat oil in large skillet over medium heat until hot. Add zucchini, mushrooms, onion and garlic. Cook and stir 5 minutes or until vegetables are tender. Set aside.

Combine ricotta cheese, Parmesan cheese, eggs, Italian seasoning, garlic salt and black pepper in medium bowl. Combine tomatoes and spaghetti sauce in another medium bowl.

Spread about ¾ cup tomato mixture in prepared dish. Place layer of noodles over tomato mixture, overlapping noodles. Spread half of vegetable mixture over noodles; top with half of ricotta mixture. Sprinkle 1 cup mozzarella over ricotta mixture. Place second layer of noodles over mozzarella. Spread about 1 cup tomato mixture over noodles. Top with remaining vegetable and ricotta cheese mixtures. Sprinkle 1 cup mozzarella over ricotta mixture. Place third layer of noodles over mozzarella. Spread remaining tomato mixture over noodles. Sprinkle remaining 2 cups mozzarella evenly over top.

Cover tightly with foil and bake 1 hour or until noodles in center are soft. Uncover; bake 5 minutes or until cheese is melted and lightly browned. Remove from oven; cover and let stand 15 minutes before serving.   *Makes 6 servings*

MIAMI RICE AND BEAN BURRITOS

1 medium packaged cored fresh pineapple,
   coarsely chopped
2 tablespoons olive oil, divided
1 cup chopped seeded tomatoes
2 tablespoons light brown sugar
⅓ cup chopped fresh cilantro
3 tablespoons balsamic vinegar, divided
1 cup canned chicken broth
⅔ cup prepared mild or hot salsa
¾ cup uncooked long-grain rice
2 cloves garlic, minced
1½ teaspoons ground cumin
½ teaspoon ground allspice
1 can (16 ounces) pinto beans, rinsed and
   drained
8 flour tortillas (7-inch diameter)
   Sour cream
   Sliced green onions

1. Preheat oven to 400°F.

2. Toss pineapple and 1 tablespoon oil on large nonstick baking sheet. Bake 20 minutes or until pineapple is lightly browned, stirring halfway through baking time. Turn oven off.

3. Transfer pineapple to large bowl; stir in tomatoes and brown sugar. Let cool to room temperature. Stir in cilantro and 1 tablespoon vinegar.

4. Bring chicken broth and salsa to a boil in heavy medium saucepan over high heat. Stir in rice. Reduce heat to low; simmer, covered, 20 minutes or until rice is tender and liquid is absorbed.

5. Heat remaining 1 tablespoon oil in large saucepan over medium heat. Add garlic, cumin and allspice; cook and stir 3 minutes. Add beans and remaining 2 tablespoons vinegar; cook and stir 2 minutes or until heated through. Coarsely mash bean mixture with potato masher.

6. Preheat oven to 350°F. Spread about 3 tablespoons bean mixture evenly on bottom half of each tortilla; top with rice mixture. Roll tortillas up to enclose filling.

7. Place burritos in ungreased 12×8×2-inch baking dish. Cover; bake 20 minutes or until heated through. Serve with pineapple salsa, sour cream and sliced green onions. Garnish as desired.

Makes 4 servings

Miami Rice and Bean Burritos

MAIN DISHES

POLENTA LASAGNA

1½ cups whole-grain yellow cornmeal
4 teaspoons finely chopped fresh marjoram
1 teaspoon olive oil
1 pound fresh mushrooms, sliced
1 cup chopped leeks
1 clove garlic, minced
½ cup (2 ounces) shredded part-skim
    mozzarella cheese
2 tablespoons chopped fresh basil
1 tablespoon chopped fresh oregano
⅛ teaspoon black pepper
2 red bell peppers, chopped
¼ cup water
¼ cup freshly grated Parmesan cheese,
    divided

1. Bring 4 cups water to a boil in medium saucepan over high heat. Slowly add cornmeal to water, stirring constantly with wire whisk. Reduce heat to low; stir in marjoram. Simmer 15 to 20 minutes or until polenta thickens and pulls away from side of saucepan. Spread in 13×9-inch ungreased baking pan. Cover and chill about 1 hour or until firm.

2. Heat oil in medium nonstick skillet. Cook and stir mushrooms, leeks and garlic over medium heat 5 minutes or until vegetables are crisp-tender. Stir in mozzarella, basil, oregano and black pepper.

3. Place bell peppers and water in food processor or blender; process until smooth. Preheat oven to 350°F. Spray 11×7-inch baking dish with nonstick cooking spray.

4. Cut cold polenta into 12 (3½-inch) squares; arrange 6 squares in bottom of prepared pan. Spread with half of bell pepper mixture, half of vegetable mixture and 2 tablespoons Parmesan cheese. Place remaining 6 squares polenta over Parmesan cheese; top with remaining bell pepper mixture, vegetable mixture and Parmesan cheese. Bake 20 minutes or until cheese is melted and polenta is hot. *Makes 6 servings*

Cook's Tip

Polenta, an essential part of northern Italian cuisine, is made by combining cornmeal and water and cooking it to a thick, spoonable consistency. It can be served hot, usually with butter or Parmesan cheese. When allowed to cool, polenta becomes firm and can be sliced or cut into squares and fried, broiled or baked.

Polenta Lasagna

MAIN DISHES

RAVIOLI WITH HOMEMADE TOMATO SAUCE

3 cloves garlic, peeled
½ cup fresh basil leaves
3 cups seeded peeled tomatoes, cut into quarters
2 tablespoons tomato paste
2 tablespoons fat-free Italian salad dressing
1 tablespoon balsamic vinegar
¼ teaspoon black pepper
1 package (9 ounces) refrigerated reduced-fat cheese ravioli
2 cups shredded spinach leaves
1 cup (4 ounces) shredded part-skim mozzarella cheese

MICROWAVE DIRECTIONS

1. To prepare tomato sauce, process garlic in food processor until coarsely chopped. Add basil; process until coarsely chopped. Add tomatoes, tomato paste, salad dressing, vinegar and pepper; process using on/off pulsing action until tomatoes are chopped.

2. Spray 9-inch square microwavable dish with nonstick cooking spray. Spread 1 cup tomato sauce in dish. Layer half of ravioli and spinach over tomato sauce. Repeat layers with 1 cup tomato sauce and remaining ravioli and spinach. Top with remaining 1 cup tomato sauce.

3. Cover with plastic wrap; refrigerate 1 to 8 hours. Vent plastic wrap. Microwave at MEDIUM (50%) 20 minutes or until pasta is tender and hot. Sprinkle with cheese. Microwave at HIGH 3 minutes or just until cheese melts. Let stand, covered, 5 minutes before serving. *Makes 6 servings*

"WILD" BLACK BEANS

2 cups cooked wild rice
1 can (15 ounces) black beans, undrained
1 cup canned or thawed frozen corn, drained
½ cup chopped red bell pepper
1 small jalapeño pepper*, seeded and chopped
1 tablespoon red wine vinegar
1 cup (4 ounces) shredded Monterey Jack cheese
¼ cup chopped fresh cilantro

Jalapeño peppers can sting and irritate the skin; wear rubber gloves when handling peppers and do not touch your eyes. Wash hands after handling jalapeño peppers.

Preheat oven to 350°F. In 1½-quart baking dish, combine wild rice, beans, corn, bell pepper, jalapeño and vinegar. Cover; bake 20 minutes. Top with cheese; bake, uncovered, 10 minutes. Garnish with cilantro. *Makes 6 to 8 servings*

Favorite recipe from **Minnesota Cultivated Wild Rice Council**

Ravioli with Homemade Tomato Sauce

ROASTED GARLIC PARMESAN PENNE PRIMAVERA

1 box (16 ounces) penne pasta
1 medium carrot, cut into very thin strips
1 cup snow peas
1 small red bell pepper, cut into very thin strips
1 jar (17 ounces) RAGÚ® Cheese Creations!™ Roasted Garlic Parmesan Pasta Sauce
½ cup chicken broth
⅛ teaspoon ground black pepper
⅛ teaspoon ground nutmeg (optional)

Cook pasta according to package directions, adding vegetables during last 3 minutes of cooking; drain. Return to saucepan and stir in Ragú® Cheese Creations!™ Pasta Sauce, chicken broth, black pepper and nutmeg; heat through. Sprinkle, if desired, with grated Parmesan cheese.

Makes 8 servings

Recipe Tip: To reheat leftovers (as if there'll be any!), microwave in a covered dish on HIGH (100% power) for about 1 minute. If not heated through, stir and continue cooking, checking at 15-second intervals.

GARDEN LINGUINE

8 ounces linguine or rotini pasta
3 tablespoons olive oil
1 tablespoon butter
1 cup sliced mushrooms
½ cup sliced onions
2 cups snow peas, cut into halves
2 cups diced zucchini
½ red pepper, cut into strips (optional)
1 teaspoon dried basil leaves *or* 3 tablespoons fresh basil
1 teaspoon salt
½ teaspoon garlic powder
½ teaspoon black pepper
½ cup Parmesan cheese

Cook linguine as directed on package; drain. Set aside. Heat oil and butter in saucepan; sauté mushrooms, onions, snow peas, zucchini and bell pepper, if desired, until crisp-tender. Remove saucepan from heat. Add seasonings to vegetable mixture. Toss with linguine. Sprinkle Parmesan cheese over top.

Makes 4 servings

Favorite recipe from **North Dakota Wheat Commission**

Roasted Garlic Parmesan Penne Primavera

VEGETABLE LASAGNA

Tomato Sauce (recipe follows)
8 ounces uncooked lasagna noodles
 (9 noodles)
2 teaspoons olive oil
⅓ cup finely chopped carrot
2 cloves garlic, minced
2 cups coarsely chopped fresh mushrooms
3 cups coarsely chopped broccoli, including
 stems
1 package (10 ounces) frozen chopped
 spinach, thawed and drained
⅛ teaspoon ground nutmeg
1 container (15 ounces) nonfat ricotta
 cheese
2 tablespoons minced fresh parsley
1 tablespoon minced fresh basil
1 tablespoon minced fresh oregano
2 teaspoons cornstarch
¼ teaspoon ground black pepper
1½ cups (6 ounces) shredded part-skim
 mozzarella cheese, divided
2 tablespoons grated Parmesan cheese

1. Prepare Tomato Sauce. Set aside. Cook noodles according to package directions. Drain and rinse well under cold water. Set aside.

2. Heat olive oil in large nonstick skillet over medium heat. Add carrot and garlic; cook until garlic is soft, about 3 minutes. Add mushrooms; cook and stir until moisture is evaporated. Reduce heat. Add broccoli; cover and simmer 3 to 5 minutes or until broccoli is crisp-tender. Remove from heat; stir in spinach and nutmeg.

3. Preheat oven to 350°F. Combine ricotta cheese, parsley, basil, oregano, cornstarch and black pepper in small bowl. Stir in 1¼ cups mozzarella cheese.

4. Lightly spray 13×9-inch baking dish with nonstick cooking spray. Spread 2 tablespoons Tomato Sauce in bottom of dish. Arrange 3 noodles in dish. Spread with ½ cheese mixture and ½ vegetable mixture. Pour ⅓ tomato sauce over vegetable layer. Repeat layers, ending with noodles. Pour remaining ⅓ tomato sauce over noodles. Sprinkle with Parmesan cheese and remaining mozzarella. Cover; bake 30 minutes. Uncover; continue baking 10 to 15 minutes or until bubbly and heated through. Let stand 10 minutes. *Makes 10 servings*

TOMATO SAUCE

2 cans (16 ounces each) whole, peeled
 tomatoes, undrained
2 cans (6 ounces each) no-salt-added tomato
 paste
1 medium onion, finely chopped
¼ cup red wine
2 cloves garlic, minced
1 tablespoon Italian seasoning blend

Combine tomatoes, tomato paste, onion, red wine, garlic and Italian seasoning blend in medium saucepan. Cover. Bring to a boil; reduce heat. Simmer 20 minutes.

Vegetable Lasagna

SPINACH–STUFFED MANICOTTI

1 package (10 ounces) frozen spinach
8 uncooked manicotti shells
1½ teaspoons olive oil
1 teaspoon dried rosemary
1 teaspoon dried sage leaves
1 teaspoon dried oregano leaves
1 teaspoon dried thyme leaves
1 teaspoon chopped garlic
1½ cups chopped fresh tomatoes
½ cup ricotta cheese
½ cup fresh whole wheat bread crumbs
2 egg whites, lightly beaten
Yellow pepper rings and sage sprig for garnish

1. Cook spinach according to package directions. Drain and cool. Squeeze spinach to remove excess moisture. Set aside.

2. Cook pasta according to package directions; drain and cool.

3. Preheat oven to 350°F. Heat oil in small saucepan over medium heat. Cook and stir rosemary, sage, oregano, thyme and garlic in hot oil about 1 minute. Do not let herbs brown. Add tomatoes; reduce heat to low. Simmer, uncovered, 10 minutes, stirring occasionally.

4. Combine spinach, ricotta cheese and crumbs in bowl. Fold in egg whites. Fill shells with spinach mixture.

5. Place one third of tomato mixture on bottom of 13×9-inch baking dish. Arrange manicotti over tomato mixture. Pour remaining tomato mixture over stuffed shells. Cover with foil. Bake 30 minutes or until bubbly. Garnish, if desired.

Makes 4 servings

BAKED ZITI WITH WALNUTS

1 cup uncooked ziti pasta
1 box (10 ounces) BIRDS EYE® frozen Peas & Pearl Onions
1 cup tomato sauce
½ cup chopped walnuts
1 tablespoon olive oil
2 tablespoons grated Parmesan cheese

• Preheat oven to 350°F.

• Cook ziti according to package directions; drain and set aside.

• In large bowl, combine vegetables, tomato sauce, walnuts and oil. Add ziti; toss well.

• Place mixture in 13×9-inch baking pan. Sprinkle with cheese.

• Bake 20 minutes or until heated through.

Makes 4 servings

Prep Time: 10 minutes
Cook Time: 20 minutes

Spinach-Stuffed Manicotti

THREE-CHEESE PENNE

2 cups uncooked penne pasta
  Nonstick cooking spray
2 slices whole wheat bread, cubed
2 cups nonfat cottage cheese
2 cups (8 ounces) shredded reduced-fat
  Cheddar cheese
1 cup chopped Roma tomatoes, divided
⅓ cup sliced green onions
¼ cup grated Parmesan cheese
¼ cup reduced-fat (2%) milk

1. Cook pasta according to package directions. Drain and rinse well under cold water until pasta is cool; drain well.

2. Spray large skillet with nonstick cooking spray; heat over medium heat until hot. Place bread cubes in skillet; spray bread cubes lightly with cooking spray. Cook and stir 5 minutes or until bread cubes are browned and crisp.

3. Preheat oven to 350°F. Combine pasta, cottage cheese, Cheddar cheese, ¾ cup tomatoes, green onions, Parmesan cheese and milk in medium bowl. Spray 2-quart casserole with cooking spray. Place pasta mixture in casserole. Top with remaining ¼ cup tomatoes and cooled bread cubes.

4. Bake 20 minutes or until heated through. Garnish, if desired. *Makes 6 servings*

VEGETARIAN LENTIL CASSEROLE

1 pound lentils, cooked
¾ cup honey
½ cup soy sauce
2 teaspoons dry mustard
1 teaspoon pepper
½ teaspoon ground ginger
½ cup chopped onion
½ cup sliced carrot
½ cup sliced celery
3 tablespoons vegetable oil
8 cups cooked white rice

Place lentils in 2½-quart casserole. Combine honey, soy sauce, mustard, pepper and ginger in small bowl. Gently stir into lentils. Cook and stir onion, carrot and celery in oil in small skillet over medium-high heat until onion is translucent. Add to lentils. Cover and bake at 350°F 45 minutes. Uncover and bake 15 minutes more. Serve over rice.

Makes 8 servings

Favorite recipe from **National Honey Board**

Three-Cheese Penne

Seafood SUPPERS

CHESAPEAKE CRAB STRATA

4 tablespoons butter or margarine
4 cups unseasoned croutons
2 cups (8 ounces) shredded Cheddar cheese
2 cups milk
8 eggs, beaten
½ teaspoon dry mustard
½ teaspoon seafood seasoning
   Dash black pepper
1 pound crabmeat, picked over to remove any
   shells or cartillage

Preheat oven to 325°F. Place butter in 11×7-inch baking dish. Heat in oven until melted, tilting to coat dish. Remove dish from oven; spread croutons over melted butter. Top with cheese; set aside.

Combine milk, eggs, dry mustard, seafood seasoning, salt and black pepper; mix well. Pour egg mixture over cheese in dish; sprinkle with crabmeat. Bake 50 minutes or until mixture is set. Remove from oven and let stand about 10 minutes. Garnish, if desired. *Makes 6 to 8 servings*

Left: *Chesapeake Crab Strata*

Above: *Baked Fish with Potatoes and Onions (page 316)*

SHRIMP LA LOUISIANA

1 tablespoon butter
1½ cups uncooked long-grain white rice
1 medium onion, chopped
1 green bell pepper, chopped
2¾ cups beef broth
¼ teaspoon salt
¼ teaspoon ground black pepper
¼ teaspoon hot pepper sauce
1 pound medium shrimp, peeled and deveined
1 can (4 ounces) sliced mushrooms, drained
3 tablespoons snipped parsley
¼ cup sliced green onions for garnish (optional)

Melt butter in 3-quart saucepan. Add rice, onion, and bell pepper. Cook 2 to 3 minutes. Add broth, salt, black pepper, and pepper sauce; bring to a boil. Cover and simmer 15 minutes. Add shrimp, mushrooms, and parsley. Cook 5 minutes longer or until shrimp turn pink. Garnish with green onions.

Makes 8 servings

Favorite recipe from **USA Rice Federation**

EGGPLANT & SHRIMP OVER FUSILLI

2 tablespoons olive or vegetable oil, divided
1 large eggplant (about 1½ pounds), peeled and cut into 1-inch cubes (about 6 cups)
⅔ cup water, divided
1 medium onion, chopped
2 cloves garlic, finely chopped
¾ teaspoon salt
¼ teaspoon ground black pepper
1 jar (27.5 ounces) RAGÚ® Light Pasta Sauce
8 ounces uncooked shrimp, peeled and deveined
1 box (16 ounces) fusilli pasta or spaghetti, cooked and drained
1 cup crumbled feta cheese (optional)

In 12-inch nonstick skillet, heat 1 tablespoon oil over medium heat and cook eggplant with ⅓ cup water, covered, stirring occasionally, 15 minutes or until eggplant is tender. Remove eggplant and set aside.

In same skillet, heat remaining 1 tablespoon oil over medium heat and cook onion, garlic, salt and pepper 2 minutes or until onion is tender. Stir in Ragú® Light Pasta Sauce, remaining ⅓ cup water and eggplant. Reduce heat to low and simmer covered, stirring occasionally, 6 minutes. Stir in shrimp and simmer, stirring occasionally, 4 minutes or until shrimp turn pink. Serve over hot pasta and sprinkle with crumbled feta cheese, if desired.

Makes 6 servings

Eggplant & Shrimp over Fusilli

CRAB AND CORN ENCHILADA CASSEROLE

Spicy Tomato Sauce (recipe follows), divided
10 to 12 ounces fresh crabmeat or flaked or chopped surimi crab
1 package (10 ounces) frozen corn, thawed, drained
1½ cups (6 ounces) shredded reduced-fat Monterey Jack cheese, divided
1 can (4 ounces) diced mild green chilies
12 (6-inch) corn tortillas
1 lime, cut into 6 wedges
Sour cream (optional)

Preheat oven to 350°F. Prepare Spicy Tomato Sauce.

Combine 2 cups Spicy Tomato Sauce, crabmeat, corn, 1 cup cheese and chilies in medium bowl. Cut each tortilla into 4 wedges. Place one-third of tortilla wedges in bottom of shallow 3- to 4-quart casserole, overlapping to make solid layer. Spread half of crab mixture on top. Repeat with another layer tortilla wedges, remaining crab mixture and remaining tortillas. Spread remaining Spicy Tomato Sauce over top; cover.

Bake 30 to 40 minutes or until heated through. Sprinkle with remaining ½ cup cheese and bake uncovered 5 minutes or until cheese melts. Squeeze lime over individual servings. Serve with sour cream, if desired. *Makes 6 servings*

SPICY TOMATO SAUCE

2 cans (15 ounces each) no-salt-added stewed tomatoes, undrained *or* 6 medium tomatoes
2 teaspoons olive oil
1 medium onion, chopped
1 tablespoon minced garlic
2 tablespoons chili powder
2 teaspoons ground cumin
2 teaspoons dried oregano leaves
1 teaspoon ground cinnamon
¼ teaspoon crushed red pepper
¼ teaspoon ground cloves

Combine tomatoes with liquid in food processor or blender; process until finely chopped. Set aside.

Heat oil over medium-high heat in large saucepan or Dutch oven. Add onion and garlic. Cook and stir 5 minutes or until onion is tender. Add chili powder, cumin, oregano, cinnamon, red pepper and cloves. Cook and stir 1 minute. Add tomatoes; reduce heat to medium-low. Simmer, uncovered, 20 minutes or until sauce is reduced to 3 to 3¼ cups.

Crab and Corn Enchilada Casserole

JAMBALAYA

1 teaspoon vegetable oil
½ pound smoked deli ham, cubed
½ pound smoked sausage, cut into
    ¼-inch-thick slices
1 large onion, chopped
1 large green bell pepper, chopped
3 ribs celery, chopped
3 cloves garlic, minced
1 can (28 ounces) diced tomatoes,
    undrained
1 can (10½ ounces) chicken broth
1 cup uncooked rice
1 tablespoon Worcestershire sauce
1 teaspoon salt
1 teaspoon dried thyme leaves
½ teaspoon black pepper
¼ teaspoon ground red pepper
1 package (12 ounces) frozen ready-to-cook
    shrimp, thawed
    Fresh chives (optional)

Preheat oven to 350°F. Spray 13×9-inch baking dish with nonstick cooking spray.

Heat oil in large skillet over medium-high heat until hot. Add ham and sausage. Cook and stir 5 minutes or until sausage is lightly browned on both sides. Remove from skillet and place in prepared dish. Place onion, bell pepper, celery and garlic in same skillet; cook and stir 3 minutes. Add to sausage mixture.

Combine tomatoes with juice, broth, rice, Worcestershire sauce, salt, thyme and black and red peppers in same skillet; bring to boil over high heat.

Reduce heat to low and simmer 3 minutes. Pour over sausage mixture and stir until combined.

Cover tightly with foil and bake 45 minutes or until rice is almost tender. Remove from oven; place shrimp on top of rice mixture. Bake, uncovered, 10 minutes or until shrimp are pink and opaque. Garnish with chives, if desired.   *Makes 8 servings*

CRAB AND BROWN RICE CASSEROLE

1 pound Florida blue crab meat, fresh, or
    frozen, thawed
3 eggs, slightly beaten
1 cup mayonnaise
1 cup cooked brown rice
¾ cup evaporated milk
¾ cup (3 ounces) shredded Cheddar cheese
¼ teaspoon hot pepper sauce

Preheat oven to 350°F. Grease 1½-quart casserole; set aside. Remove any pieces of cartilage from crab meat. Set aside.

Combine eggs, mayonnaise, brown rice, milk, cheese and hot pepper sauce in large bowl. Stir in crab meat. Bake 30 to 35 minutes or until knife inserted 1 inch from center comes out clean.

Makes 6 servings

Favorite recipe from **Florida Department of Agriculture and Consumer Services, Bureau of Seafood and Aquaculture**

Jambalaya

SEAFOOD LASAGNA

1 package (16 ounces) lasagna noodles, cooked
½ pound flounder fillets
½ pound bay scallops
2 tablespoons butter or margarine
1 large onion, minced
1 package (8 ounces) cream cheese, cubed
1½ cups cream-style cottage cheese
2 teaspoons dried basil leaves
½ teaspoon salt
⅛ teaspoon black pepper
1 egg, lightly beaten
2 cans (10¾ ounces each) cream of mushroom soup
⅓ cup milk
1 clove garlic, minced
½ pound medium raw shrimp, peeled and deveined
½ cup dry white wine
1 cup (4 ounces) shredded mozzarella cheese
2 tablespoons grated Parmesan cheese

1. Rinse fish fillets and scallops. Pat dry with paper towels. Cut fillets into ½-inch cubes. Set aside.

2. Melt butter in large skillet over medium heat and cook onion. Stir in cream cheese, cottage cheese, basil, salt and pepper; mix well. Stir in egg; set aside.

3. Combine soup, milk and garlic in large bowl until well blended. Stir in fish fillets, scallops, shrimp and wine.

4. Preheat oven to 350°F. Grease 13×9-inch baking pan. Place layer of noodles in prepared pan, overlapping the noodles.

Spread half of cheese mixture over noodles. Place layer of noodles over cheese mixture and top with half of seafood mixture. Repeat layers. Sprinkle with mozzarella and Parmesan cheeses. Bake 45 minutes or until bubbly. Let stand 10 minutes before cutting.

Makes 8 to 10 servings

SWANSON® GARLIC SHRIMP & PASTA

1 can (14½ ounces) SWANSON® Chicken Broth
2 cloves garlic, minced
3 tablespoons chopped fresh parsley *or* 1 tablespoon dried parsley flakes
2 tablespoons cornstarch
2 tablespoons lemon juice
⅛ teaspoon ground red pepper
1 pound medium shrimp, shelled and deveined
4 cups hot cooked thin spaghetti (about 8 ounces uncooked)

1. In medium saucepan mix broth, garlic, parsley, cornstarch, lemon juice and pepper. Over medium-high heat, heat to a boil. Cook until mixture thickens, stirring constantly.

2. Add shrimp. Cook 5 minutes more or until shrimp turn pink, stirring often. Toss with spaghetti.

Makes 4 servings

Prep Time: 15 minutes
Cook Time: 10 minutes

Seafood Lasagna

Seafood
SUPPERS

CREAMY "CRAB" FETTUCCINE

1 pound imitation crabmeat sticks
6 ounces uncooked fettuccine
3 tablespoons butter or margarine, divided
1 small onion, chopped
2 ribs celery, chopped
½ medium red bell pepper, chopped
2 cloves garlic, minced
1 cup reduced-fat sour cream
1 cup reduced-fat mayonnaise
1 cup (4 ounces) shredded sharp Cheddar
    cheese
2 tablespoons chopped fresh parsley
¼ teaspoon salt
⅛ teaspoon black pepper
½ cup cornflake crumbs

Preheat oven to 350°F. Spray 2-quart square baking dish with nonstick cooking spray. Cut crabmeat into bite-size pieces. Cook pasta according to package directions. Drain and set aside.

Meanwhile, melt 1 tablespoon butter in large skillet over medium-high heat. Add onion, celery, bell pepper and garlic; cook and stir 2 minutes or until vegetables are tender.

Combine sour cream, butter, cheese, parsley, salt and black pepper in large bowl. Add crabmeat, pasta and vegetable mixture, stirring gently to combine. Pour into prepared dish.

Melt remaining 2 tablespoons butter. Combine cornflake crumbs and margarine in small bowl; sprinkle evenly over casserole. Bake, uncovered, 30 minutes or until hot and bubbly.   *Makes 6 servings*

FILLETS STUFFED WITH CRABMEAT

1 envelope LIPTON® RECIPE SECRETS®
    Savory Herb with Garlic Soup Mix
½ cup fresh bread crumbs
1 package (6 ounces) frozen crabmeat,
    thawed and well-drained
½ cup water
2 teaspoons lemon juice
4 fish fillets (about 1 pound)
1 tablespoon butter or margarine, melted

Preheat oven to 350°F.

In medium bowl, combine soup mix, bread crumbs, crabmeat, water and lemon juice.

Top fillets evenly with crabmeat mixture; roll up fillets and secure with wooden toothpicks. Place in lightly greased 2-quart oblong baking dish. Brush fish with butter and bake 25 minutes or until fish flakes. Remove toothpicks before serving.

Makes 4 servings

*Also terrific with LIPTON® RECIPE SECRETS® Golden Herb with Lemon or Golden Onion Soup Mix.

Creamy "Crab" Fettuccine

STIR–FRIED SCALLOPS WITH VEGETABLES

1 pound sea scallops
¼ teaspoon salt
⅛ teaspoon black pepper
½ cup vegetable broth
1 tablespoon cornstarch
3 tablespoons butter or margarine, divided
1 package (6 ounces) red radishes, sliced
¼ cup dry white wine
1 package (6 ounces) frozen snow peas, partially thawed
½ cup sliced bamboo shoots
   Hot cooked couscous

1. Rinse scallops and pat dry with paper towels. Sprinkle with salt and black pepper.

2. Stir broth into cornstarch in cup until smooth; set aside.

3. Heat 1½ tablespoons butter in large skillet or wok over high heat. Arrange half of scallops in single layer in skillet, leaving ½ inch between. Cook scallops until browned on both sides. Remove scallops to large bowl. Repeat with remaining 1½ tablespoons butter and scallops. Reduce heat to medium-high.

4. Add radishes to wok; stir-fry about 1 minute or until crisp-tender. Remove to bowl with scallops.

5. Add wine and broth mixture to wok. Add snow peas and bamboo shoots; stir-fry until hot. Return scallops and radishes to wok; stir-fry until hot. Serve over couscous.
Makes 4 servings

SHRIMP NOODLE SUPREME

1 package (8 ounces) spinach noodles, cooked and drained
1 package (3 ounces) cream cheese, cubed and softened
1½ pounds medium shrimp, peeled and deveined
½ cup butter, softened
   Salt and pepper to taste
1 can (10¾ ounces) condensed cream of mushroom soup
1 cup sour cream
½ cup half-and-half
½ cup mayonnaise
1 tablespoon chopped chives
1 tablespoon chopped parsley
½ teaspoon Dijon mustard
¾ cup (6 ounces) shredded sharp Cheddar cheese

Preheat oven to 325°F. Combine noodles and cream cheese in medium bowl. Spread noodle mixture into bottom of greased 13×9-inch glass casserole. Cook shrimp in butter in large skillet over medium-high heat until pink and tender, about 5 minutes. Season with salt and pepper. Spread shrimp over noodles.

Combine soup, sour cream, half-and-half, mayonnaise, chives, parsley and mustard in another medium bowl. Spread over shrimp. Sprinkle Cheddar cheese over top. Bake 25 minutes or until hot and cheese is melted. Garnish, if desired.
Makes 6 servings

Shrimp Noodle Supreme

SOUTHERN–STYLE JAMBALAYA

2 teaspoons olive or vegetable oil, divided
4 boneless, skinless chicken thighs (about 12 ounces), cut into ¾-inch chunks
8 ounces uncooked medium shrimp, peeled
1 clove garlic, finely chopped
¼ to ½ teaspoon crushed red pepper flakes
1 medium onion, chopped
1 cup RAGÚ® Chunky Gardenstyle Pasta Sauce
½ cup chicken broth
½ cup water
2 tablespoons dry white wine (optional)
¼ teaspoon ground cumin (optional)
¼ teaspoon dried oregano leaves, crushed
1 cup frozen peas, partially thawed
3 cups hot cooked rice

In 12-inch skillet, heat 1 teaspoon oil over medium-high heat and lightly brown chicken 3 minutes. Add shrimp, garlic and red pepper flakes and cook 2 minutes or until shrimp turn pink. Remove chicken-shrimp mixture and set aside.

In same skillet, heat remaining 1 teaspoon oil over medium heat and cook onion 3 minutes or until tender. Stir in Ragú® Chunky Gardenstyle Pasta Sauce, chicken broth, water, wine, cumin and oregano. Reduce heat to low and simmer covered 8 minutes. Return chicken-shrimp mixture to skillet and stir in peas. Bring to a boil over high heat. Reduce heat to medium and cook 1 minute or until peas are tender and chicken is no longer pink. Serve with hot rice.   *Makes 4 servings*

SHRIMP PRIMAVERA POT PIE

1 can (10¾ ounces) condensed cream of shrimp soup, undiluted
1 package (12 ounces) frozen peeled and uncooked medium shrimp
2 packages (1 pound each) frozen mixed vegetables, such as green beans, potatoes, onions and red peppers, thawed and drained
1 teaspoon dried dill weed
¼ teaspoon salt
¼ teaspoon black pepper
1 package (11 ounces) refrigerated soft breadstick dough

1. Preheat oven to 400°F. Heat soup in large ovenproof skillet over medium-high heat 1 minute. Add shrimp; cook and stir 3 minutes or until shrimp begin to thaw. Stir in vegetables, dill, salt and pepper; mix well. Reduce heat to medium-low; cook and stir 3 minutes.

2. Unwrap breadstick dough; separate into 8 strips. Twist strips, cutting to fit skillet. Arrange attractively over shrimp mixture. Press ends of dough lightly to edges of skillet to secure. Bake 18 minutes or until crust is golden brown and shrimp mixture is bubbly.   *Makes 4 to 6 servings*

Prep and Cook Time: 30 minutes

Shrimp Primavera Pot Pie

ZESTY SEAFOOD LASAGNA

2 packages (1.8 ounces each) white sauce
    mix
4½ cups milk
  1 teaspoon dried basil leaves
  ½ teaspoon dried thyme leaves
  ½ teaspoon garlic powder
  ¾ cup grated Parmesan cheese, divided
  3 tablespoons FRANK'S® REDHOT® Hot
    Sauce
  9 oven-ready lasagna pasta sheets
  2 packages (10 ounces each) frozen chopped
    spinach, thawed and squeezed
  ½ pound cooked shrimp
  ½ pound raw bay scallops or flaked imitation
    crabmeat
  2 cups (8 ounces) shredded mozzarella
    cheese, divided

1. Preheat oven to 400°F. Prepare white sauce according to package directions using milk and adding basil, thyme and garlic powder in large saucepan. Stir in ½ cup Parmesan cheese and RedHot® sauce.

2. Spread 1 cup sauce in bottom of greased 13×9×2-inch casserole. Layer 3 pasta sheets crosswise over sauce. (Do not let edges touch.) Layer half of the spinach and seafood over pasta. Spoon 1 cup sauce over seafood; sprinkle with ¾ cup mozzarella cheese. Repeat layers a second time. Top with final layer of pasta sheets, remaining sauce and cheeses.

3. Cover pan with greased foil. Bake 40 minutes. Remove foil; bake 10 minutes or until top is browned and pasta is fully cooked. Let stand 15 minutes before serving. *Makes 8 servings*

Tip: Splash RedHot® sauce on foods after cooking instead of salt and black pepper. RedHot® sauce perks up the flavor of all foods!

Prep Time: 30 minutes
Cook Time: 50 minutes

Food Fact

Shellfish are highly perishable; therefore, it's best to use them within 24 hours of purchase. All fresh shellfish should have a mild aroma and smell of the sea. To find the freshest shellfish available, buy from a reputable fish market or supermarket with a rapid turnover.

Zesty Seafood Lasagna

Seafood
SUPPERS

LOW-FAT SEAFOOD FETTUCCINE

8 ounces fettuccine
  Vegetable cooking spray
2 cups sliced fresh mushrooms
¾ cup chopped onion
½ cup chopped green bell pepper
1 cup evaporated skimmed milk
1 (10¾-ounce) can low-fat, low-sodium
  cream of mushroom soup
¼ teaspoon garlic salt
½ teaspoon dried parsley flakes
1 pound frozen medium shrimp, cooked
1 pound imitation crab, chopped
  Dry bread crumbs (optional)

Cook pasta according to package directions.

Spray electric skillet with cooking spray and heat to 300°F. Sauté mushrooms, onion and bell pepper until tender, about 6 minutes.

Add evaporated milk, soup, garlic salt, parsley flakes, shrimp and crab. Turn skillet temperature to simmer. Cook and stir until thoroughly heated, about 10 to 15 minutes. Serve over hot pasta. Garnish with bread crumbs, if desired. *Makes 5 servings*

Favorite recipe from **North Dakota Wheat Commission**

OLD-FASHIONED TUNA NOODLE CASSEROLE

¼ cup plain dry bread crumbs
3 tablespoons butter or margarine, melted
  and divided
1 tablespoon finely chopped parsley
½ cup chopped onion
½ cup chopped celery
1 cup water
1 cup milk
1 package LIPTON® Noodles & Sauce—
  Butter
2 cans (6 ounces each) tuna, drained and
  flaked

In small bowl, thoroughly combine bread crumbs, 1 tablespoon butter and parsley; set aside.

In medium saucepan, heat remaining 2 tablespoons butter. Cook onion and celery over medium heat, stirring occasionally, 2 minutes or until onion is tender. Add water and milk; bring to a boil. Stir in Noodles & Sauce—Butter. Continue boiling over medium heat, stirring occasionally, 8 minutes or until noodles are tender. Stir in tuna. Turn into greased 1-quart casserole, then top with bread crumb mixture. Broil until bread crumbs are golden. *Makes about 4 servings*

Seafood
SUPPERS

SALMON LINGUINI SUPPER

8 ounces linguini, cooked in unsalted water
    and drained
1 package (10 ounces) frozen peas
1 cup milk
1 can (10¾ ounces) condensed cream of
    celery soup
¼ cup (1 ounce) grated Parmesan cheese
⅛ teaspoon dried tarragon, crumbled
    (optional)
1 can (15½ ounces) salmon, drained and
    flaked
1 egg, slightly beaten
¼ teaspoon salt
¼ teaspoon pepper
1⅓ cups FRENCH'S® French Fried Onions,
    divided

Preheat oven to 375°F. Return hot pasta to
saucepan; stir in peas, milk, soup, cheese and
tarragon; spoon into 12×8-inch baking dish. In
medium bowl, using fork, combine salmon, egg, salt,
pepper and ⅔ cup French Fried Onions. Shape
salmon mixture into 4 oval patties. Place patties on
pasta mixture. Bake, covered, at 375°F for 40
minutes or until patties are done. Top patties with
remaining ⅔ cup onions; bake, uncovered, 3 minutes
or until onions are golden brown.

Makes 4 servings

SPICY SNAPPER & BLACK BEANS

1½ pounds fresh red snapper fillets, cut into
    4 portions (6 ounces each)
   Juice of 1 lime
½ teaspoon coarsely ground black pepper
   Nonstick cooking spray
1 cup GUILTLESS GOURMET® Spicy Black
    Bean Dip
½ cup water
½ cup (about 35) crushed GUILTLESS
    GOURMET® Baked Tortilla Chips
    (yellow or white corn)
1 cup GUILTLESS GOURMET® Salsa

Wash fish thoroughly; pat dry with paper towels.
Place fish in 13×9-inch glass baking dish. Pour juice
over top; sprinkle with pepper. Cover and refrigerate
1 hour.

Preheat oven to 350°F. Coat 11×7-inch glass baking
dish with cooking spray. Combine bean dip and
water in small bowl; spread 1 cup bean mixture in
bottom of prepared baking dish. Place fish over bean
mixture, discarding juice. Spread remaining bean
mixture over top of fish; sprinkle with crushed chips.

Bake about 20 minutes or until chips are lightly
browned and fish turns opaque and flakes easily
when tested with fork. To serve, divide fish among
4 serving plates; spoon ¼ cup salsa over top of each
serving.

Makes 4 servings

BAKED FISH WITH POTATOES AND ONIONS

1 pound baking potatoes, thinly sliced
1 large onion, thinly sliced
1 small red or green bell pepper, thinly sliced
 Salt
 Black pepper
½ teaspoon dried oregano leaves, divided
1 pound lean fish fillets, cut 1 inch thick
¼ cup butter or margarine
¼ cup all-purpose flour
2 cups milk
¾ cup (3 ounces) shredded Cheddar cheese

Preheat oven to 375°F.

Arrange half of potatoes in buttered 3-quart casserole. Top with half of onion and half of bell pepper. Season with salt and black pepper. Sprinkle with ¼ teaspoon oregano. Arrange fish in one layer over vegetables. Arrange remaining potatoes, onion and bell pepper over fish. Season with salt, black pepper and remaining ¼ teaspoon oregano.

Melt butter in medium saucepan over medium heat. Stir in flour; cook until bubbly, stirring constantly. Gradually stir in milk. Cook until thickened, stirring constantly. Pour white sauce over casserole. Cover and bake at 375°F 40 minutes or until potatoes are tender. Sprinkle with cheese. Bake, uncovered, about 5 minutes more or until cheese is melted.

Makes 4 servings

VEGGIE MAC AND TUNA

1½ cups (6 ounces) elbow macaroni
3 tablespoons butter or margarine
1 small onion, chopped
½ medium red bell pepper, chopped
½ medium green bell pepper, chopped
¼ cup all-purpose flour
1¾ cups milk
8 ounces cubed light pasteurized process cheese product
½ teaspoon dried marjoram leaves
1 package (10 ounces) frozen peas
1 can (9 ounces) tuna in water, drained

SLOW COOKER DIRECTIONS

Cook macaroni according to package directions until just tender; drain. Melt butter in medium saucepan over medium heat. Add onion and bell peppers. Cook and stir 5 minutes or until tender. Add flour. Stir constantly over medium heat 2 minutes. Stir in milk and bring to a boil. Boil, stirring constantly, until thickened. Reduce heat to low; add cheese and marjoram. Stir until cheese is melted.

Combine macaroni, cheese sauce, peas and tuna in slow cooker. Cover and cook on LOW 2½ hours or until bubbly at edge.

Makes 6 servings

Baked Fish with Potatoes and Onions

Seafood
SUPPERS

TUNA NOODLE CASSEROLE

1 tablespoon **CRISCO® Oil*** plus additional
    for oiling baking dish
1 cup sliced celery
⅓ cup chopped onion
¼ cup chopped green bell pepper
1 can (6 ounces) chunk white tuna packed in
    water, drained and flaked
6 ounces egg noodles (3½ cups dry), cooked
    and well drained
½ cup sour cream
1 jar (2 ounces) sliced pimientos, drained
    (optional)
½ teaspoon salt
1 can (10¾ ounces) condensed cream of
    celery soup
½ cup milk
4 slices (¾ ounce each) Cheddar or
    American cheese, chopped
2 tablespoons plain dry bread crumbs

*Any Crisco® Oil can be substituted.

1. Heat oven to 425°F. Oil 2-quart baking dish
lightly.

2. Heat one tablespoon oil in large skillet on medium
heat. Add celery, onion and green pepper. Cook and
stir until tender. Add tuna, noodles, sour cream,
pimientos and salt. Stir to blend. Remove from heat.

3. Combine soup and milk in small saucepan. Stir on
medium heat until warmed. Add cheese. Stir until
cheese melts. Stir into noodle mixture. Spoon into
baking dish. Sprinkle with bread crumbs.

4. Bake at 425°F for 20 to 25 minutes or until hot
and bubbly. *Makes 6 servings*

BROCCOLI–FISH ROLLUPS

1 can (10¾ ounces) cream of broccoli soup
½ cup milk
2 cups seasoned stuffing crumbs
¾ pound flounder fillets (4 medium)
1 box (10 ounces) broccoli spears, thawed
    Paprika

1. Preheat oven to 375°F. Grease 9×9-inch baking
pan. Combine soup and milk in medium bowl. Set
aside ½ cup soup mixture.

2. Combine stuffing crumbs and remaining soup
mixture. Pat into prepared pan.

3. Place fish on clean work surface. Arrange
1 broccoli spear across narrow end of fish. Starting
at narrow end, gently roll up fish. Place over stuffing
mixture, seam side down. Repeat with remaining
fish and broccoli.

4. Arrange any remaining broccoli spears over
stuffing mixture. Spoon reserved ½ cup soup
mixture over broccoli-fish rollups. Sprinkle with
paprika. Bake 20 minutes or until fish flakes easily
when tested with fork. *Makes 4 servings*

Broccoli-Fish Rollups

Seafood
SUPPERS

CHILLED SEAFOOD LASAGNA WITH HERBED CHEESE

8 (2-inch wide) uncooked lasagna noodles
2 cups ricotta cheese
1½ cups mascarpone cheese
2 tablespoons lemon juice
1 tablespoon minced fresh basil leaves
1 tablespoon minced dill
1 tablespoon minced fresh tarragon leaves
¼ teaspoon white pepper
1 pound lox, divided
4 ounces Whitefish caviar, gently rinsed
   Lox and fresh tarragon sprigs for garnish

1. Cook lasagna noodles according to package directions until tender but still firm. Drain and set aside.

2. Process ricotta cheese, mascarpone cheese, lemon juice, basil, dill, tarragon and pepper in food processor or blender until well combined.

3. Line terrine mold* with plastic wrap, allowing wrap to extend 5 inches over sides of mold.

4. Place 1 noodle in bottom of mold. Spread ½ cup cheese mixture over noodle. Cover cheese mixture with 2 ounces lox; spread 2 rounded teaspoons caviar over lox. Repeat layers with remaining ingredients, ending with noodle. Set aside remaining 2 ounces lox for garnish.

5. Cover; refrigerate several hours or until firm. Carefully lift lasagna from mold and remove plastic wrap.

6. Garnish with remaining strips of lox rolled to look like roses and fresh tarragon sprigs, if desired. Slice with warm knife.   *Makes 24 first-course servings*

Can be prepared without terrine mold. Layer lasagna on plastic wrap. Cover and wrap with foil.

SAUMON AU FOUR (BAKED SALMON)

5 tablespoons butter, divided
1½ pounds salmon steaks
15 frozen artichoke hearts, cooked, halved
   Juice of 1 large lemon
   Salt and pepper
1 (4-ounce) package ALOUETTE® Garlic et Herbes Cheese
1 teaspoon dried basil leaves, crushed

Preheat oven to 375°F. Grease casserole dish with 1 tablespoon butter. Arrange salmon steaks and artichoke hearts in dish; sprinkle with lemon juice. Melt remaining 4 tablespoons butter; pour over salmon and artichokes. Season with salt and pepper.

Spread Alouette® generously over salmon and artichokes; sprinkle with basil. Bake about 20 minutes or until fish flakes easily when tested with fork and cheese is melted.   *Makes 4 servings*

Chilled Seafood Lasagna with Herbed Cheese

FESTIVE STUFFED FISH

2 whole red snappers, about 2½ pounds each (or substitute any firm white fish), cleaned
Lemon and lime wedges
2 tablespoons olive oil
2 medium onions, finely chopped
2 cloves garlic, minced
1 cup seeded and chopped medium-hot pepper (such as poblano, serrano, or Anaheim) or green bell pepper
1 cup chopped red bell pepper
8 ounces JARLSBERG or JARLSBERG LITE™ Cheese, shredded
12 tomatillos, thinly sliced, then chopped
1 cup dry white wine or unsweetened apple juice

Score flesh on each fish ¼ inch deep on the diagonal every 1½ inches. Insert lemon and lime wedges, peel side out. Heat olive oil in medium skillet over medium-high heat. Add onions and garlic; cook until translucent. Add peppers; cook 2 minutes. Place in large bowl; stir in cheese and tomatillos. Stuff fish cavity with cheese mixture. Use kitchen string to tie each fish closed every 2 inches (3 or 4 ties). Set aside. Preheat oven to 375°F.

In same skillet, bring wine to a boil. Place fish in large glass or enamel baking dish. Pour hot wine over fish and cover tightly.

Bake 30 minutes or until fish is opaque. Transfer to serving platter and remove string.

Makes 4 to 6 servings

TUNA POT PIE

1 tablespoon butter or margarine
1 small onion, chopped
1 can (10¾ ounces) condensed cream of potato soup, undiluted
¼ cup milk
½ teaspoon dried thyme leaves
¼ teaspoon salt
⅛ teaspoon black pepper
2 cans (6 ounces each) albacore tuna in water, drained
1 package (16 ounces) frozen vegetable medley, such as broccoli, green beans, carrots and red peppers, thawed
2 tablespoons chopped fresh parsley
1 can (8 ounces) refrigerated crescent roll dough

Preheat oven to 350°F. Spray 11×7-inch baking dish with nonstick cooking spray.

Melt butter in large skillet over medium heat. Add onion; cook and stir 2 minutes or until onion is tender. Add soup, milk, thyme, salt and pepper; cook and stir 3 to 4 minutes or until thick and bubbly. Stir in tuna, vegetables and parsley. Pour mixture into prepared dish.

Unroll crescent roll dough and divide into triangles. Place triangles over tuna filling without overlapping dough.

Bake, uncovered, 20 minutes or until triangles are golden brown. Let stand 5 minutes before serving.

Makes 6 servings

Tuna Pot Pie

LEMONY DILL SALMON AND SHELL CASSEROLE

6 ounces uncooked medium shell pasta
  Nonstick cooking spray
1½ cups sliced mushrooms
⅓ cup sliced green onions
1 clove garlic, minced
2 cups fat-free (skim) milk
3 tablespoons all-purpose flour
1 tablespoon grated lemon peel
¾ teaspoon dried dill weed
¼ teaspoon salt
⅛ teaspoon ground black pepper
1½ cups frozen green peas
1 can (7½ ounces) salmon, drained and flaked

1. Preheat oven to 350°F. Cook pasta according to package directions. Rinse; drain. Set aside.

2. Spray large nonstick saucepan with cooking spray; heat over medium heat until hot. Add mushrooms, onions and garlic; cook and stir 5 minutes or until vegetables are tender.

3. Combine milk and flour in medium bowl; mix until smooth. Stir in lemon peel, dill weed, salt and pepper. Add to vegetable mixture; heat over medium-high heat 5 to 8 minutes or until thickened, stirring constantly. Remove saucepan from heat. Stir in pasta, peas and salmon. Pour pasta mixture into 2-quart casserole.

4. Bake, covered, 35 to 40 minutes. Serve immediately. Garnish as desired.

Makes 6 servings

Food Fact

Although salmon has a higher fat content than most fish, it is still very nutritious. Salmon's fat content is made up primarily of omega-3 fatty acids. There is a wealth of research available today that links consumption of omega-3 fatty acids with the reduced risk of heart attack and heart disease.

Lemony Dill Salmon and Shell Casserole

Seafood
SUPPERS

FISH CREOLE

1 pound fresh or thawed frozen snapper or sole fillets

1 bag (16 ounces) BIRDS EYE® frozen Farm Fresh Mixtures Broccoli, Green Beans, Pearl Onions & Red Peppers

1 can (16 ounces) tomato sauce

1 tablespoon dried oregano or Italian seasoning

1 tablespoon vegetable oil

1½ teaspoons salt

• Preheat oven to 350°F.

• Place fish in 13×9-inch baking pan.

• In large bowl, combine vegetables, tomato sauce, oregano, oil and salt.

• Pour vegetable mixture over fish.

• Bake 20 minutes or until fish flakes easily when tested with fork.   *Makes 4 servings*

Birds Eye Idea: To remove fish odor from your hands after handling fish, rub your hands with salt and then wash them with cold water.

Prep Time: 5 minutes
Cook Time: 20 minutes

ALBACORE VEGETABLE PILAF

1 cup long grain white rice

1 can (14½ ounces) chicken broth

¼ cup water

2 to 3 tablespoons lemon juice

1 teaspoon dried dill weed

½ teaspoon salt

¼ teaspoon ground black pepper

¼ teaspoon garlic powder

½ cup chopped red bell pepper

½ cup chopped green bell pepper

½ cup chopped zucchini

½ cup corn

1 cup sour cream

1 can (12 ounces) STARKIST® Solid White Tuna, drained and chunked

In medium saucepan with tight-fitting lid, combine rice, chicken broth, water, lemon juice, dill, salt, black pepper and garlic powder. Bring to a boil; cover. Reduce heat; simmer 15 minutes. Stir in vegetables; cover and continue cooking 5 to 7 more minutes or until all liquid is absorbed. Stir in sour cream and tuna. Serve hot or cold.

Makes 6 servings

Prep Time: 30 minutes

Fish Creole

BAKED FISH GALICIAN STYLE

½ cup plus 4 teaspoons **FILIPPO BERIO**®
   Olive Oil, divided
1 large onion, chopped
2 tablespoons minced fresh parsley, divided
2 cloves garlic, crushed
2 teaspoons paprika
1½ pounds new potatoes, peeled and cut into
   ⅛-inch-thick slices
1 tablespoon all-purpose flour
3 small bay leaves
½ teaspoon dried thyme leaves
   Dash ground cloves
4 orange roughy or scrod fillets, 1 inch thick
   Salt and freshly ground black pepper

Preheat oven to 350°F. In large skillet, heat ½ cup olive oil over medium heat until hot. Add onion; cook and stir 5 to 7 minutes or until softened. Stir in 1 tablespoon parsley, garlic and paprika. Add potatoes; stir until lightly coated with mixture. Sprinkle with flour. Add enough water to cover potatoes; stir gently to blend. Add bay leaves, thyme and cloves. Bring to a boil. Cover; reduce heat to low and simmer 20 to 25 minutes or until potatoes are just tender. *(Do not overcook potatoes.)*

Spoon potato mixture into large casserole. Top with fish fillets. Drizzle teaspoon of remaining olive oil over each fillet. Spoon sauce from bottom of casserole over each fillet. Bake 15 to 20 minutes or until fish flakes easily when tested with fork. Sprinkle fillets with remaining 1 tablespoon parsley. Season to taste with salt and pepper. Remove bay leaves before serving. *Makes 4 servings*

IMPOSSIBLY EASY SALMON PIE

1 can (7½ ounces) salmon packed in water,
   drained and deboned
½ cup grated Parmesan cheese
¼ cup sliced green onions
1 jar (2 ounces) chopped pimiento, drained
½ cup low-fat (1%) cottage cheese
1 tablespoon lemon juice
1½ cups low-fat (1%) milk
¾ cup reduced-fat baking and pancake mix
2 eggs
2 egg whites *or* ¼ cup egg substitute
¼ teaspoon dried dill weed
¼ teaspoon salt
¼ teaspoon paprika (optional)

1. Preheat oven to 375°F. Spray 9-inch pie plate with nonstick cooking spray. Combine salmon, Parmesan cheese, onions and pimiento in prepared pie plate.

2. Combine cottage cheese and lemon juice in blender or food processor; blend until smooth. Add milk, baking mix, eggs, egg whites, dill and salt. Blend 15 seconds. Pour over salmon mixture. Sprinkle with paprika, if desired.

3. Bake 35 to 40 minutes or until lightly golden and knife inserted halfway between center and edge comes out clean. Cool 5 minutes before serving. Garnish as desired. *Makes 8 servings*

Impossibly Easy Salmon Pie

Seafood
SUPPERS

TUNA NOODLE CASSEROLE

1 can (10¾ ounces) condensed cream of
   mushroom soup
1 cup milk
3 cups hot cooked rotini pasta (2 cups
   uncooked)
1 can (12.5 ounces) tuna packed in water,
   drained and flaked
1⅓ cups FRENCH'S® French Fried Onions,
   divided
1 package (10 ounces) frozen peas and
   carrots
½ cup (2 ounces) shredded Cheddar or
   grated Parmesan cheese

Combine soup and milk in 2-quart microwavable
shallow casserole. Stir in pasta, tuna, ⅔ cup French
Fried Onions, vegetables and cheese. Cover;
microwave on HIGH 10 minutes* or until heated
through, stirring halfway through cooking time. Top
with remaining ⅔ cup onions. Microwave 1 minute
or until onions are golden.   *Makes 6 servings*

Or, bake, covered, in 350°F oven 25 to 30 minutes.

Tip: Garnish with chopped pimiento and parsley
sprigs, if desired.

Prep Time: 10 minutes
Cook Time: 11 minutes

PEPPERIDGE FARM® SEAFOOD & MUSHROOM SHELLS

1 package (10 ounces) PEPPERIDGE FARM®
   Frozen Puff Pastry Shells
4 tablespoons unsalted butter
2½ cups thinly sliced mushrooms (about
   8 ounces)
1 can (10¾ ounces) CAMPBELL'S®
   Condensed Cream of Mushroom Soup *or*
   98% Fat Free Cream of Mushroom Soup
½ cup dry white wine *or* vermouth
1 tablespoon lemon juice
1 pound firm white fish (cod, haddock or
   halibut), cut into 1-inch pieces
½ cup grated Parmesan cheese

1. Bake pastry shells according to package
directions.

2. In medium skillet over medium heat, heat butter.
Add mushrooms and cook until tender.

3. Add soup, wine, lemon juice and fish. Cook
5 minutes or until fish flakes easily when tested
with a fork.

4. Serve in pastry shells. Sprinkle with cheese.
                              Makes 4 servings

Bake Time: 30 minutes (Bake pastry shells while
preparing fish mixture.)
Prep/Cook Time: 20 minutes

Tuna Noodle Casserole

JUMBO SHELLS SEAFOOD FANCIES

1 package (16 ounces) uncooked jumbo pasta shells
1 can (7½ ounces) crabmeat
1 cup (4 ounces) grated Swiss cheese
1 can (2½ ounces) tiny shrimp, drained
½ cup salad dressing or mayonnaise
2 tablespoons thinly sliced celery
1 tablespoon finely chopped onion
1 tablespoon finely chopped pimiento
Celery leaves for garnish

1. Cook shells according to package directions until tender but still firm; drain. Rinse under cold running water; drain again. Invert shells on paper towel-lined plate and cool.

2. Drain and discard liquid from crabmeat. Place crabmeat in large bowl; flake with fork into small pieces. Remove any bits of shell or cartilage.

3. Add Swiss cheese, shrimp, salad dressing, celery, onion and pimiento to crabmeat. If mixture seems too dry, add more salad dressing.

4. Using large spoon, stuff cooled shells with seafood mixture. Cover; refrigerate until chilled. Garnish, if desired. *Makes 4 servings*

TUNA–SWISS PIE

2 cups cooked unsalted regular rice (⅔ cup uncooked)
1 tablespoon butter or margarine
¼ teaspoon garlic powder
3 eggs
1⅓ cups FRENCH'S® French Fried Onions, divided
1 cup (4 ounces) shredded Swiss cheese
1 can (9 ounces) water-packed tuna, drained and flaked
1 cup milk
¼ teaspoon salt
¼ teaspoon pepper

Preheat oven to 400°F. To hot rice in saucepan, add butter, garlic powder and 1 slightly beaten egg; mix thoroughly. Spoon rice mixture into ungreased 9-inch pie plate. Press rice mixture firmly across bottom and up side of pie plate to form a crust. Layer ⅔ *cup* French Fried Onions, ½ cup cheese and the tuna evenly over rice crust. In small bowl, combine milk, remaining eggs and the seasonings; pour over tuna filling. Bake, uncovered, at 400°F for 30 to 35 minutes or until center is set. Top with remaining cheese and ⅔ *cup* onions; bake, uncovered, 1 to 3 minutes or until onions are golden brown. *Makes 4 to 6 servings*

Jumbo Shells Seafood Fancies

Seafood
SUPPERS

HERB–BAKED FISH & RICE

1½ cups hot chicken bouillon
½ cup uncooked regular rice
¼ teaspoon Italian seasoning
¼ teaspoon garlic powder
1 package (10 ounces) frozen chopped
    broccoli, thawed and drained
1⅓ cups FRENCH'S® French Fried Onions,
    divided
1 tablespoon grated Parmesan cheese
1 pound unbreaded fish fillets, thawed if
    frozen
    Paprika (optional)
½ cup (2 ounces) shredded Cheddar cheese

Preheat oven to 375°F. In 12×8-inch baking dish,
combine hot bouillon, uncooked rice and seasonings.
Bake, covered, at 375°F for 10 minutes. Top with
broccoli, ⅔ cup French Fried Onions and the
Parmesan cheese. Place fish fillets diagonally down
center of dish; sprinkle fish lightly with paprika.
Bake, covered, at 375°F for 20 to 25 minutes or
until fish flakes easily with fork. Stir rice. Top fish
with Cheddar cheese and remaining ⅔ cup onions;
bake, uncovered, 3 minutes or until onions are
golden brown.   *Makes 3 to 4 servings*

Microwave Directions: In 12×8-inch microwave-
safe dish, prepare rice mixture as above, except
reduce bouillon to 1¼ cups. Cook, covered, on
HIGH 5 minutes, stirring halfway through cooking
time. Stir in broccoli, ⅔ cup onions and the
Parmesan cheese. Arrange fish fillets in single layer
on top of rice mixture; sprinkle fish lightly with
paprika. Cook, covered, on MEDIUM (50-60%)

18 to 20 minutes or until fish flakes easily with fork
and rice is done. Rotate dish halfway through
cooking time. Top fish with Cheddar cheese and
remaining ⅔ cup onions; cook, uncovered, on HIGH
1 minute or until cheese melts. Let stand 5 minutes.

FLOUNDER FILLETS OVER ZESTY LEMON RICE

¼ cup margarine or butter
3 tablespoons fresh lemon juice
2 teaspoons chicken bouillon granules
½ teaspoon black pepper
1 cup cooked rice
1 package (10 ounces) frozen chopped
    broccoli, thawed
1 cup (4 ounces) shredded sharp Cheddar
    cheese
1 pound flounder fillets
½ teaspoon paprika

Preheat oven to 375°F. Spray 2-quart square
casserole with nonstick cooking spray.

Melt margarine in small saucepan over medium
heat. Add lemon juice, bouillon and pepper; cook
and stir 2 minutes or until bouillon dissolves.

Combine rice, broccoli, cheese and ¼ cup lemon
sauce in medium bowl; spread on bottom of
prepared dish. Place fillets over rice mixture. Pour
remaining lemon sauce over fillets.

Bake, uncovered, 20 minutes or until fish flakes
easily when tested with fork. Sprinkle evenly with
paprika.   *Makes 6 servings*

Flounder Fillets over Zesty Lemon Rice

TUNA–STUFFED SOLE WITH LIME SAUCE

½ **cup carrot strips**
½ **cup zucchini or yellow squash strips**
2 **green onions, cut into thin strips**
1 **can (9 ounces) STARKIST® Tuna, drained and flaked**
2 **tablespoons lemon juice**
1 **teaspoon dried basil leaves**
½ **teaspoon dried dill weed**
8 **thin sole or other white fish fillets (about 1½ pounds)**
16 **large fresh spinach leaves, washed**

LIME SAUCE

½ **cup chicken broth**
2 **tablespoons butter or margarine**
2 **tablespoons lime juice**
1 **tablespoon cornstarch**
¼ **teaspoon black pepper**
  Lemon or lime peel for garnish (optional)

In 1-quart microwavable bowl, combine carrots, zucchini and onions. Cover with waxed paper; microwave at HIGH 2 to 3 minutes or until nearly tender, stirring once during cooking. Stir in tuna, lemon juice, basil and dill. Arrange one sole fillet on microwavable roasting rack or plate. Top with two spinach leaves, overlapping if necessary. Spoon equal portion of vegetable mixture over each fillet; roll up each fillet from short side, enclosing filling. Secure with wooden toothpicks; transfer to shallow microwavable dish, filling sides up. Repeat with remaining fillets and filling.

Cover dish with vented plastic wrap. Microwave at HIGH 8 to 11 minutes, or until fish flakes easily, rotating dish once during cooking. Remove wooden toothpicks. Let stand while making Lime Sauce.

For Lime Sauce, in medium microwavable bowl, combine all sauce ingredients except garnish until well blended. Microwave, covered, at HIGH 1 to 3 minutes, or until thickened, stirring once. Serve fish with sauce. Garnish, if desired.

Makes 4 servings

Prep Time: 15 minutes

Food Fact

Sole, also known as Dover Sole or English Sole, is a saltwater flat fish. It is further classified as a lean fish. Lean fish are low in fat, have white flesh and a mild, delicate flavor.

Tuna-Stuffed Sole with Lime Sauce

Seafood
SUPPERS

SOLE FLORENTINE

1¼ pounds washed fresh spinach or
    2 packages (10 ounces each) frozen
    spinach, thawed
¼ teaspoon salt or to taste
¼ teaspoon white pepper or to taste
½ cup dry white wine or chicken broth
1½ pounds boneless sole fillets (about 6)
6 ounces (1 carton) Alpine Lace® Fat Free
    Cream Cheese with Garlic & Herbs
½ cup fat free sour cream
3 tablespoons unsalted butter substitute
¼ cup (1 ounce) shredded Alpine Lace® Fat
    Free Pasteurized Process Skim Milk
    Cheese Product—For Parmesan Lovers
Paprika

1. Preheat the oven to 350°F. Spray an 8-inch square baking dish with nonstick cooking spray.

2. In a large saucepan, bring 1 inch of water to a boil. Add the spinach and steam just until wilted; drain well. Line the bottom of the baking dish with the spinach, then sprinkle with the salt and pepper.

3. In a large nonstick skillet, bring the wine to a simmer over medium-high heat. Slide in the sole fillets, cover and poach for 4 minutes or until opaque and springy to the touch. Using a slotted spatula, remove the fillets and arrange on top of the spinach.

4. In a small bowl, blend the cream cheese with the sour cream, then spread on top of the fillets. Dot with the butter and sprinkle with the Parmesan and paprika. Bake, uncovered, for 20 minutes or until the cheese mixture is bubbly. *Makes 6 servings*

PASTA WITH SALMON AND DILL

6 ounces mafalda pasta, cooked
1 tablespoon olive oil
2 ribs celery, sliced
1 small red onion, chopped
1 can (10¾ ounces) condensed cream of
    celery soup, undiluted
¼ cup reduced-fat mayonnaise
¼ cup dry white wine
3 tablespoons chopped fresh parsley
1 teaspoon dried dill weed
1 can (7½ ounces) pink salmon, drained
½ cup dry bread crumbs
1 tablespoon butter or margarine, melted
Fresh dill sprigs (optional)

Preheat oven to 350°F. Spray 1-quart square baking dish with nonstick cooking spray.

Heat oil in medium skillet over medium-high heat until hot. Add celery and onion; cook and stir 2 minutes or until vegetables are tender. Set aside.

Combine soup, mayonnaise, wine, parsley and dill weed in large bowl. Stir in pasta, vegetables and salmon until pasta is well coated. Pour salmon mixture into prepared dish.

Combine bread crumbs and butter in small bowl; sprinkle evenly over casserole. Bake, uncovered, 25 minutes or until hot and bubbly. Garnish with dill sprigs, if desired. *Makes 4 servings*

Pasta with Salmon and Dill

Seafood
SUPPERS

BAJA FISH AND RICE BAKE

  3 tablespoons vegetable oil
¾ cup chopped onion
½ cup chopped celery
  1 clove garlic, minced
½ cup uncooked white rice
  2 cans (14½ ounces each) **CONTADINA**®
     Stewed Tomatoes, cut up, undrained
  1 teaspoon lemon pepper seasoning
½ teaspoon salt
⅛ teaspoon cayenne pepper
  1 pound fish fillets (any firm white fish)
¼ cup finely chopped fresh parsley
     Lemon slices (optional)

1. Heat oil in large skillet over medium heat; sauté onion, celery and garlic.

2. Stir in rice; sauté about 5 minutes, or until rice browns slightly. Add tomatoes with juice, lemon pepper, salt and cayenne pepper.

3. Place fish fillets in bottom of 12×7½×2-inch baking dish. Spoon rice mixture over fish.

4. Cover with foil; bake in preheated 400°F oven for 45 to 50 minutes or until rice is tender. Allow to stand 5 minutes before serving. Sprinkle with parsley. Garnish with lemon slices, if desired.

Makes 6 servings

Microwave Directions:
1. Combine onion, celery and garlic in microwave-safe bowl. Microwave at HIGH (100%) for 3 minutes. Stir in rice, tomatoes and juice, lemon pepper, salt and cayenne pepper. Microwave at HIGH power for an additional 5 minutes.

2. Place fish fillets in 12×7½×2-inch microwave-safe baking dish. Spoon tomato mixture over fish. Cover tightly with plastic wrap, turning up corner to vent. Microwave at HIGH for 20 to 25 minutes or until rice is tender. Allow to stand 5 minutes before serving. Serve as above.

BAKED STUFFED SNAPPER

  1 red snapper (1½ pounds)
  2 cups hot cooked rice
  1 can (4 ounces) sliced mushrooms, drained
½ cup diced water chestnuts
¼ cup thinly sliced green onions
¼ cup diced pimiento
  2 tablespoons chopped parsley
  1 tablespoon finely shredded lemon peel
½ teaspoon salt
⅛ teaspoon black pepper
  1 tablespoon margarine, melted

Preheat oven to 400°F. Clean and butterfly fish. Combine rice, mushrooms, water chestnuts, onions, pimiento, parsley, lemon peel, salt and pepper; toss lightly. Fill cavity of fish with rice mixture; close with wooden toothpicks soaked in water. Place fish in 13×9-inch baking dish coated with nonstick cooking spray; brush fish with margarine. Bake 18 to 20 minutes or until fish flakes easily when tested with fork. Wrap any remaining rice in foil and bake in oven with fish. *Makes 4 servings*

Favorite recipe from **USA Rice Federation**

Baked Stuffed Snapper

TUNA NOODLE CASSEROLE

7 ounces uncooked elbow macaroni
2 tablespoons butter or margarine
¾ cup chopped onion
½ cup thinly sliced celery
½ cup finely chopped red bell pepper
2 tablespoons all-purpose flour
1 teaspoon salt
⅛ teaspoon ground white pepper
1½ cups milk
1 can (6 ounces) albacore tuna in water, drained
½ cup grated Parmesan cheese, divided
Fresh dill sprigs (optional)

Preheat oven to 375°F. Spray 8-inch square baking dish with nonstick cooking spray.

Cook pasta according to package directions. Drain and set aside.

Meanwhile, melt butter in large deep skillet over medium heat. Add onion; cook and stir 3 minutes. Add celery and bell pepper; cook and stir 3 minutes. Sprinkle flour, salt and white pepper over vegetables; cook and stir 1 minute. Gradually stir in milk; cook and stir until thickened. Remove from heat.

Add pasta, tuna and ¼ cup cheese to skillet; stir until pasta is well coated. Pour tuna mixture into prepared dish; sprinkle evenly with remaining ¼ cup cheese.

Bake, uncovered, 20 to 25 minutes or until hot and bubbly. Garnish with dill, if desired.

Makes 4 servings

Food Fact

Canned tuna is precooked and packed in either water or oil. Like other food products, it is available in various quality grades. Fancy is the highest grade, containing large pieces of meat; followed by chunk, with smaller pieces; and finally flake, which contains even smaller bits and pieces.

Tuna Noodle Casserole

Casseroles
ON THE SIDE

SPINACH–CHEESE PASTA CASSEROLE

8 ounces uncooked pasta shells
2 eggs
1 cup ricotta cheese
1 package (10 ounces) frozen chopped spinach,
**   thawed and squeezed dry**
1 jar (26 ounces) marinara sauce
1 teaspoon salt
1 cup (4 ounces) shredded mozzarella cheese
¼ cup grated Parmesan cheese

Preheat oven to 350°F. Spray 1½-quart round casserole with nonstick cooking spray.

Cook pasta according to package directions. Drain.

Meanwhile, whisk eggs in large bowl until blended. Add ricotta and spinach to eggs; stir until combined. Stir in pasta, marinara sauce and salt until pasta is well coated. Pour into prepared dish. Sprinkle mozzarella and Parmesan cheeses evenly over casserole.

Bake, covered, 30 minutes. Uncover and bake 15 minutes or until hot and bubbly. *Makes 6 to 8 servings*

344

*Left:
Spinach-Cheese
Pasta Casserole*

*Above: Wild
Rice Mushroom
Stuffing (page
364)*

345

ON THE SIDE

PENNSYLVANIA DUTCH POTATO FILLING

6 medium Idaho Potatoes, peeled and
    quartered
¼ cup margarine
½ medium onion, diced
1 large rib celery, diced
8 slices soft white bread, diced
2 eggs, lightly beaten
2 tablespoons chopped parsley
½ teaspoon salt
¼ teaspoon pepper

1. Preheat oven to 350°F. Lightly spray 2-quart casserole with nonstick cooking spray.

2. Boil potatoes 15 to 20 minutes or until potatoes are tender when pierced with a fork. Drain.

3. Place potatoes in medium mixing bowl. Mash potatoes by hand or with electric mixer. Mix until smooth.

4. In small skillet over medium heat, melt margarine. Add onion and celery; cook, stirring occasionally, about 5 minutes or until onion is translucent and celery has softened. Add onion and celery to potato mixture; mix to combine.

5. Add bread, eggs, parsley, salt and pepper to potato mixture; mix to combine.

6. Place mixture into casserole and bake, uncovered, 40 to 45 minutes or until lightly browned on top. *Makes 8 (1-cup) servings*

Favorite recipe from **Idaho Potato Commission**

RICE CHILI VERDE

1 tablespoon butter or margarine
¼ cup finely chopped onion
1 cup small-curd cottage cheese
1 cup (½ pint) sour cream
½ teaspoon salt
⅛ teaspoon white pepper
1 can (7 ounces) whole green chilies,
    drained and cut into 1-inch pieces
3 cups cooked rice
1 cup (4 ounces) shredded Monterey Jack
    cheese
1 cup (4 ounces) shredded Cheddar cheese

Preheat oven to 350°F. Melt butter in small skillet over medium heat. Add onion; cook until tender. Combine onion, cottage cheese, sour cream, salt and pepper in medium bowl; mix well. Stir in chilies. Butter 1½-quart casserole. Spoon in half of the rice; cover with half of the cottage cheese mixture. Top with half of the Monterey Jack cheese and half of the Cheddar cheese. Repeat layering with remaining ingredients. Bake 25 to 30 minutes or until rice is hot and cheese is melted. *Makes 6 servings*

ON THE SIDE

BAKED BEANS WITH HAM

1 cup chopped onion
2 tablespoons vegetable oil
2 cans (16 ounces each) beans with tomato
  sauce
1½ cups diced lean ham
6 tablespoons honey
3½ tablespoons prepared mustard
  Salt and pepper to taste

Cook and stir onions in oil in large skillet over medium heat until tender. Add remaining ingredients; mix thoroughly. Spoon into 1½-quart baking dish. Bake, covered, at 350°F 45 minutes. Uncover during last 15 minutes of cooking if drier beans are desired. *Makes 6 servings*

Favorite recipe from **National Honey Board**

BARBECUED BAKED BEANS

1 can (15¼ ounces) kidney beans, drained
1 can (15 ounces) pinto beans, drained
1 cup barbecue sauce
1⅓ cups FRENCH'S® French Fried Onions,
  divided
2 strips uncooked bacon, diced

Preheat oven to 350°F. Combine beans, barbecue sauce and ⅔ cup French Fried Onions in 1½-quart baking dish. Sprinkle with bacon. Bake, uncovered, 45 minutes or until hot and bubbly. Stir; sprinkle with remaining ⅔ cup onions. Bake 5 minutes or until onions are golden. *Makes 6 servings*

Prep Time: 5 minutes
Cook Time: 50 minutes

Food Fact

The color and flavor of honey is determined by the type of flower from which the nectar originated. The color of honey ranges form pale gold to deep amber. In general, the lighter the color, the milder the flavor.

BEAN POT MEDLEY

1 can (15½ ounces) black beans, rinsed and drained
1 can (15½ ounces) red beans, rinsed and drained
1 can (15½ ounces) Great Northern beans, rinsed and drained
1 can (15½ ounces) black-eyed peas, rinsed and drained
1 can (8½ ounces) baby lima beans, rinsed and drained
1½ cups ketchup
1 cup chopped onion
1 cup chopped red bell pepper
1 cup chopped green bell pepper
½ cup packed brown sugar
½ cup water
2 to 3 teaspoons cider vinegar
1 teaspoon dry mustard
2 bay leaves
⅛ teaspoon black pepper

SLOW COOKER DIRECTIONS

Combine all ingredients in slow cooker; stir. Cover and cook on LOW 6 to 7 hours or until onion and peppers are tender. Remove and discard bay leaves.

Makes 8 servings

SPANISH POTATOES

2½ pounds Idaho Potatoes, sliced into bite-sized pieces
1 (8-ounce) package sliced lean bacon
1 (10-ounce) package frozen diced sweet peppers
1 (15-ounce) can crushed tomatoes
2 cups water
½ cup chopped Spanish olives with pimiento
1 to 3 tablespoons chili powder
½ teaspoon onion powder
¼ teaspoon garlic powder
1 to 2 tablespoons chopped capers*

*Additional capers may be used for garnish

1. In large heavy skillet, cook bacon until well done and crisp. Remove from skillet. Drain on paper towel. Crumble and reserve.

2. Pour off drippings; add peppers to skillet. Cook 5 minutes or until liquid has evaporated.

3. Add potatoes, tomatoes, water, olives, chili powder and onion powder. Bring to a boil and cook uncovered, stirring occasionally, 20 minutes or until fork-tender. Stir in capers.

4. Let stand 5 minutes to allow liquids to absorb. Stir in crumbled bacon and serve.

Makes 8 servings (about 9 cups)

Favorite recipe from **Idaho Potato Commission**

Bean Pot Medley

PEPPERIDGE FARM® VEGETABLE STUFFING BAKE

4 cups PEPPERIDGE FARM® Herb Seasoned Stuffing
2 tablespoons margarine *or* butter, melted
1 can (10¾ ounces) CAMPBELL'S® Condensed Cream of Mushroom Soup *or* 98% Fat Free Cream of Mushroom Soup
½ cup sour cream
2 small zucchini, shredded (about 2 cups)
2 medium carrots, shredded (about 1 cup)
1 small onion, finely chopped (about ¼ cup)

1. Mix *1 cup* stuffing and margarine. Set aside.

2. Mix soup, sour cream, zucchini, carrots and onion. Add remaining stuffing. Mix lightly. Spoon into 1½-quart casserole. Sprinkle with reserved stuffing mixture.

3. Bake at 350°F. for 35 minutes or until hot.

Makes 6 servings

Prep Time: 15 minutes
Cook Time: 35 minutes

CAMPBELL'S® CREAMED ONION BAKE

4 tablespoons margarine *or* butter
1½ cups PEPPERIDGE FARM® Corn Bread Stuffing
2 tablespoons chopped fresh parsley *or* 2 teaspoons dried parsley flakes
3 large onions, cut in half and sliced (about 3 cups)
1 can (10¾ ounces) CAMPBELL'S® Condensed Cream of Mushroom Soup *or* 98% Fat Free Cream of Mushroom Soup
¼ cup milk
1 cup frozen peas
1 cup shredded Cheddar cheese (4 ounces)

1. Melt *2 tablespoons* margarine and mix with stuffing and parsley. Set aside.

2. In medium skillet over medium heat, heat remaining margarine. Add onions and cook until tender.

3. Stir in soup, milk and peas. Spoon into 2-quart shallow baking dish. Sprinkle cheese and stuffing mixture over soup mixture.

4. Bake at 350°F. for 30 minutes or until hot.

Makes 6 servings

Prep Time: 15 minutes
Cook Time: 30 minutes

Top to bottom: Pepperidge Farm® Vegetable Stuffing Bake and Campbell's® Creamed Onion Bake

ON THE SIDE

BROCCOLI–CHEESE RICE PILAF

Nonstick cooking spray
¼ cup minced onion
¼ cup diced red bell pepper
2 cups uncooked instant rice
1⅓ cups water
1 can (10¾ ounces) condensed broccoli & cheese soup
1 tablespoon minced fresh parsley
½ teaspoon salt

Coat medium saucepan with nonstick cooking spray. Add onion and pepper; cook and stir until tender. Stir in rice. Add water, soup, parsley and salt; mix well. Bring to a boil; reduce heat to low. Cover and cook 10 minutes or until liquid is absorbed and rice is tender.

Makes 6 servings

CHEDDAR SPOONBREAD

2 cups milk
1 cup quick cooking hominy grits
¼ cup butter or margarine
¾ teaspoon LAWRY'S® Seasoned Salt
¼ teaspoon LAWRY'S® Garlic Powder with Parsley
¼ teaspoon nutmeg
3 eggs, lightly beaten
1½ cups (8 ounces) shredded cheddar cheese
¼ cup grated Parmesan cheese

In heavy saucepan, bring milk just to a boil over medium-high heat; slowly stir in grits. Reduce heat to low and cook 3 minutes, stirring constantly, until thick. Stir in remaining ingredients; mix well. Pour into 1-quart buttered casserole. Bake, uncovered, in 350°F 40 minutes until puffed and golden. Serve immediately.

Makes 6 servings

Food Fact

Grits, also known as hominy grits, is a cereal made of dried, milled white or yellow corn kernels. Grits can be boiled in water or milk. When cooked, it has a consistency similar to oatmeal. Although sold throughout the country, it is most popular in the South, where it is standard breakfast fare.

Broccoli-Cheese Rice Pilaf

Casseroles
ON THE SIDE

PEPPERIDGE FARM®
SCALLOPED APPLE BAKE

¼ cup margarine *or* butter, melted
¼ cup sugar
2 teaspoons grated orange peel
1 teaspoon ground cinnamon
1½ cups PEPPERIDGE FARM® Corn Bread
    Stuffing
½ cup coarsely chopped pecans
1 can (16 ounces) whole berry cranberry
    sauce
⅓ cup orange juice *or* water
4 large cooking apples, cored and thinly
    sliced (about 6 cups)

1. Lightly mix margarine, sugar, orange peel, cinnamon, stuffing and pecans and set aside.

2. Mix cranberry sauce, juice and apples. Add *half* the stuffing mixture. Mix lightly. Spoon into 8-inch square baking dish. Sprinkle remaining stuffing mixture over apple mixture.

3. Bake at 375°F. for 40 minutes or until apples are tender.   *Makes 6 servings*

Tip: To melt margarine, remove wrapper and place in microwave-safe cup. Cover and microwave on HIGH 45 seconds.

Prep Time: 25 minutes
Cook Time: 40 minutes

SOUR CREAM
TORTILLA CASSEROLE

2 tablespoons vegetable oil
½ cup chopped onion
1 can (1 pound 12 ounces) whole tomatoes,
    cut up
¼ cup chunky salsa
1 package (1.25 ounces) LAWRY'S® Taco
    Spices & Seasonings
12 corn tortillas
    Vegetable oil
¾ cup chopped onion
4 cups (1 pound) shredded Monterey Jack
    cheese
1½ cups dairy sour cream
    LAWRY'S® Seasoned Pepper

In medium skillet, heat 2 tablespoons oil; add ½ cup onion and cook over medium high heat until tender. Add tomatoes, salsa and Taco Spices & Seasonings. Bring to a boil over medium-high heat; reduce heat to low and simmer, uncovered, 15 minutes. In small skillet, fry tortillas lightly, one at a time, in small amount of oil, 10 to 15 seconds on each side. In bottom of 13×9×2-inch baking dish, pour ½ cup sauce. Arrange layer of tortillas over sauce; top with ⅓ of sauce, onion and cheese. Repeat layers 2 times. Spread sour cream over cheese. Sprinkle lightly with Seasoned Pepper. Bake in 325°F oven 25 to 30 minutes.   *Makes 10 to 12 servings*

ON THE SIDE

CAMPBELL'S® HEALTHY REQUEST® VEGETABLE–RICE PILAF

Vegetable cooking spray
¼ cup chopped green *or* red bell pepper
2 cloves garlic, minced
½ teaspoon dried basil leaves, crushed
⅛ teaspoon black pepper
1 cup *uncooked* regular long-grain white rice
1 can (16 ounces) CAMPBELL'S® HEALTHY REQUEST® Ready to Serve Chicken Broth
¾ cup frozen mixed vegetables

1. Spray medium skillet with cooking spray and heat over medium heat 1 minute. Add green pepper, garlic, basil, black pepper and rice. Cook until rice is browned and green pepper is tender-crisp, stirring constantly.

2. Stir in broth. Heat to a boil. Reduce heat to low. Cover and cook 10 minutes.

3. Stir in vegetables. Cover and cook 10 minutes more or until rice is done and most of liquid is absorbed.   *Makes 4 servings*

Tip: Try this delicious side dish as a healthier alternative to high-sodium packaged rice dishes.

Prep Time: 5 minutes
Cook Time: 20 minutes

WILD ONION PIE

¼ cup butter, divided
½ cup crushed soda crackers
8 cups sliced sweet onions
3 cups cooked wild rice
2 cups shredded Swiss cheese, divided
1½ cups milk
2 large eggs, well beaten
2 teaspoons dried Greek seasoning
1 teaspoon dried rosemary, crushed
Fresh rosemary, garnish

Preheat oven to 350°F. Melt 2 tablespoons butter; combine with crackers. Press into buttered 8×8-inch pan; set aside. In large skillet, sauté onions in remaining 2 tablespoons butter 15 minutes or until light golden brown; set aside. Layer crust with wild rice, 1 cup cheese, onions and remaining 1 cup cheese. In small saucepan, scald milk and cool; add eggs and seasonings. Pour over cheese; bake 30 to 40 minutes or until golden brown. Cut into squares; garnish with rosemary.   *Makes 6 servings*

Favorite recipe from **Minnesota Cultivated Wild Rice Council**

NEW ENGLAND BAKED BEANS

½ **pound uncooked navy beans**
¼ **pound salt pork, trimmed**
 1 **small onion, chopped**
2 **cloves garlic, minced**
3 **tablespoons firmly packed brown sugar**
3 **tablespoons maple syrup**
3 **tablespoons unsulphured molasses**
½ **teaspoon salt**
½ **teaspoon dry mustard**
⅛ **teaspoon black pepper**
½ **bay leaf**
⅓ **cup canned diced tomatoes, well drained**

1. Place beans in large bowl; cover with 4 inches water. Soak for at least 8 hours, or overnight; drain.

2. Cut pork into 4 (¼-inch-thick) slices. Score pork with knife; set aside.

3. Bring 3 cups water to a boil in 1-quart saucepan. Place pork in water; boil 1 minute. Remove from saucepan to medium plate. Slice and set aside. Discard liquid.

4. Place beans in heavy 3-quart saucepan. Cover beans with 2 inches cold water. Bring beans to a boil over high heat. Reduce heat to low; simmer, covered, 30 to 35 minutes until tender. Drain; reserve liquid.

5. Preheat oven to 350°F. Line bottom of large casserole with ½ of pork slices. Spoon beans over pork slices.

6. Place 2 cups reserved bean liquid into 1½-quart saucepan. Bring to a boil over high heat. Add onion, garlic, brown sugar, maple syrup, molasses, salt, mustard, pepper and bay leaf; simmer 2 minutes. Stir in tomatoes; cook 1 minute. Pour onion mixture over beans in casserole. Top with remaining pork slices.

7. Cover casserole with foil. Bake 2½ hours. Remove foil; bake 30 minutes or until thickened. Skim fat from surface. Discard top 2 pork slices and bay leaf before serving.   *Makes 4 to 6 servings*

WILD RICE APPLE SIDE DISH

 1 **cup uncooked wild rice**
3½ **cups chicken broth**
½ **teaspoon ground nutmeg**
 1 **cup dried apple slices**
 1 **cup chopped onion**
 1 **jar (4½ ounces) sliced mushrooms, drained**
½ **cup thinly sliced celery**

In large saucepan, simmer wild rice, broth and nutmeg 20 minutes. Add remaining ingredients; cover and simmer 20 to 30 minutes, stirring occasionally, until wild rice reaches desired doneness.   *Makes 6 servings*

Favorite recipe from **Minnesota Cultivated Wild Rice Council**

New England Baked Beans

POTATO GORGONZOLA GRATIN

1 pound (2 medium-large) Colorado baking potatoes, unpeeled and very thinly sliced, divided
Salt
Black pepper
Ground nutmeg
½ medium onion, thinly sliced
1 medium tart green apple, such as pippin or Granny Smith, or 1 medium pear, unpeeled, cored and very thinly sliced
1 cup low-fat milk or half-and-half
¾ cup (3 ounces) Gorgonzola or other blue cheese, crumbled
2 tablespoons freshly grated Parmesan cheese

Preheat oven to 400°F. In 8- or 9-inch square baking dish, arrange half the potatoes. Season with salt and pepper; sprinkle lightly with nutmeg. Top with onion and apple. Arrange remaining potatoes on top. Season again with salt and pepper; add milk. Cover dish with aluminum foil. Bake 30 to 40 minutes or until potatoes are tender. Remove foil; top with both cheeses. Bake, uncovered, 10 to 15 minutes or until top is lightly browned.   *Makes 4 to 6 servings*

Favorite recipe from **Colorado Potato Administrative Committee**

CRUNCHY ONION STUFFING

1 package (8 ounces) herb-seasoned stuffing
1⅓ cups FRENCH'S® French Fried Onions, divided
½ cup finely chopped celery
½ cup finely chopped carrots
1 can (14½ ounces) reduced-sodium chicken broth
1 egg, beaten

Combine stuffing, ⅔ cup French Fried Onions and vegetables in 2-quart microwavable shallow casserole. Mix broth and egg in small bowl; pour over stuffing. Stir to coat evenly. Cover; microwave on HIGH 10 minutes* or until vegetables are tender, stirring halfway through cooking time. Sprinkle with remaining ⅔ cup onions. Microwave 1 minute or until onions are golden.   *Makes 6 servings*

Or, bake, covered, in preheated 350°F oven 40 to 45 minutes.

Tip: For a moister stuffing, add up to ½ cup water to chicken broth. You may add ½ cup cooked sausage or 2 tablespoons crumbled, cooked bacon to stuffing, if desired.

Prep Time: 10 minutes
Cook Time: 11 minutes

Potato Gorgonzola Gratin

FRUIT AND SPICY SAUSAGE STUFFING

¼ cup dried cranberries, chopped
¼ cup dried apricots, chopped
1 tangerine, peeled, sectioned, seeded and diced
Grated zest of 1 tangerine
Juice from 3 tangerines
1 pound HILLSHIRE FARM® Smoked Sausage, casing removed and chopped
1 onion, diced
2 ribs celery, chopped
¼ cup diced cored peeled pear
6 to 8 cups bread crumbs
1 tablespoon chopped fresh tarragon *or*
   1 teaspoon dried tarragon leaves
Salt and black pepper to taste
1 cup vegetable or chicken broth, heated

Preheat oven to 400°F.

Combine cranberries, apricots, diced tangerine, tangerine zest and tangerine juice in small bowl; set aside to plump dried fruit. Sauté Smoked Sausage, onion, celery and pear in small skillet over medium-high heat until pear is barely tender.

Toss sausage mixture with cranberry mixture, bread crumbs, tarragon, salt and pepper in large bowl; add hot broth to moisten. Turn mixture into greased casserole or baking pan; bake, uncovered, 45 minutes or until browned on top.

Makes 6 to 8 servings

VEGETABLE–STUFFED BAKED POTATOES

1 jar (17 ounces) RAGÚ® Cheese Creations!™ Roasted Garlic Parmesan Pasta Sauce or Double Cheddar Pasta Sauce
1 bag (16 ounces) frozen assorted vegetables, cooked and drained
6 large baking potatoes, unpeeled and baked

In 2-quart saucepan, heat Ragú® Cheese Creations!™ Pasta Sauce. Stir in vegetables; heat through.

Cut a lengthwise slice from top of each potato. Lightly mash pulp in each potato. Evenly spoon sauce mixture onto each potato. Sprinkle, if desired, with ground black pepper.   *Makes 6 servings*

Vegetable-Stuffed Baked Potato

ON THE SIDE

CAMPBELL'S® GREEN BEAN BAKE

1 can (10¾ ounces) CAMPBELL'S®
   Condensed Cream of Mushroom Soup *or*
   98% Fat Free Cream of Mushroom Soup
½ cup milk
1 teaspoon soy sauce
   Dash pepper
4 cups cooked cut green beans
1 can (2.8 ounces) French fried onions
   (1⅓ cups)

1. In 1½-quart casserole mix soup, milk, soy sauce, pepper, beans and ½ *can* onions.

2. Bake at 350°F. for 25 minutes or until hot.

3. Stir. Sprinkle remaining onions over bean mixture. Bake 5 minutes more or until onions are golden.

Makes 6 servings

Tip: Use 1 bag (16 to 20 ounces) frozen green beans, 2 packages (9 ounces *each*) frozen green beans, 2 cans (about 16 ounces *each*) green beans *or* about 1½ pounds fresh green beans for this recipe.

Prep Time: 10 minutes
Cook Time: 30 minutes

MAPLE LINK SWEET POTATOES AND APPLES

4 medium to large sweet potatoes
2 Granny Smith or other tart apples
1 (12-ounce) package BOB EVANS® Maple
   Links
½ teaspoon salt
¾ cup packed brown sugar, divided
¼ teaspoon ground nutmeg
¼ teaspoon ground cinnamon
¼ cup butter or margarine
1 cup apple juice

Cook unpeeled potatoes in 4 quarts boiling water 15 minutes. Drain and cool slightly. Peel and cut into ¼-inch slices. Peel, core and cut apples into ¼-inch slices. Preheat oven to 350°F. Cook sausage in large skillet until browned. Drain off any drippings; place on paper towels. Cut each sausage link into 3 pieces. Arrange potatoes, apples and sausage alternately in buttered 13×9-inch (or similar size) baking dish. Sprinkle with salt, ½ cup brown sugar, nutmeg and cinnamon. Dot with butter. Pour apple juice over top. Cover and bake 30 minutes. Remove from oven; sprinkle with remaining ¼ cup brown sugar. Bake, uncovered, 25 to 30 minutes more or until lightly browned and potatoes are tender. Refrigerate leftovers.

Makes 8 servings

Campbell's® Green Bean Bake

ON THE SIDE

WILD RICE MUSHROOM STUFFING

½ cup uncooked wild rice
 Day-old French bread (about 4 ounces)
½ cup butter or margarine
 1 large onion, chopped
 1 clove garlic, minced
 3 cups sliced fresh mushrooms
½ teaspoon rubbed sage
½ teaspoon dried thyme leaves, crushed
½ teaspoon salt
¼ teaspoon freshly ground black pepper
 1 cup chicken broth
½ cup coarsely chopped pecans
 Thyme sprigs for garnish

Rinse and cook rice according to package directions; set aside.

Cut enough bread into ½-inch cubes to measure 4 cups. Spread in single layer on baking sheet. Broil 5 to 6 inches from heat 4 minutes or until lightly toasted, stirring after 2 minutes; set aside.

Melt butter in large skillet over medium heat. Add onion and garlic. Cook and stir 3 minutes. Add mushrooms; cook 3 minutes, stirring occasionally. Add sage, dried thyme leaves, salt and pepper. Add cooked rice; cook 2 minutes, stirring occasionally. Stir in broth. Add pecans and toasted bread cubes; toss lightly.

Transfer to 1½-quart casserole. Preheat oven to 325°F. Cover casserole with lid or foil. Bake 40 minutes or until heated through. Garnish, if desired.

Makes 6 to 8 servings

SAUCY SKILLET POTATOES

 1 tablespoon MAZOLA® Margarine
 1 cup chopped onion
½ cup HELLMANN'S® or BEST FOODS®
 Real or Light Mayonnaise or Low Fat
 Mayonnaise Dressing
⅓ cup cider vinegar
 1 tablespoon sugar
 1 teaspoon salt
¼ teaspoon freshly ground pepper
 4 medium potatoes, cooked, peeled and sliced
 1 tablespoon chopped parsley
 1 tablespoon crumbled cooked bacon or real bacon bits

1. In large skillet, melt margarine over medium heat. Add onion; cook 2 to 3 minutes or until tender-crisp.

2. Stir in mayonnaise, vinegar, sugar, salt and pepper. Add potatoes; cook, stirring constantly, 2 minutes or until hot (do not boil).

3. Sprinkle with parsley and bacon.

Makes 6 to 8 servings

Wild Rice Mushroom Stuffing

CHEESY RICE CASSEROLE

2 cups hot cooked rice
1⅓ cups FRENCH'S® French Fried Onions,
  divided
1 cup sour cream
1 jar (16 ounces) medium salsa, divided
1 cup (4 ounces) shredded Cheddar or taco
  blend cheese, divided

Combine rice and ⅔ *cup* French Fried Onions in large bowl. Spoon half of the rice mixture into microwavable 2-quart shallow casserole. Spread sour cream over rice mixture.

Layer half of the salsa and half of the cheese over sour cream. Sprinkle with remaining rice mixture, salsa and cheese. Cover loosely with plastic wrap. Microwave on HIGH 8 minutes or until heated through. Sprinkle with remaining ⅔ *cup* onions. Microwave 1 minute or until onions are golden.

Makes 6 servings

Prep Time: 15 minutes
Cook Time: 9 minutes

CURRIED BAKED BEANS

1 pound small dry white beans
6 cups water
1 teaspoon salt
2 medium apples, cored, pared and diced
½ cup golden raisins
1 small onion, minced
⅓ cup sweet pickle relish
⅔ cup honey
1 tablespoon prepared mustard
1 teaspoon curry powder (or to taste)

Combine beans, water and salt in large saucepan. Let stand overnight. Bring to a boil over high heat. Reduce heat to low and simmer 2 hours, adding water, if needed. Drain beans, reserving liquid. Combine beans with remaining ingredients. Pour into 2½-quart casserole. Add enough bean liquid to barely cover. Bake, covered, at 300°F 1 hour. Remove cover; bake about 30 minutes, adding more liquid, if needed.

Makes 8 servings

Favorite recipe from **National Honey Board**

Cheesy Rice Casserole

ON THE SIDE

NEW–FASHIONED SPAM™ SCALLOPED POTATOES

Nonstick cooking spray
1 (10¾-ounce) can 99% fat-free condensed cream of mushroom soup
½ cup skim milk
1 (2-ounce) jar diced pimiento, drained
¼ teaspoon black pepper
1 (12-ounce) can SPAM® Lite Luncheon Meat, cubed
1 cup chopped onion
½ cup frozen peas
4½ cups thinly sliced, peeled potatoes
2 tablespoons dry bread crumbs
1 tablespoon chopped fresh parsley

Preheat oven to 350°F. Spray 2-quart casserole with nonstick cooking spray. In medium bowl, combine soup, milk, pimiento and pepper. In casserole, layer half of each of SPAM®, onion, peas, potatoes and sauce. Repeat layers. Cover. Bake 1 hour or until potatoes are nearly tender. Combine bread crumbs and parsley; sprinkle over casserole. Bake, uncovered, 15 minutes longer or until potatoes are tender. Let stand 10 minutes before serving.

Makes 6 servings

OLD–FASHIONED STUFFING

½ cup (1 stick) butter or margarine
1½ cups coarsely chopped celery
1½ cups coarsely chopped carrots
½ cup chopped parsley
1 pound day-old bread, cut into cubes (about 3 quarts)
3 cups (6-ounce can) FRENCH'S® French Fried Onions, divided
1 can (10½ ounces) condensed chicken broth
1¼ cups water
2 teaspoons poultry seasoning
1 teaspoon seasoned salt
¼ teaspoon ground black pepper
1 egg, beaten

Preheat oven to 350°F. Grease 3-quart baking dish. Melt butter in 12-inch nonstick skillet; stir in vegetables, parsley, bread and *1½ cups* French Fried Onions.

Combine broth, water, seasonings and egg; mix well. Pour over bread mixture; stir until moistened. Spoon stuffing into baking dish. Cover; bake 25 minutes. Uncover; bake 10 minutes or until heated and top is crusty. Sprinkle with remaining *1½ cups* onions. Bake, uncovered, 5 minutes or until onions are golden.

Makes 8 servings

Prep Time: 20 minutes
Cook Time: 40 minutes

CHEESY MUSHROOM AU GRATIN

3 tablespoons Wisconsin butter, divided
¼ cup all-purpose flour
3 cups hot, not scalded, milk
½ cup (2 ounces) shredded Wisconsin Colby cheese
½ cup (2 ounces) shredded Wisconsin Muenster cheese
¾ teaspoon salt
¾ teaspoon hot pepper sauce
¼ teaspoon ground nutmeg
8 ounces sliced fresh mushrooms
6 ounces sliced shiitake mushrooms
½ cup sliced green onions
1½ teaspoons dried fines herbes, crumbled *or* ½ teaspoon *each*: dried parsley flakes, dried chervil leaves, dried tarragon leaves and freeze-dried chives
12 slices bread, toasted
¼ cup plus 2 tablespoons grated Wisconsin Asiago cheese
   Cooked asparagus tips for garnish
   Additional shredded Wisconsin cheese for garnish

1. In large skillet, melt 2 tablespoons butter; whisk in flour. Cook on low heat 3 to 4 minutes. Slowly whisk in hot milk, stirring well. Bring sauce to a boil; reduce heat and simmer 5 to 6 minutes, stirring occasionally.

2. Stir in Colby and Muenster until melted. Stir in salt, hot pepper sauce and nutmeg; set aside.

3. In separate large skillet, melt remaining 1 tablespoon butter; add mushrooms, green onions and fines herbes. Cook on medium-high heat until mushrooms are golden brown, 10 to 12 minutes. Stir mushroom mixture into cheese sauce.

4. Lightly butter six individual shallow ramekins or single-serving casserole dishes. Place 2 slices toasted bread in each dish; top with ½ cup mushroom sauce and sprinkle with 1 tablespoon Asiago. Repeat with remaining toast slices and mushroom sauce. Bake in preheated 400°F oven 8 to 10 minutes or until browned and bubbly.

5. To serve, top with asparagus and additional cheese. *Makes 6 servings*

Favorite recipe from **Wisconsin Milk Marketing Board**

ON THE SIDE

APPLE STUFFING

1 cup finely chopped onion
½ cup finely chopped celery
½ cup finely chopped unpeeled apple
1½ cups MOTT'S® Natural Apple Sauce
1 (8-ounce) package stuffing mix (original or cornbread)
1 cup low-fat reduced-sodium chicken broth
1½ teaspoons dried thyme leaves
1 teaspoon ground sage
½ teaspoon salt
½ teaspoon black pepper

1. Spray medium skillet with nonstick cooking spray. Heat over medium heat until hot. Add onion and celery; cook and stir about 5 minutes or until transparent. Add apple; cook and stir about 3 minutes or until golden. Transfer to large bowl. Stir in apple sauce, stuffing mix, broth, thyme, sage, salt and black pepper.

2. Loosely stuff chicken or turkey just before roasting or place stuffing in greased 8-inch square pan. Cover pan; bake in preheated 350°F oven 20 to 25 minutes or until hot. Refrigerate leftovers.

Makes 8 servings

Note: Cooked stuffing can also be used to fill centers of cooked acorn squash.

COUNTRY CORN BREAD DRESSING

WESSON® No-Stick Cooking Spray
1 (12-ounce) package seasoned corn bread stuffing
2½ cups dry bread crumbs
2 cups chopped celery
1 cup finely chopped onion
¼ cup (½ stick) butter
½ teaspoon poultry seasoning
¼ teaspoon pepper
2 (14½-ounce) cans chicken broth
¼ cup WESSON® Vegetable Oil

Preheat oven to 375°F. Spray a 13×9×2-inch baking dish with Wesson® Cooking Spray; set aside. Combine stuffing mix and bread crumbs in a large bowl; set aside. In a medium saucepan, sauté celery and onion in butter until crisp-tender; blend in poultry seasoning and pepper. Add broth and Wesson® Oil; bring to boil for 1 minute. Add to corn bread mixture; toss lightly to coat. Spoon corn bread mixture into baking dish; bake, uncovered, for 35 to 45 minutes or until golden brown.

Makes 10 to 12 servings

Apple Stuffing

Casseroles
ON THE SIDE

HONEY NOODLE KUGEL

8 ounces medium noodles
¼ cup butter or margarine, melted
4 eggs, lightly beaten
½ cup honey
½ cup raisins
4 apples, coarsely grated
1 teaspoon salt
1 teaspoon ground cinnamon
   Crisp Topping (recipe follows)

Cook noodles according to package directions. Drain and place in large bowl. Add butter; mix well. Cool 10 minutes. Add eggs, honey, raisins, apples, salt and cinnamon; mix well. Place noodle mixture in greased 9-inch square baking pan. Top with Crisp Topping and cover with foil. Bake at 350°F 50 minutes. Uncover and bake 10 to 15 minutes more or until browned on top.   *Makes 8 servings*

Crisp Topping: Combine ⅓ cup bread crumbs and 1 teaspoon ground cinnamon; mix well. Drizzle ¼ cup honey over mixture and stir until crumbs are coated. Makes ⅓ cup.

Favorite recipe from **National Honey Board**

PEPPERIDGE FARM® CREAMY VEGETABLES IN PASTRY SHELLS

1 package (10 ounces) PEPPERIDGE FARM® Frozen Puff Pastry Shells
1 can (10¾ ounces) CAMPBELL'S® Condensed Cream of Mushroom Soup *or* 98% Fat Free Cream of Mushroom Soup
⅓ cup milk *or* water
1 bag (16 ounces) frozen vegetable combination (broccoli, cauliflower, carrots), cooked and drained

1. Prepare pastry shells according to package directions.

2. In medium saucepan mix soup and milk. Over medium heat, heat through, stirring often. Divide vegetables among pastry shells. Spoon sauce over vegetables and pastry shells.   *Makes 6 servings*

Tip: Substitute 2 cups broccoli flowerets, 1 cup cauliflowerets and 2 medium carrots, sliced (about 2 cups), cooked and drained, for the frozen vegetable combination.

Bake Time: 30 minutes (Bake pastry shells while preparing sauce mixture.)
Prep/Cook Time: 15 minutes

Pepperidge Farm® Creamy Vegetables in Pastry Shells

ACKNOWLEDGMENTS

The publisher would like to thank the companies and organizations listed below for the use of their recipes and photographs in this publication.

American Lamb Council
BC-USA, Inc.
Bestfoods
Birds Eye®
Bob Evans®
Butterball® Turkey Company
Campbell Soup Company
Colorado Potato Administrative Committee
Del Monte Corporation
Delmarva Poultry Industry, Inc.
Filippo Berio Olive Oil
Florida Department of Agriculture and Consumer Services, Bureau of Seafood and Aquaculture
Golden Grain®
Grey Poupon® Mustard
Guiltless Gourmet®
Hebrew National®
Heinz U.S.A.
Hillshire Farm®
Hormel Foods Corporation
Hunt-Wesson, Inc.
The HV Company
Idaho Potato Commission
Kraft Foods, Inc.

Land O' Lakes, Inc.
Lawry's® Foods, Inc.
Lipton®
McIlhenny Company (TABASCO® brand Pepper Sauce)
Minnesota Cultivated Wild Rice Council
MOTT'S® Inc., a division of Cadbury Beverages Inc.
National Cattlemen's Beef Association
National Honey Board
National Pasta Association
National Pork Producers Council
National Turkey Federation
Newman's Own, Inc.®
Norseland, Inc.
North Dakota Wheat Commission
The Procter & Gamble Company
Reckitt & Colman Inc.
The J.M. Smucker Company
StarKist® Seafood Company
Sunkist Growers
Uncle Ben's Inc.
USA Rice Federation
Washington Apple Commission
Wisconsin Milk Marketing Board

INDEX

INDEX

INDEX

INDEX

INDEX

INDEX

INDEX

INDEX

INDEX

METRIC CHART

VOLUME MEASUREMENTS (dry)

$\frac{1}{8}$ teaspoon = 0.5 mL
$\frac{1}{4}$ teaspoon = 1 mL
$\frac{1}{2}$ teaspoon = 2 mL
$\frac{3}{4}$ teaspoon = 4 mL
1 teaspoon = 5 mL
1 tablespoon = 15 mL
2 tablespoons = 30 mL
$\frac{1}{4}$ cup = 60 mL
$\frac{1}{3}$ cup = 75 mL
$\frac{1}{2}$ cup = 125 mL
$\frac{2}{3}$ cup = 150 mL
$\frac{3}{4}$ cup = 175 mL
1 cup = 250 mL
2 cups = 1 pint = 500 mL
3 cups = 750 mL
4 cups = 1 quart = 1 L

VOLUME MEASUREMENTS (fluid)

1 fluid ounce (2 tablespoons) = 30 mL
4 fluid ounces ($\frac{1}{2}$ cup) = 125 mL
8 fluid ounces (1 cup) = 250 mL
12 fluid ounces (1$\frac{1}{2}$ cups) = 375 mL
16 fluid ounces (2 cups) = 500 mL

WEIGHTS (mass)

$\frac{1}{2}$ ounce = 15 g
1 ounce = 30 g
3 ounces = 90 g
4 ounces = 120 g
8 ounces = 225 g
10 ounces = 285 g
12 ounces = 360 g
16 ounces = 1 pound = 450 g

DIMENSIONS

$\frac{1}{16}$ inch = 2 mm
$\frac{1}{8}$ inch = 3 mm
$\frac{1}{4}$ inch = 6 mm
$\frac{1}{2}$ inch = 1.5 cm
$\frac{3}{4}$ inch = 2 cm
1 inch = 2.5 cm

OVEN TEMPERATURES

250°F = 120°C
275°F = 140°C
300°F = 150°C
325°F = 160°C
350°F = 180°C
375°F = 190°C
400°F = 200°C
425°F = 220°C
450°F = 230°C

BAKING PAN SIZES

Utensil	Size in Inches/Quarts	Metric Volume	Size in Centimeters
Baking or Cake Pan (square or rectangular)	8×8×2	2 L	20×20×5
	9×9×2	2.5 L	23×23×5
	12×8×2	3 L	30×20×5
	13×9×2	3.5 L	33×23×5
Loaf Pan	8×4×3	1.5 L	20×10×7
	9×5×3	2 L	23×13×7
Round Layer Cake Pan	8×1½	1.2 L	20×4
	9×1½	1.5 L	23×4
Pie Plate	8×1¼	750 mL	20×3
	9×1¼	1 L	23×3
Baking Dish or Casserole	1 quart	1 L	—
	1½ quart	1.5 L	—
	2 quart	2 L	—